DAUGHTERS AND GRANDDAUGHTERS OF FARMWORKERS

Families in Focus

Series Editors

Anita Ilta Garey, University of Connecticut

Naomi R. Gerstel, University of Massachusetts, Amherst

Karen V. Hansen, Brandeis University

Rosanna Hertz, Wellesley College

Margaret K. Nelson, Middlebury College

DAUGHTERS AND GRANDDAUGHTERS OF FARMWORKERS

Emerging from the Long Shadow of Farm Labor

Barbara Wells

RUTGERS UNIVERSITY PRESS
NEW BRUNSWICK, NEW JERSEY, AND LONDON

Library of Congress Cataloging-in-Publication Data

Wells, Barbara, 1950–

  Daughters and granddaughters of farmworkers : emerging from the long shadow of farm labor / Barbara Wells.

       pages cm. — (Families in focus)

  Includes bibliographical references and index.

  ISBN 978–0–8135–6285–8 (hardcover : alk. paper) — ISBN 978–0–8135–6284–1 (pbk. : alk. paper) — ISBN 978–0–8135–6286–5 (e-book)

  1. Mexican American women agricultural laborers—California. 2. Mexican American women—Social conditions—California. 3. Mexican American women—Social life and customs. I. Title.

  HQ1166.W45 2013

  305.8968'72073—dc23   2013000428

A British Cataloging-in-Publication record for this book is available from the British Library.

Visit our website: http://rutgerspress.rutgers.edu

Manufactured in the United States of America

For Valentina and Maya Garcia Wells

CONTENTS

PREFACE AND
ACKNOWLEDGMENTS

As an Anglo graduate student in sociology, I was honored and privileged to work with a leading Latina family sociologist, Maxine Baca Zinn. I learned from her that to be a successful scholar, one must ask the right questions and be committed to the virtue of hard work. In working with Maxine, I became convinced of the explanatory power of a structural analysis that takes into account the intersection of race, social class, and gender. The honor continued as we collaborated on what is by now a well-known analysis of Latino families, "Diversity within Latino Families: New Lessons for Family Social Science" (2000). Beyond specific Latina/o concerns, I have been privileged to work with Maxine and D. Stanley Eitzen on a diversity-based approach to family sociology in the textbook, *Diversity in Families.* It is the convergence of these two themes in my intellectual development—seeing the analytical promise of structural analysis and developing an interest in Latino families—that brought me to the present project.

My decision to undertake this research project was further encouraged by what I perceived to be a challenge put forward by authors of an article in a leading journal in the field of family studies, the *Journal of Marriage and Family.* In a review of the research on ethnic families from the 1990s, "Marital Processes and Parental Socialization in Families of Color: A Decade Review of Research" (2000), McLoyd and her coauthors concluded that if one had to deduce the current demographic realities of the United States from the quantity of research on Latino families, one would conclude that these families were a "miniscule" percentage of the population. The authors called for more and better research on Latino families. The circumstances have changed in ensuing years as more research has centered on Latino families. Much of the new research is excellent, but it has been clear that more qualitative research is needed. This book is the product of a process of thinking carefully about how I might contribute to the body of research on this important segment of the U.S. population.

My greatest thanks go to the women, daughters and granddaughters of farm-workers, who participated in my research. As I prepared to launch this project in Imperial County, I did not know whether the Latinas I hoped to interview would share their family histories and the stories of their own lives with me. A research fellowship in the summer of 2005 allowed me to explore that question. During this time, I made many community contacts and pretested my interview with Mexican American mothers who met my criteria for research participation. I found then, and in every subsequent research trip to the Imperial Valley, that local residents—both Anglo and Mexican American—were entirely gracious with their time and encouraging of my work.

In concluding my interviews, I always asked the participants if they had questions for me. Sometimes women asked me for advice or asked me to tell them about Tennessee, where I work and live. But the most common question to me, an Anglo woman from someplace else, was, "Why are you doing this?" The subtext to their question was, "Why would you care?" When I told them that my goal was to help all of us in the United States better understand families like theirs, most simply said, "Thank you." Some gave me a hug and a few shed a tear. As I wrote this manuscript, I have tried to honor my commitment.

Special thanks go to several Imperial County women who supported my work in ways that truly made a difference. Kimberly Collins, Director of CCBRES (California Center for Border and Regional Economic Studies) at San Diego State University–Imperial Valley, gave me research associate status, provided an office, and helped me understand a complex research setting. Gloria Arrington, site supervisor of the Brawley One Stop, provided me with a space for conducting interviews in a private setting and patiently explained the intricacies of social service programs in California. Maria Solano and Norma Gamez also provided important assistance.

I must also acknowledge the Hernandez family of Brawley. Julian and Maria Hernandez were immigrant farmworkers who picked and packed melons. The Hernandez home continues to be the gathering place for large extended family celebrations of holidays and other hallmark events for the Hernandez, Garcia, and Duarte families and others. I first learned of the Hernandez family of Brawley and about the Imperial Valley more generally from my daughter-in-law, who is one of Julian and Maria's granddaughters.

The time I have spent in field research in the Imperial Valley has been my most satisfying professional work to date. I have never failed to be fascinated by the people and the place. My time in the Valley was all the more dynamic because my husband, a historian, was at the same time working on his own research, which overlapped mine in some ways. His project, centered on religious aspects of the Latino civil rights movement in California associated with the career of Cesar Chavez, brought the lives of farmworkers to his mind as well as mine. We found in this research, as in life, that sociology and history are compatible pursuits, with perspectives that complement and support each other.

I am indebted to funding from Maryville College's Faculty Development Committee for this research. I also acknowledge the support of the Appalachian College Association, first for a John B. Stephenson Fellowship and second for a Ledford Award to support Caitlin Teaster as a research assistant for the project. Caitlin's meticulous work in transcribing and coding many of the interviews was vital in moving this project forward.

I am grateful to Peter Mickulas at Rutgers University Press for guiding me through the publication process. I thank Rosanna Hertz, the Families in Focus series editor for my book, for her thorough engagement and careful review of the manuscript. This book is the better for her efforts. I also thank Maxine Baca Zinn and Ann Tickamyer for their helpful suggestions.

DAUGHTERS AND GRANDDAUGHTERS OF FARMWORKERS

INTRODUCTION

For me, my goal for my kids is that you don't have to suffer like Mom suffered. And you have to be better than Mom because it's getting harder. And you don't have to go to the fields—unless you become a bum and then that's where you're going to end up. But God forbid. You play it smart, stay out of trouble.
—*Rosa Navarra, second-generation Mexican American*

Rosa Navarra is a thirty-eight-year-old mother of two who grew up in a farmworker household. Rosa has reason to celebrate. She has achieved her long-term goals of completing an associate's degree and getting a good job in border security. She hopes her sons will find an easier path than hers to financial stability.

Farm labor framed the first twenty-five years of Rosa's life. She remembers helping her parents in the fields as a young child. Her first job was in farm labor and she continued in that work until she was in her mid-twenties. She resolved early on to get the education that would provide her with a better life, but these plans were initially derailed by a pregnancy. She attributes her eventual achievement to her own determination and the support of her family. She says, "So I got pregnant, and I knew it was going to be hard. But I always told myself in the back of my mind and in my heart—I will finish. I will at least get my associate's of science. Someday I will do it. Whether it's with the kids or not, I'm going to do it. And I thank the Lord that I did something, you know." For a number of years Rosa worked and took classes at the local community college. When she was out of work, she attended school and received welfare. She frequently worked the graveyard shift to minimize her time away from her boys. She has relied heavily on her father and brothers to step in and care for sons. She explains their assistance in these terms: "We're real united as a family, so it is cool."

Rosa's achievement is impressive. Neither of her parents, a U.S.-born father and a Mexico-born mother, ever attended school; both speak mainly Spanish. Her father and two brothers continue in farm work. Rosa relishes her own accomplishments, but fears that if her sons are not careful, they might yet end up in farm labor.

In contrast to Rosa Navarra, Claudia Gomez and her family, husband Manuel and five children, are currently experiencing hard times. The couple had been hopeful about their economic situation when Manuel moved from field labor to construction work a few years ago, but he has had a disabling accident and Claudia is currently unemployed. In better days, when Manuel did construction by day, she worked at night. As she says, "I don't want to leave my children with no one." Now Claudia is especially frustrated because her husband, who cannot work, will not take much responsibility for housework at home. She states, "He won't make breakfast, not clean, no nothing. He says, 'That's not a man's job, that a girl's job.'"

Claudia, a thirty-year-old second-generation Mexican American, tries to be realistic about her job prospects. She believes that her lack of education and family size work against her. She says, "When I apply for jobs, I haven't tried to apply for the good-paying jobs, more than the minimum [wage]. I don't have my high school diploma. I didn't go to college. And then, on top of that, I have to say that I am a mother of five children. If I were hiring, I would say, why would I hire this person? I would hire the gal that is out of college, or no kids, no nothing, you know what I mean?" Claudia's current circumstances are related, at least in part, to what she calls a difficult home life as a child. Her immigrant farmworker parents, adjusting as they were to a new environment, did not understand the importance of education in their new setting. They did not encourage her to do well in school, and, in fact, impeded her educational progress. Claudia explains that when she had homework to do, her parents would turn off the lights and force her to go to bed before she finished her work. She "messed up" and became pregnant at age seventeen, then dropped out of school.

Although discouraged, Claudia is not without hope. She enjoys being an informal mentor for certain of her children's friends, whose parents, she believes, are inattentive to their children's needs. She aspires to work with troubled teens who might benefit from her support.

I met Rosa and Claudia in Brawley, California, where, in 2005, I began a research project and was interviewing Mexican American women about their work and family lives. I returned in 2007 and 2010 for additional research. I had come to the Imperial Valley, one of the great agricultural valleys of California, to explore the work and family experience of U.S.-born Mexican American women. I was particularly interested in native-born women precisely because they were born, raised, and educated in the United States. My interest in this group was due, in part, to what I perceived to be a national climate of public fear and suspicion regarding Mexican immigrants. The concern of many seemed to be that Mexican immigrants had little desire to integrate into American society, whatever that might mean. With anti-immigrant sentiment on the rise, it seemed important for me to ask how it was that second- and third-generation Mexican Americans, children and grandchildren of immigrants, were going about their lives in the United States.

My initial research questions might have been asked of any group of women in any community in the United States. First, how do women who are mothers negotiate their work and family responsibilities? Second, how do their families manage to sustain themselves economically in a particular social and economic context (in this case, a disadvantaged rural place)? And third, to what extent have the families represented by these women experienced intergenerational upward mobility?

Those general research questions connect to a number of related questions about the Mexican American experience in the United States. Questions about labor force experience and responsibilities for children connect to persistent stereotypes about family traditionality and rigid gender roles among this population. Questions about how families make ends meet connect to the concept of "familism," which is a strong orientation toward and obligation to the family. Familism among Mexican Americans has sometimes been critiqued as a deterrent to economic well-being among this population. And, finally, millions of Mexican immigrants have entered the United States as economic migrants. They have come in hopes of a better life for themselves and their children. A large segment of these were drawn by the availability of jobs in western agriculture. To what extent have these hopes been realized across generations of Mexican-origin families?

The women in my study are not, of course, just any group of women. They are Mexican American women, daughters and granddaughters of farmworkers, who live in a poor agriculture-reliant county at the Mexican border. They are members of a racial-ethnic group whose historical place has been to provide low-wage, temporary labor in the United States. The permanent settlement of Mexican-origin families in the United States has been controversial and frequently unwelcome. As to social class origins, the labor niche that Mexican immigrants have historically been most likely to fill is farm labor. This work is arguably the lowest-paid and most marginal work among all job categories.

At the heart of the national understanding of the United States as a "nation of immigrants" is the assumption of upward mobility. Immigrants leave home and country in pursuit of the American Dream in the Land of Opportunity. The American Dream most hope to achieve is "not the excessive wealth of the very rich, but the middle-class standard of decency implicit in a family's ability to own its own home, live in a decent neighborhood, have access to good transportation, and send its children to good schools" (Pedraza 1996, 479). Immigrants hope for a better life for themselves but count on it for their children. The assumption is that with hard work, each generation will better its socioeconomic position relative to the last.

The prospects for upward mobility among the Mexican-origin population have been a topic of considerable scholarly conversation, with a substantial body of research focused on the consequences of immigration for second- and third-generation Mexican Americans (see, for example, Fry and Lowell 2006; López and Stanton-Salazar 2001; Telles and Ortiz 2008; Vasquez 2011; Waldinger, Lim, and Cort 2007). Scholars now recognize that the old "straight line" assimilation model was oversimplified. This model derived from the European-based immigration of the late nineteenth and early twentieth centuries and assumed that each succeeding generation became more integrated into U.S. society, which contributed to their experience of upward mobility (Foner and Kasinitz 2007). Upon examination, this model does not apply to the post-1965 "new immigration," in which most immigrants are people of color from Latin America and Asia.[1] They join a racially stratified society in which racial-ethnics experience unequal access to social opportunities and privileges. Systematic racial disadvantage compounds the challenges of integration—especially economic integration—of Mexican Americans into U.S. society.

My analytic strategy in this book is, as Maxine Baca Zinn has written, to "locate family experience in societal arrangements that extend beyond the family and allocate social and economic rewards" (1990, 72). Here I take into account social structures of race, social class, gender, and other systems of inequality. Thus a gender-based analysis of women's individual and family experiences is inadequate on its own, because social class and race/ethnicity will also powerfully shape their work and family lives. Increasingly, scholars use the concept of social location, that is, where one is located on hierarchies of race, social class, and gender, to uncover and understand diversity in individual and family experiences (Baca Zinn and Wells 2000).[2] This means that I look for the structural antecedents to individual outcomes.

Further, I assume that spatial location matters. Social, political, and economic forces create environments for family life that vary across geographic space. One of the tasks of rural sociology has come to be contesting the overgeneralization of research findings that are based on urban analyses but tacitly assumed to describe all spatial contexts. Research in many other fields of social research, including the family field, typically does not emphasize locale as an explanatory factor. My research incorporates the methodology of rural social science in that it includes a strong spatial component. The rural border setting of this study provides both an opportunity and a necessity to connect women's experience to place.

Ruth Zambrana critiques conventional research on Latino families as "largely reactive, seldom identifying root causes of social problems and rarely providing an in-depth understanding of the structural and historical factors that shaped the experience of Latino groups in the United States" (2011, 244). I share Zambrana's concern and have very intentionally been attentive to the structural factors and historical circumstances influencing the families represented in this research. Two major issues came to the forefront as I interacted with the Imperial County women. Most important was the degree to which farm labor—as past and present reality—was formative as they narrated their lives. A close second in importance, and quite obvious from looking at a map, is how their lives were deeply affected by their proximity to the U.S.-Mexico border.

I found that the legacy of a farmworker past took center stage in explaining the work and family struggles experienced by these women. The organization of western agriculture was experienced as an oppressive structure that created barriers to mobility not only for immigrant Mexican farmworkers but also for succeeding generations. We see the pervasive nature of the ways that agricultural production continued to influence the lives of these second- and third-generation Mexican American women and structure their opportunities. A focus on farm labor proved central to understanding how inequality is created and sustained in this context. The everyday challenges associated with life in this agriculture-reliant community are exacerbated by its location at the border.

The stories of Rosa and Claudia forecast, in part, the direction of my research findings. Both are daughters of farmworkers. Neither expected that becoming a mother meant staying out of the labor force; it was clear to both women that their earnings were needed to supplement their husbands' incomes. As a young woman, Rosa had aspirations for her own education as a way to leave farmwork behind. A pregnancy intervened and the marriage it precipitated eventually dissolved, but with the help of her family, she has created a far more economically stable life for herself and her sons. Claudia's experience has been different. She had expected her husband to be the family's primary breadwinner. As a mother of five without a high school diploma, her family's main economic chance was for her husband to move out of farm work and into higher-paying construction work. She tried to resolve the need for her own continued labor force participation by split-shift parenting and expecting her husband to share the household work. Her husband's resistance to "helping her" at home has been a great burden. Claudia works on filing her husband's disability claim and looks for a job herself, but without extended-family assistance, this family relies on welfare, subsidized housing, and food stamps. She is beginning to wonder about her long-term obligation to this man.

Rosa, Claudia, and the other women I interviewed grapple with the same work and family issues facing mothers across the United States. These concerns include unplanned pregnancy, single parenthood, marriage, negotiating housework, earning a living, and concerns for children's care and education. The lives of the women I interviewed, mostly working class, are in some ways similar to those of other groups of women similarly situated in American society. But they are also different. Many second- and third-generation women experienced obstacles to "getting ahead" that are clearly related to the recentness of their family's immigrant experience. Many are building their adult lives without a clear road map. Immigrant parents, some with little English language proficiency and no formal education, have frequently not been able to assist children in setting educational goals and working to achieve them. Some women now express deep regret for circumstances that brought them to teen pregnancy, early marriage, and a limited ability to support their families.

Figure 1. Irrigation canals provide water for Imperial Valley agriculture (*Credit:* Johno Wells)

A discussion of work and family requires us to engage the subject of gender as a system of inequality. Many of the women I interviewed actively contest patriarchal assumptions or deeply regret their concessions to them in hindsight. For example, Ana Ramirez resisted the family assumption that she would always work in her aunt and uncle's local restaurant, and she attended college over her father's objections; she is now a teacher. Christina Gilbert refers to herself as "stupid me, the typical Mexican wife" when she allows her husband to make a decision with which she fundamentally disagrees. Like Christina, many connect traditional expectations about men's and women's roles to Mexican culture.

THE SETTING

The setting for this research is Imperial County, California, located in the southeastern corner of the state of California and bounded by Mexico to the south and Arizona to the east. With scant rainfall and scorching summer days, it is part of a region that has been said to be singularly unsuitable for human population (Ducheny 2004, xi). Although it initially may seem an unlikely destination for immigrant farmworkers, its harsh climate belies the reality that it is also one of the most productive agricultural areas in California. This seeming incongruity follows from the diversion of the Colorado River by a system of canals early in the twentieth century that enabled this region, called the Colorado Desert, to become an important center of agribusiness (Collins 2004). The desert area, from the Mexican border to the Salton Sea, was virtually uninhabited when

Anglo settlers arrived around 1900. The Colorado River had deposited good top-soil in the area for many centuries before climate change, occurring hundreds of years ago, dried up the land and drove away native people. All that was needed to make this rich, fertile soil bloom again was water. The main canal, called the All-American Canal, and its derivative smaller canals carry water from the Colorado River, enabling irrigation and productivity previously unimaginable.

Imperial County is a large county (4,175 square miles), sparsely settled for its size with a population of 153,000 in 2005 (population density 37 per square mile) (U.S. Census Bureau 2010).[3] A first-time visitor finds the Imperial Valley visually stunning. Field after field of lettuce and sugar beets are a wonder to see, and they are all the more arresting against the starkness of the desert that surrounds them. Also intriguing to the visitor is the realization that much of the valley is below sea level. There are numerous reference points to indicate the relationship of particular places to sea level. For example, the county's sugar refinery marks the location of sea level with a line painted high on a tower in its processing plant. Entering the town of Brawley from the south one finds a sign indicating its population and noting that the elevation is 113 feet below sea level.

A majority of the county's population lives within twenty-five miles of the international border in and around the county's three largest towns: Calexico, El Centro, and Brawley. The U.S.-Mexico border crossing is at Calexico, population 35,000, a town that revolves principally around serving the needs of Mexican border crossers. Calexico is also the site for San Diego State University–Imperial Valley, a small satellite campus. Ten miles north is El Centro, population 39,000,

Figure 2. The Holly Sugar plant, a beet sugar refinery, Brawley (*Credit:* Johno Wells)

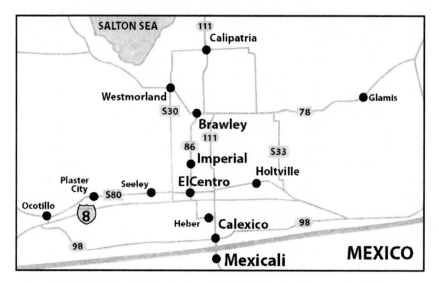

Map 1. Imperial Valley research setting

the Imperial County seat and the county's main commercial center. El Centro is also the location for a major center for border control operations. Eleven miles farther north is Brawley, population 22,000. Brawley is oriented toward agriculture and is the place of residence for most of the major growers in the Valley; it is home to Cattle Call, an annual rodeo-based cultural event that brings significant tourism to the area.

The raison d'être for settlement in this area is agriculture. Agriculture brought Anglo Americans from across the United States to this place to seek their fortunes, and it subsequently brought Mexicans and Asians to the area as workers. A service economy is emerging, but it was—and is—agriculture that makes the Imperial Valley what it is. Prior to 1970, county workers were more likely to be employed in agriculture than in any other sector of private employment. Recent decades have seen a shift in the distribution of jobs, with more employment now provided by the commercial or service sector than by agriculture. As of 2000, the government services sector became the largest employer in the county. More than one-third of workers hold public sector employment in the form of city, county, state, or federal government jobs (Fimbres Durazo 2004). Despite numerical shifts in employment sector, few would deny the region's continued reliance on agriculture. Imperial County ranks tenth among California counties in agricultural production, with a total value of production approaching $1.3 billion in 2005. Its leading commodities are cattle, alfalfa, lettuce, carrots, and livestock (California Deptartment of Finance 2007).

A majority of the growers in the Imperial Valley are themselves descendents of those who settled the Valley about a century ago. The history museum in the county, located near El Centro, is called Pioneers Museum. It suggests the fairly recent origins of Anglo settlement in the region. The general hospital in Brawley is named Pioneers Memorial Hospital. One elderly, prominent grower I interviewed is the son of an original settler; such is the sense of recentness in the area. In common parlance, Mexican farm laborers are often referred to as migrants. But there is a way in which Anglo settlers, recent newcomers, historically speaking, may also be thought of as migrants. Fimbres Durazo writes of these Anglos, who came from various regions of the United States, "These migrants were pioneers who colonized the Imperial Valley" (2004, 45).

The majority of the population of Imperial County today is Hispanic (76 percent) and native born (68 percent). Historically, Mexicans have migrated to the United States to do agricultural labor in this area; a significant number of these workers and their families settled permanently in the county. The representation of Hispanics in the population has increased rapidly over the past fifty years. In 1950, Hispanics were 14 percent of the population of Imperial County. That figure rose to 31 percent in 1970 and 64 percent in 1990 (Fimbres Durazo 2004, 47). The women who participated in my research were daughters or granddaughters of immigrant farmworkers. Immigration legislation from the 1960s and 1980s had enabled many of these families to settle permanently or regularize their immigration status and remain in the U.S. legally. The increasingly Hispanic makeup of Imperial County mirrors the Hispanicization of most U.S. counties positioned at the Mexico border.

Imperial County presents challenges to sustaining an economically stable family life. It has the highest unemployment rate in the state of California: 16.0 percent in 2005, in comparison to unemployment rates of 5.4 percent for the state of California and 5.1 percent for the United States overall (U.S. Department of Labor 2007). The poverty rate for Imperial County was 21 percent in 2005, compared to 13 percent for both California and the nation overall (U.S. Census Bureau 2007).

The Economic Research Service (ERS) of the U.S. Department of Agriculture classifies all U.S. counties by their economic and social characteristics. This typology is especially useful in that it provides a means for comparing the characteristics of counties nationwide. This typology classifies Imperial County economically as a farming-dependent county. As to policy-relevant social characteristics, Imperial County is classified as a low-employment, low-education county with housing stress (Parker 2005).[4]

The women I interviewed lived in and around the town of Brawley. Brawley is bisected by two streets, Main Street, running east–west, and Imperial Avenue, running north–south. The intersection of these streets divides the town into four quadrants. Historically, the Mexican-origin population was concentrated in the southeast quadrant of town. The Miguel Hidalgo School, named for a hero of the Mexican Revolution, is located there. Cesar Chavez attended this school while his family did agricultural labor in the area, and he is the subject of a mural on

Figure 3. Miguel Hidalgo Elementary School, Brawley (*Credit:* Johno Wells)

the front of the school. As the composition of the town has become increasingly Mexican American, this group has become the dominant population group in the northern quadrants as well. In the southwestern quadrant of Brawley is a neighborhood with mature trees and large homes. Here prosperous growers, many of whom are descendants of those called "pioneers," live. Wealth and an understated elegance not to be found in other towns in the Valley are evident here.

The municipal and commercial center of Brawley is located at the intersection of Main Street and Imperial Avenue. This is the site of Plaza Park, an attractive park where community festivals and other events take place. The public library, city hall, and chamber of commerce are located in this area. As in many rural towns, downtown businesses struggle to remain viable. Many older community residents describe the glory days of Brawley as having been in the past, when the community had a vitality that they perceive to be greatly diminished today. Many point to the absence of a local commercial center where families can buy clothing and household goods. One woman I interviewed pointed out that aside from the grocery stores, the largest retail establishment in town is a dollar-type store. Another noted with some exasperation that she could no longer buy a set of sheets in Brawley.[5]

THE PARTICIPANTS

I sometimes refer to the thirty-eight women who are at the center of this research as the Imperial County women. Table 1 provides descriptive information about

Figure 4. Entering Brawley from the south, at an elevation of 113 feet below sea level (*Credit:* Johno Wells)

them; the names used are pseudonyms.[6] All women self-identify as Mexican American, but some complexity underlies that designation. One woman (Julie Peña) has an Anglo mother. A few women mention an Asian, Native American, or Anglo grandparent or great-grandparent. Twenty-six women (68 percent) are second-generation Mexican Americans while twelve (32 percent) are third-generation Mexican Americans.[7] The women range in age from twenty-one to forty-nine years old; a majority are in their thirties. Twenty-two women are age thirty to thirty-nine (58 percent); eleven are age twenty to twenty-nine (30 percent); five are age forty to forty-nine (13 percent). None spoke about her sexual orientation; to my knowledge, all are heterosexual. These women are mothers to between one and seven children each; a large majority (76 percent) have between one and three children. Ten women have one child, seven women have two children, and twelve women have three children. A minority (24 percent) have larger families: five women have four children and four women have five or more children.

Nearly all research participants are in the labor force; that is, they are employed or looking for work. Just over half of the women I interviewed were currently employed. Most of the women not employed were looking for a job; a few were working to complete a GED or attending the county's community college, Imperial Valley College. Several women who were underemployed were looking for a better job or a second job. Seventy-nine percent (30) of women have at least a high school diploma or GED; of these, five (13 percent) have graduated from college with B.A. degrees. None have advanced degrees.

TABLE 1

DEMOGRAPHIC CHARACTERISTICS OF RESEARCH PARTICIPANTS

Pseudonym	Age	Number of children	Generation in U.S.	Occupation*	Marital/ household status
Ana Ramirez	37	1	2nd	Teacher	Single
Angelica Perez	25	3	2nd	Home health aide (CNA)	Separated
Antonia Alivar	35	3	2nd	[Housekeeping]	Married
Beatrice Padilla	40	4	2nd	Bookkeeper, seasonal	Widowed
Carmen Silva	38	3	2nd	Clerical, county	Cohabiting
Cecilia Diaz	37	7	3rd	[Gas station cashier]	Divorced
Celia Roberts	35	3	2nd	[Instructional aide]	Married
Christina Gilbert	31	2	2nd	Retail manager (part-time)	Divorced
Claudia Gomez	30	5	2nd	[Customer service]	Married
Consuela Reyes	28	2	2nd	[Cashier]	Married
Cynthia Mateo	26	1	3rd	Retail	Separated
Daniela Rosales	22	1	2nd	[Restaurant cashier]	Single
Denise Ortiz	28	1	2nd	[Human resources clerk]	Married
Elena Sanchez	30	3	3rd	[Medical billing]	Married
Erica Martinez	33	3	2nd	Customer service, county	Separated
Esther Valdez	39	6	2nd	Cashier	Married
Eva Vallejo	44	3	3rd	School secretary	Married
Francesca Alvarez	21	1	2nd	[Customer service]	Cohabiting
Gloria Espinoza	24	1	2nd	[Grocery cashier]	Single
Helen Estrada	28	4	3rd	[Cashier]	Cohabiting
Jennifer Castillo	35	3	2nd	Clerical, on-call	Married
Julie Pena	34	4	3rd	Instructional aide	Married

(Continued)

TABLE 1

DEMOGRAPHIC CHARACTERISTICS OF RESEARCH PARTICIPANTS (*continued*)

Pseudonym	Age	Number of children	Generation in U.S.	Occupation*	Marital/ household status
Lisa Cabrillo	34	1	2nd	Social worker, county	Married
Lucia Hernandez	40	4	2nd	Home health aide	Married
Margarita Campos	35	3	2nd	[Fast food cashier]	Divorced
Marina Mendez	23	2	2nd	Retail, home health aide	Cohabiting
Marjorie Salas	31	3	3rd	Teacher	Married
Marta Lujan	37	3	2nd	[Child care provider]	Married
Miranda Flores	43	2	2nd	Homemaker	Separated
Monica Rodriquez	31	2	2nd	Teacher	Separated
Natalie Torres	22	1	3rd	[Preschool teacher aide]	Single
Patricia Ochoa	49	5	3rd	Food service	Separated
Priscilla Ortega	30	2	2nd	Vocation ed instructor	Married
Rosa Navarra	38	2	2nd	Border security	Divorced
Rosemary Correa	30	4	3rd	[Medical records tech]	Divorced
Stephanie Ruiz	26	1	3rd	[Stocker]	Single
Sylvia Moreno	30	3	3rd	Shift supervisor	Cohabiting
Theresa Romero	31	1	2nd	Optical technician	Single

*Brackets indicate most recent job for someone currently unemployed.

Marital or partner status is an important predictor of a family's economic situation. Married or cohabiting couples have, at least theoretically, the option of dual earning. Alternatively, much of the economic disadvantage of single-parent families derives from their reliance on the earnings of one worker. Just over half of research participants (53 percent) were married or living with a male partner. Of these, fifteen women were married and five were unmarried and living with a partner. Just under half of the women (47 percent) were single parents. Among these, six were never married, six were separated, five were divorced, and one was widowed.

Analyses of family formation and fathers' continuing involvement in their children's lives increasingly consider men's employment situations. The central issue of concern is the problem of "too little" work because employment difficulties and low earnings serve to disconnect men from family life; men who are unable to provide for their children oftentimes lose contact with them (Bianchi and Milkie 2010, 709). Finding a high rate of single mothers among research participants in this poor place is not unexpected.

The economic well-being of these families was associated with marital or partner status. Among women who were married or living with a partner, in only three of twenty cases (15 percent) did neither adult have employment. In most cases, both adults were employed, but one might have seasonal employment. Among single parents (not living with a partner), eight of eighteen mothers (44 percent) are not presently employed. A job is not a guarantee of economic stability, but in general, the most economically deprived families were jobless.

The families of women participants have varying degrees of labor market success, but a majority of families struggle economically. A large segment, nearly two-thirds (63 percent), has annual family incomes lower than $30,000. One-quarter (26 percent) are in serious financial distress, with earnings of less than $10,000 yearly. The matter of family income is complicated by a high rate of extended family households. Sixteen families (42 percent) live in extended family households. The family incomes reported by these families do not include all income coming into the household. Women generally did not know how much other household members earned.[8]

THE LEGACY OF FARM WORK: MEMORY, MEANING, AND EXPERIENCE

A farmworker past is a deeply held aspect of the identity of the women who participated in this research. Farm work explains something important about their family lives. Perhaps most obviously, it explains why their parents or grandparents left Mexico to come to the United States. Agricultural labor had provided a previous generation with their initial experience in the United States, and the women knew at least something of the family immigration story. I also found that farm work had set, at least partially, the parameters for the childhood experiences of most of the women. Although in some cases their parents left agricultural employment before the interviewee was born, in two-thirds of cases women had grown up in farmworker households. These women are not sentimental or nostalgic about farm labor. Many family stories revolved around the physical debilitation of family members who did this work.

Their general perspective is that farm labor is the work of last resort. No one aspires to be a farmworker. Everyone agrees that getting ahead in the United

States means leaving farm labor behind. Angelica Perez, who is separated from a farmworker husband, sums up the perspective of research participants on the undesirability of farm work when she says, "I think everyone that does farm work would like a better job." These women know from experience that it is next to impossible to build an economically stable family life on farm labor wages. While some women have been able to distance themselves from their farmworker origins, farm labor and its legacy continues to shape the experiences of many of them. For example, women may themselves have been farmworkers; women may have partners who were or are farmworkers; and women may work in jobs providing county services to current and former farmworkers.

In many cases the legacy of farm labor affects women's roles as daughters and parents. Some women provide care and support for their disabled or economically disadvantaged farmworker parents. Many women, in their parental role of encouraging their children's educational achievement, do so in reaction to the undesirability of farm work. As second- and third-generation Mexican Americans, one of their strongest wishes is that their children have options for employment that will never require them to do farm work.

THE INTERPLAY OF STRUCTURE AND CULTURE

The field of family studies originally approached the subject of the Mexican American family from a cultural deficiency perspective. Traditional cultural norms were believed to interfere with "normal" patterns of acculturation observed in other immigrant groups. Rigid male dominance (machismo) and dysfunctional clannishness (familism) were believed to reinforce traditional Mexican ways, including large family size, strict gender role segregation, and retention of Spanish language usage. Remnants of that perspective remain, but much of the newer research uses a structural perspective. A structural perspective assumes that all families are patterned by the varying opportunities, resources, and rewards present in the environments in which they are embedded. Within environments, social opportunities—distributed unequally by factors including race or ethnicity, gender, social class, sexual orientation, immigration status, and language—will shape employment status, marital patterns, and household structure. Thus, variation in family patterns is viewed as produced by structural factors rather than cultural factors (Baca Zinn and Wells 2000).

The approach used in this book considers the interplay of structure and culture. This means that I analyze the family experience of the households represented in this research using a structural perspective while at the same time considering the continuing relevance of Mexican culture in explaining or failing to explain the organization of gender roles within the family, work patterns, and household structure. Two examples illustrate the direction in which this line of inquiry might lead: women's employment and extended family households.

First, in assessing women's employment, I will examine the structure of employment in Imperial County and consider ways in which the structure of local opportunity shapes women's job prospects. The women, in general, stated that the option of staying out of the labor force did not really exist for them. The low wage structure—for both women and men—requires two incomes to sustain a family. Furthermore, the organization of welfare does not permit single mothers to opt out of work. While assumptions about traditional gender roles as an aspect of Mexican culture might predict that women would be at home taking responsibility for the domestic realm, structural realities did not support that possibility for most women.

A second example is the high rate of extended family households among research participants. Four of every ten families live in extended family households. Does this reflect a cultural preference that is an artifact of traditional Mexican life, or is it better described as a strategy precipitated by an unstable or inadequate resource base? In grappling with this question, it will be important to note that household extension is an adaptive strategy used by working-class and poor families of all racial groups when low earnings cannot support nuclear families in private households. At the same time, research over several decades has identified an extended family system as a characteristic of Mexican culture (Baca Zinn and Wells 2000; Pyke 2004). Both structural and cultural elements may be seen in the high incidence of this household type. Household extension was clearly an adaptation to structural constraints. It frequently functioned as a way of reducing the risk of unstable housing in a labor market in which employment in low-skill jobs was frequently seasonal and paid minimum wage. The cultural component may be seen in the generally unquestioned sense of obligation to share housing with relatives. Household extension is a dimension of familism that may be seen to be a cultural resource facilitating positive outcomes within and across generations of Mexican American households.

Organization of the Book

This book examines the work and family lives of U.S.-born Mexican-origin women in a disadvantaged rural community near the Mexican border. Their families' immigration narratives are stories of deprivation on the Mexican side of the border or the indignities of fieldwork on the U.S. side. None of these women is interested in living in Mexico or working in the fields. The American side of the border is home and the way forward is building the best lives possible for themselves and their families in the United States.

Chapter 1, "The Structure of Agriculture and the Organization of Farm Labor," examines developments in U.S. agriculture, with a focus on California agriculture. It considers the relationship between the labor-intensive model of agriculture that typifies California and the availability of a large pool of available labor from Mexico. Farm labor is viewed as highly undesirable work. Generations of farmworkers and their children have moved out of this employment as soon as possible.

Chapter 2, "Farmworker Origins," shows how a farmworker past has shaped the lives of the Imperial County women and members of their families. Farm labor is central to their families' immigration stories and to the childhood experience of most women. In the context of family narratives about the financial hardships and physical debilitation experienced by farmworkers, and their own experiences growing up in farmworker families, women perceive farm labor to be the work of last resort.

Chapter 3, "Life in a Border Community," considers how living in proximity to the border shapes community and family life. Examining the cross-border activities of people on both sides of the Imperial-Mexicali border reveals the dynamic nature of the border region. This border is a major site for both authorized and unauthorized border crossings. Mexicans cross the border to work and shop in the United States, while Imperial County residents cross the border to access low-cost services and to visit family members on the Mexican side. Imperial County is home to one of the major centers of U.S. border enforcement operations, the El Centro Sector. Observing border control activities is part of daily life in the county. A cause for considerable border-related concern for the Imperial County women is the high volume of illegal drugs crossing from Mexico into the county.

Chapter 4, "Negotiating Work and Family," examines how women create and sustain their family lives. This chapter considers the work-family interface and the construction of gender in their families. It examines women's decisions about labor force participation and the child care-related issues they encounter. Most women rely on extended family members or state-subsidized programs for child care. In integrating work and family, women take into account both the needs of their children and obligations to their extended families, which, in this setting, constitute both a resource and a responsibility. Familism is evident in the day-to-day lives of these women and their families. Many women have higher educational attainment and occupational status than their husbands and partners. Women are frequently outperforming the men with whom they are associated. As a result, many women are not economically reliant on their partners. Some have separated from or divorced men who were thought not to be good role models for their children.

Chapter 5, "The Legacy of Farm Labor," probes the extent to which farm labor continues to shape the lives of these daughters and granddaughters of farmworkers. Some families have been able to distance themselves from their farmworker origins, but farm labor continues to inform the experiences of many women. Women may themselves have been farmworkers; women may have partners who were or are farmworkers; and women may work in jobs providing county services to current and former farmworkers. Women desire not only to leave farm work behind, but also to achieve a more economically stable life. This proves to be difficult for most in a context of stiff competition for all jobs, including low-wage jobs.

Chapter 6, "Surviving Now and Building a Better Life for Later," examines, first, how women manage to sustain their families in this agriculture-reliant, Hispanic-majority county at the U.S.-Mexico border, and, second, their progress and prospects related to upward mobility. This chapter finds women strategizing to support their families in a poor local labor market. A majority of families are not self-sufficient and rely on extended family network support and public assistance. The Imperial County women understand that "getting an education" is central to building a more economically secure future. Many women pursue additional education, hoping that it will land them a better job. Few finish their degree programs. In reflecting on their current circumstances, many women recognize that an early birth interfered with attaining their educational goals. They are now actively promoting their children's educational attainment.

Chapter 7 asks the question, "Why Do They Stay?" California's Imperial Valley is a difficult place to sustain a family economically. Most women express dissatisfaction with the local economy and understand the obstacles to upward mobility in this place. But still they stay. They stay because their extended family network is here and because they are genuinely attached to the community. Some cite family responsibilities and others cite the family support they receive. For many, the two are connected. Several stay to assist parents who are now disabled farm laborers and are unable to work. As to community attachment, they appreciate the small-town environment and the sense of community they experience in Brawley. They believe it is easier to raise a family in the Valley than in an urban setting.

The concluding chapter returns to the questions and concerns that have guided this research. Upward mobility is an elusive goal for these daughters and granddaughters of Mexican farmworkers. All have improved their situations since their families entered the United States on the lowest rung of the occupational ladder, but few have been able to achieve the middle-class lives of the American Dream. One of the challenges in understanding and explaining unequal outcomes in U.S. society is articulating how processes of inequality actually work. Scholars and others use the language of "barriers" and "obstacles" experienced by certain demographic groups, but showing how social advantage and disadvantage are created and perpetuated is difficult. This research connects microlevel family interactions and processes to macrolevel social structures to understand the experience of women participating in the research. I find that the structure of agriculture, including assumptions about who will do the work, hazards of the work, and patterns of remuneration, creates impediments to upward mobility that are multigenerational in impact. In addition, living at the border in a poor rural community with few jobs provides little opportunity to join the economic mainstream.

CHAPTER 1

THE STRUCTURE
OF AGRICULTURE
AND THE ORGANIZATION
OF FARM LABOR

The work and family experience of the Imperial County women cannot be understood without taking into account their farmworker origins. An essential thread woven into the interviews was the centrality of farm work to the women's lives. Family immigration stories were framed in terms of farm labor. Two-thirds of the women grew up in farmworker households. Their ideas about good jobs and bad jobs are referenced to farm work. Their aspirations for their children are to avoid farm work at all costs. Farm work is central to their family and personal narratives, but their antipathy to it is palpable. It is perhaps counterintuitive to find that the current experience of many women continues to be shaped by farm work, but that is the case. Their husbands may be farmworkers. Their own employment may be related to providing social services to immigrant farmworkers. They may be providing physical care or economic support to parents who have been disabled by farm work.

This chapter is intended to provide a larger social context for the narratives that will follow in subsequent chapters. The purpose of this book is not only to illumine the lives of these daughters and granddaughters of farmworkers by sharing stories of their struggles, triumphs, and everyday experiences. The analytical strategy is also to view these stories on a larger canvas that includes the social structures that create the barriers, constraints, and opportunities that have shaped their lives. If farm work has cast a shadow on the experience of these women and their families, it is incumbent on us to examine the assumptions, understandings, and decisions that have created the institution they are contending with today. Thus the historical, political, and economic forces that have shaped the structure of agriculture and the organization of farm labor must be taken into account.

This chapter contextualizes several important public issues related to this research. It describes transformations in agriculture and provides historic perspective on governmental and nongovernmental actions affecting the status of farm laborers. It traces the relationship that has developed between agriculture, specifically California agriculture, and Mexican-origin workers. Further, it describes the situation of contemporary farmworkers and the propensity of most to shift into nonfarm employment as soon as possible.

U.S. agriculture today is utterly reliant on Mexican labor, with Mexican-born individuals constituting approximately 90 percent of U.S. farmworkers (Martin 2002). The current concentration of Mexican-origin individuals in farm work reflects the relationship between the structure of agriculture as it evolved in the twentieth century and the availability of a large pool of unskilled workers across the U.S. border with Mexico. Since the late nineteenth century, Mexicans have responded to labor shortages in the United States by crossing their northern border for work. Mexican workers have constituted a flexible, contingent labor force ready to meet the needs of U.S. employers, particularly in western agriculture. It is their availability for physically demanding, seasonal work that has cemented the relationship between Mexican workers and U.S. agriculture.

The reliance of U.S. agriculture on Mexican farmworkers has implications that extend far beyond today's farmworkers whose labor meets this industry's demand for cheap labor. Telles and Ortiz's important analysis of the continuing economic disadvantage of the Mexican-origin population over several generations comes down to one overarching cause. They write, "We argue that American capitalists' desire to quench its persistent thirst for cheap Mexican labor for over a century, which is supported by the American state and enabled by Mexico's proximity and its large labor supply, can largely account for the persistent low status and ethnic retention of Mexican Americans. For an entire century, inexpensive and easily disposable Mexican labor has filled the labor needs of Southwest agriculture as well as those of Southwest urban employers" (2008, 285–286). The essential point these authors make is that stereotypes of Mexicans as "cheap labor" who are appropriately consigned to society's "dirty work" stigmatize the entire group and create barriers to the economic integration of all Mexican Americans.

THE ORGANIZATION OF U.S. AGRICULTURE

While nostalgia for a landscape dotted by family farms remains, industrial agriculture is the dominant model for producing food and other agricultural commodities in the United States. Over the past century, farming has become a large-scale, capital-intensive enterprise that is increasingly corporate in nature (England and Brown 2003, 327). An important characteristic of industrial farming is reliance on nonowner farmworkers.[1]

The transition of American farming to an industrial model, sometimes called corporate or capitalist agriculture, has occurred unevenly. The subsistence model of family farm agriculture never really described the structure of agriculture in California. California agriculture was not developed by homesteaders growing their own food while also hoping to produce a surplus for sale. Instead, California farmers were entrepreneurs who produced agricultural products to make a profit by efficiently meeting market demands. Arguably, an industrial model has dominated California agriculture since statehood (Du Bry 2007, 4). In California, agribusiness—the production, processing, and distribution of farm products—has always been big business.

A key feature of agricultural labor is its seasonality. Over the course of the calendar year, farming is more labor-intensive at certain times than others. The seasonal nature of agricultural employment has always presented challenges to farmers. Throughout U.S. history, family farmers addressed this problem by diversification, usually by both growing crops and raising livestock. In the West, where large farms dominated, the response to seasonality was migrant and seasonal workers. This labor strategy met the needs of growers for large numbers of seasonal workers for short periods of time and held down production costs (Martin 2002, 1127). While reliance on seasonal and migrant workers suited employers' requirements, the characteristics of this employment are undesirable for workers.[2]

In California, marginalized newcomers without other prospects were willing to take temporary farmworker jobs at low wages. From the 1870s to the beginning of the Bracero Program in 1942, this included a succession of racial and ethnic groups. The Chinese were followed by Japanese immigrants, Indians and Pakistanis, Dust Bowl migrants [Anglos], and Mexicans (Martin 2002, 1128). From the bracero period to the present, growers have depended heavily on Mexican farm labor.

A general trend in U.S. agriculture is the use of technology to increase production and reduce the need for hand labor. California has been a significant exception to the trend of declining farm labor. The continuing availability of a Mexican workforce, willing to work for California growers at low wages, created incentives for relying on manual labor and disincentives for mechanizing labor processes (Taylor, Martin, and Fix 1997, 37).[3]

The nation's collective memory of farms as small-scale entrepreneurial enterprises continued past the Great Depression and contributed to the disinclination of Congress to include farmworkers in pending legislation to protect worker's interests. Farmworkers were written out of New Deal legislation that provided economic supports and worker protection for employees. Farmworkers were excluded from the Fair Labor Standards Act (1938), which established the minimum wage and set standards for overtime pay, the Social Security Act (1935), and the National Labor Relations Act (NLRA, 1935), which granted workers the right to organize and bargain collectively.[4]

One of the results of U.S. entry into World War II was a shortage of agricultural labor. White Dust Bowl refugees left migrant field work to join the military or moved to jobs in urban areas. While some Mexican-origin farmworkers remained on the scene, hundreds of thousands had been deported or repatriated during the Great Depression. Farmers were then successful in pushing for a contract guest worker program that would fill the gap and produce "food to win the war" (Martin 2002, 1128). This program, the Bracero Program of 1942, was intended as a wartime measure, but growers became dependent on Mexican workers and the program was renewed in various versions until 1964 (Camarillo 2007, 508).[5] Over this time period, 4.6 million labor contracts brought between 1 and 2 million Mexican workers to U.S. farms, the majority of which were in California.[6]

The consequences of the Bracero Program for agriculture continue to the present. First, this program established Mexican-origin workers as the default category for field labor in western agriculture. In addition to establishing patterns of remuneration, the presence of bracero workers shaped how farm work was done. American growers had contracted with a set of workers who would, on a seasonal basis, do the most physically demanding tasks in agricultural work for the lowest wages. When farm owners asked for the extension of the Bracero Program after World War II ended, their rationale was that domestic workers would not do the "stoop labor" the braceros regularly did (Carrasco 2005, 222). Other observers pointed out that domestic workers had better employment options, while Mexican laborers did not.

THE POST-BRACERO PERIOD

Despite the end of the Bracero Program in 1964, California agricultural workers continued to be predominantly people of Mexican origin. The end of the program set off a new wave of immigration, both documented and undocumented. Farmers were able to achieve some continuity in their work force by an immigration policy that permitted some ex-braceros to become legal immigrants. Growers retained the services of their most valued bracero workers by offering them continuing employment in the post-bracero period. A grower's written offer of employment almost guaranteed that former braceros would receive legal immigrant status (M. Wells 1996, 63). Thus, the number of legal Mexican immigrants with green cards certifying them to live and work in the United States increased markedly after 1964. This policy served the interests of farm owners and dramatically altered the status of one group of Mexican workers from temporary guest workers to legal permanent residents.

During the post-bracero period years of 1965 through 1980, three factors—higher wages, labor protections, and unionization—improved the employment situations of agricultural workers. New labor legislation, passed in the 1960s and

1970s, provided a number of provisions for farmworkers, thereby eliminating the earlier exclusion of farmworkers from most of the earlier worker protection legislation.[7] But by the 1980s the context was shifting. Major changes included a new political climate that supported growers' interests, reduced union effectiveness, and growing labor surpluses produced by a rising presence of undocumented Mexican workers (M. Wells 1996, 90).[8]

Concern over illegal immigration became an important public issue in the United States in the 1980s. Estimates of unauthorized Mexican immigrants rose from 2 million in 1980 to 3.1 million in 1986 (Hondagneu-Sotelo 1994, 24). At least 25 percent of California agriculture workers were thought to be illegal immigrants. In 1986, the U.S. Congress passed the Immigration Reform and Control Act (IRCA), legislation designed to stem the growth of illegal immigration by stringent border control and employer sanctions. The legislation also contained provisions to enable some unauthorized residents to regularize their immigration status and become permanent legal residents (De Genova 2005, 356).

Two key provisions of IRCA related specifically to farm labor: the Special Agricultural Worker (SAW) program and the H-2A certification program. Both were included as part of a political compromise ensuring that the agricultural lobby would support the bill. The SAW program provided a lenient plan for the legalization of current unauthorized farmworkers. It stipulated that undocumented workers who could prove they had done ninety days of farm labor in the prior year could become legal immigrants (Martin 2002, 1131). The U.S. Department of Agriculture had estimated the presence of approximately 350,000 undocumented farmworkers at this time, but 1.3 million illegal immigrants applied for SAW status. In examining the effects of IRCA, the Commission on Agricultural Workers concluded in 1992 that nearly all SAW-eligible workers gained legal status through this program, but that a vast group of ineligible workers used false documents to gain legal status. It concluded that the SAW program was "one of the most extensive immigration frauds ever perpetrated against the U.S. government" (quoted in Martin 2002, 1133). The H-2A program enables farmers to contract with foreign workers to perform seasonal or temporary agricultural work, but it is little utilized and heavily criticized by potential employers for excessive "red tape" (Valdes 2005, 150).[9]

A major goal of the agriculture-related provisions of IRCA was to stabilize and legalize the agricultural workforce. With aggressive border enforcement and penalties for employers hiring illegal workers, it was hoped that wages would rise and newly legalized Special Agricultural Workers (SAWs) would become a stable domestic agricultural work force. What occurred, however, was that most of the SAW program immigrants left farm labor. By 1998, only 15 percent of crop workers were SAWs, while an estimated 55 percent were undocumented workers (Martin 2002, 1133). As former-agricultural workers (now legal immigrants) took jobs outside the farm sector, they were quickly replaced by a new wave of Mexican undocumented workers. The policies and procedures instituted by IRCA did not substantially close the border or deter employers from hiring illegal workers.

Theoretically, but superficially, guest worker programs are attractive because they secure the labor of individuals who will not be permanently added to the population. In fact, the practice is far more complicated. One of the main legacies of the Bracero Program is the establishment of patterns of labor migration that have now extended across several generations of Mexican workers. In 1969, five years after the end of the Bracero Program, Cesar Chavez noted that the program "lives on in the annual parade of thousands" of documented and undocumented Mexican workers to U.S. farms (quoted in Carrasco 2005, 224). Forty years later, the pattern carries on as indigenous workers from Mexico's southern states continue to use the same routes established during the bracero period as they migrate to jobs on California farms (Maier 2006). In assessing the outcome of guest worker programs, J. Edward Taylor and his colleagues cite this aphorism: "[T]here is nothing more permanent than temporary workers" (1997, 91). The unintended consequences of guest worker programs are the settlement of supposedly temporary migrants and unauthorized migration.

Farm labor contractors play an increasing role in the agricultural labor market as more farmers rely on contractor services to recruit, supervise, transport, and pay workers.[10] The increasing use of labor contractors is disadvantageous for agricultural workers because farm labor contractors frequently reduce wages by hiring undocumented workers, a practice that is specifically prohibited by law but has been minimally enforced (Vaupel and Martin 1986). In general, farmworkers employed by labor contractors are paid less per hour and work fewer weeks annually than is the case for farmworkers hired directly by farmers (Martin 2009).

Contemporary Farmworkers

More than one in three U.S. farmworkers are employed in California. On an annual basis, this means that approximately 648,000 individuals work in California agriculture (Aguirre International 2005). This high demand for farm labor is explained by the unique structure of California agriculture, namely, the dominance of high-value labor-intensive crops such as strawberries, table grapes, almonds, and lettuce. To provide the specific context for understanding the circumstances of the farmworker families represented in this research and the agriculture-reliant community in which they live, this section focuses on California farmworkers rather than all U.S. farmworkers.

The National Agricultural Workers Survey (NAWS) has been the primary source of data on the demographic and employment characteristics of farmworkers (U.S. Department of Labor 2005).[11] NAWS data are based on interviews with farmworkers in crop agriculture.[12] The California agricultural work force is

Figure 5. Farmworkers taking a break in the fields, Brawley (*Credit:* Johno Wells)

almost entirely Hispanic (99 percent), with 91 percent born in Mexico, 5 percent U.S-born, and 4 percent born in Central American nations.

The labor market experience of farmworkers is shaped by their English-language proficiency and immigration status. Spanish is the language of farm labor; it is the primary language spoken by nearly all farmworkers. A majority of NAWS participants spoke no English and were not authorized to work in the United States.[13] California farmworkers have a median age of thirty-two and have typically completed six years of education, usually in Mexico. Two-thirds may be described as "settled," that is, they live in the locale where they do farm work. This reality contradicts a common perception among the American general public—that most Mexican-origin farmworkers are migrants who return home to Mexico after the harvest. Low earnings are typical in farm labor employment, reflecting both low hourly wages and the seasonality of farm employment. Between 2005 and 2008, average hourly wages for California field workers ranged from $8.60 to $9.85 (U.S. Department of Agriculture National Agricultural Statistics Service 2005, 2006, 2007, 2008). Only one farmworker in five has year-round employment.[14]

According to the NAWS, one in four farmworkers is a woman. Relatively little is known about women farmworkers because descriptive statistics about farmworkers are not usually disaggregated by sex. Therefore, knowledge about how gender shapes the farmworker experience is limited. In general terms, most of California's women farmworkers are immigrant Latinas (94 percent), a large majority of whom are married women (72 percent) who work in the fields to contribute to the economic support of their families. For immigrant women with little formal education and limited English proficiency, farm labor is frequently the only available employment.

The patterns of work and compensation described here translate into high poverty rates for farmworkers, with 18 percent of single workers and 24 percent of families below the poverty line. For many, living in poverty or near poverty means contending with poor living conditions, inadequate nutrition, food insecurity, and stress. Housing is an especially difficult problem (Holden 2001).

Agriculture is one of the most dangerous industries (U.S. Centers for Disease Control 2008). Farmworkers are at high risk for a number of occupational injuries and diseases, including traumatic injuries, musculoskeletal problems, respiratory disease, and skin conditions. Workplace accidents such as falls, cuts, and amputations are common in agriculture (Schenker 2004; Larson 2001). Musculoskeletal injuries are the most frequently reported health problem, with a high incidence of strains and sprains. Back and neck pain are common chronic problems. The ergonomic hazards of agriculture are the main factor putting farmworkers at risk for musculoskeletal disorders. Much of the manual labor in agricultural production is concentrated in tasks that expose workers to ergonomic risk factors. The three ergonomic hazards placing farmers at most severe risk are: "lifting and carrying heavy loads (over 50 lbs.); sustained or repeated full body bending (stoop); and very highly repetitive hand work (clipping, cutting)" (Chapman and Meyers 2001). Respiratory and skin problems result from a number of environmental factors, the most serious of which is exposure to pesticides and other chemicals (Larson 2001). While more than twenty thousand disabling injuries are reported in California agriculture yearly, the actual number is likely twice that high (Schenker 2004).

The intensification of California agriculture over several decades created the context of high demand for crop workers and is now responsible for reshaping patterns of work and remuneration in the industry. The vast majority of California crop workers are employed in specialty crop production.[15] Increased acreage in these crops has implications for the organization of farm labor. Not only do they require more labor, but labor requirements are spread out on more of a year-round basis, resulting in an extension of "peak season" employment for many crops (Villarejo 2006). The production of specialty crops has created permanent year-round jobs for an increasing segment of agricultural workers (Du Bry 2007). In addition, the restructuring of agriculture has created more diversification of jobs. These changes have created a "good jobs"–"bad jobs" typology in farm labor (Palerm 2002). Some former seasonal laborers have moved into higher-skilled, permanent positions such as machine operators, foremen, and mechanics at higher wages. Seasonal field labor remains a "bad job."[16] The movement of some Latinos into jobs formerly held only by Anglos demonstrates that (limited) social mobility is possible for Latinos who remain in agriculture (Du Bry 2007).

Farm Labor's Revolving Door

This chapter brings into clear view the historic and continuing relationship between California agriculture and Mexico-origin farmworkers. The availability of a large pool of Mexican workers has encouraged the development of labor-intensive farming practices. California agriculture currently depends on a low-wage, flexible workforce. The reliance of California agriculture on Mexican immigrant farm labor is fraught with dilemmas and contradictions. J. Edward Taylor, Philip Martin, and Michael Fix refer to a paradox in *Poverty amid Prosperity: Immigration and the Changing Face of Rural California* (1997). They point out that immigrants, mostly rural Mexicans, enter the United States to fill a farm labor void. But then, because seasonal farm work is physically difficult, low-paying, and unstable, they hope to move out of seasonal farm work as soon as possible. Some immigrant farmworkers never develop the English language skills that permit them to do so. Once they arrive in the United States, however, a number of programs and services facilitate the economic integration of farmworkers' families. Farmworkers' children seek employment outside of agriculture and most find it, thus creating a continuing cycle of demand for new waves of immigrant farmworkers.

The four largest and best-known federal programs in support of migrant and seasonal farmworkers and their families are Migrant Head Start, Migrant Education, Migrant Health, and National Farmworker Jobs Program (NFJP). The total federal expenditure for programs assisting migrant farmworkers and their children is almost one billion dollars annually (Martin 2009). These programs were begun during the War on Poverty in the 1960s. At that time, mechanization was expected to reduce the agricultural work force. These programs were instituted, in part, so farmworkers could gain the skills they would need for other jobs as farm employment declined (Taylor, Martin, and Fix 1997). Although the mechanization of western agriculture did not occur as anticipated, these programs have promoted the social integration of immigrant children, facilitating their move into nonfarm jobs. The irony is that as immigrants and their children exit farm labor's revolving door, they are replaced by new immigrants who enter the United States to fill the labor void, and the cycle continues.

The seasonality of agricultural employment is arguably the reason workers are most eager to leave this work. Just one in five farmworkers has year-round, full-time employment. Agricultural economist Philip Martin examined seasonal employment in California agriculture by examining state wage and employment records.[17] He found that almost three agricultural workers share what is the equivalent of one full-time job. This means that farmworkers averaged 4.3 months of farm work annually (Martin 2009, 114). The difficulties inherent in relying on farm labor for supporting a family are obvious and the incentives to find alternative employment are great. It is unsurprising, then, that Martin also found a low rate of worker retention in farm labor jobs. Only 40 percent of farmworkers were retained over a five-year period statewide, meaning that only four of ten individuals with earnings in agriculture at one point in time also had agricultural earnings five years later.

To pursue this line of thinking, one might say that this book explores the degree to which these second and third generation Mexican American women and members of their families have exited the revolving door of farm labor. In the pages that follow, women express their antipathy for farm work. They view the work as physically grueling and economically exploitative. They present farm labor as everyone's last choice for employment. As they see it, everyone would like to leave this work behind. These daughters and granddaughters of farmworkers want something better for themselves, their partners, and, most emphatically, for their children.

The structure of U.S. agriculture and the organization of farm labor have implications extending far beyond this analysis of Mexican American women and their families. At present, three of four farm laborers in the United States were born in Mexico, as were nine of ten California farmworkers. There is every reason to believe that farm labor's revolving door will continue to operate. Today's immigrant farmworkers are no more interested in continuing in agricultural work than were those of previous generations. Neither are they more inclined to recruit their children into farm labor. The working conditions and patterns of remuneration associated with farm labor render any hopes of a stable domestic agricultural workforce to be unrealistic at this time. Immigrant farmworkers and their children who successfully exit farm labor will need to be replaced. By all accounts, it is reasonable to conclude that the next generation of U.S. farmworkers is growing up across our southwestern border in Mexico and other parts of Latin America. Given the disparity in standards of living between the U.S. and Mexico, it is realistic to expect that Mexican workers will continue to be interested in jobs on U.S. farms. On the U.S. side, growers will continue to assert that Mexican workers are necessary to sustain their operations.

CHAPTER 2

FARMWORKER ORIGINS

A farmworker past is a deeply held aspect of the identity of the women who participated in this research. For most, the past is very much present in their lives. This chapter considers the family stories and prior experiences that have shaped the sense of who these women are and where they came from, as well as their perspectives on farm work. As adult women, the personal and family lives they have created have to some extent been constructed in the context of farm work. Although they were born in the United States, the women were aware of their families' immigration experiences and ready to talk about them. These immigration stories almost always were related to farm labor. And answers to family history questions usually went back to their parents' and grandparents' experiences in farm labor. Moving forward in time, it was clear that farm work had set, at least partially, the parameters for the childhood experiences of most women.

The chapter begins with family immigration narratives told by some of the Imperial County women and the farm work–related memories surrounding these stories.[1] The focus then shifts to the experiences and perspectives of the interviewees themselves. The work that women referred to as "farm labor" took a variety of forms and included much more than field work. For example, Ana Ramirez's father worked in the same feedlot for more than thirty years. Celia Roberts' father worked year-round doing welding and other maintenance for a large farming operation while her mother picked tomatoes, cantaloupe, and lettuce locally. The mothers of Claudia Gomez and Theresa Romero packed carrots. Others had tractor jobs, forklift operator jobs, irrigation-related jobs, hay-baling jobs, and more.

The stories many women tell are variations on a gendered pattern of immigration in which men initiated the couple's or family's migration by going ahead to the United States. Eventually, when they have established employment and found appropriate housing, their wives and children join them (Pyke 2004). In these narratives, gender is paramount, with men usually presented as the principal actors, strategizing to fulfill their responsibilities for the economic support of their families. Many of the migration stories told to me harked back to the Bracero Program, which did not permit families to accompany migrant farmworkers. Frequently, entire families moved from Mexico's interior to border areas such as Mexicali where women and children awaited the return of bracero husbands and fathers. These moves often brought hardship to families who were usually impoverished, because a home in Mexicali might entail living in a shantytown or camp (Palerm 2002, 264). Several families represented in my sample migrated to the U.S. in two stages. The first stage brought them from central Mexico to Mexicali, the large metropolitan area in Mexico just across the border from Calexico in Imperial County. From here, they worked in agriculture in either northern Mexico or in the United States. A second stage brought them from Mexicali to a permanent home in Imperial County.[2]

An important storyline in my interviews is that a large majority of the mothers of women I interviewed were currently or had been farmworkers. Twenty-five of thirty-eight research participants had mothers who worked in farm labor. Six others had grandmothers in farm labor. Finding that most of the Imperial County women had a mother or grandmother in farm labor is quite surprising, given the invisibility of women in the farmworker literature.

Although nearly all bracero contracts went to men, the migration of Mexican women to the United States increased significantly with immigration reform in 1965.[3] Many of these women took jobs in agriculture. Women farmworkers generally faced a double day in which they did field work by day and then took full responsibility for children and the home at night (M. Wells 1996).

A rare portrait of farmworker women in Imperial County is provided by a classic study by the California Commission on the Status of Women (Barton 1978). This research, the first to analyze the social, economic, and employment characteristics of California's women field workers, surveyed women farmworkers in Imperial and Fresno counties. It is of special interest to my research because it was undertaken at a time when many mothers of the women I interviewed would have been working in the fields as young women. In the mid-1970s, nearly all Imperial County women farmworkers were women of Mexican origin. Two-thirds were married and more than half had a permanent residence in Imperial County. Nearly three-quarters were citizens or had a green card. Most women worked a variety of crops for a large number of employers, with three-quarters working for six or more employers a year, and lettuce providing the most weeks of employment. Most of their families had been involved in agricultural labor for several generations. This study indicates that women farmworkers of this time were a fairly settled and stable population (as compared to transient) and were more likely to be documented than were men farmworkers (Barton 1978).

IMMIGRATION STORIES AND FARMWORK

In all cases, the families represented in my research were economic migrants, that is to say, they came to the United States to work. Crossing the Mexico–United States border for farm labor constituted an economic survival strategy to provide for individuals and families. The narratives presented in this section are arranged in a kind of chronological order. I begin with stories my research participants shared about their grandparents and their migration-related decisions and activities. In some of these stories, one of the women's parents had been a child when the family immigrated to the United States. For these women, immigration happened further back in the family's history. Next I present stories that center on the immigration decisions and activities of the women's parents. In this instance, the parents had come to the United States as teenagers or adults and had, to some degree, initiated their own U.S. farmworker experience. They were, at least in part, economic actors in the stories that unfolded. For the women who told these stories, immigration had occurred more recently in the family's history.

Many women told immigration stories related to their grandparents' decisions to cross the Mexican border for farm work in the United States. Monica Rodriguez, a second-generation Mexican American teacher, explains that her maternal grandfather was chief of police in his town in Mexico. This job did not pay enough for him to support his family of ten children, so he supplemented his income with migrant farm work. He left his job for extended periods of time to work as a bracero, packing carrots in the Imperial Valley or working as a cook in a bracero camp and then returning to Mexico. He sometimes experienced danger in the line of duty in his job in law enforcement. As Monica says, "He used to chase the bandits when they stole the cows. He made some enemies. And they were trying to run over one of my uncles with a car. So that's when he decided it was time to bring the family to the United States." He then initiated a plan to eventually achieve that goal. The family first moved from the interior of Mexico to Mexicali. He then worked as a bracero and completed the necessary paperwork to bring the family to the United States. He and his family immigrated legally in 1962 and settled in Brawley. Her mother, who was ten years old when the family immigrated, has lived in the same neighborhood in Brawley for more than forty years. Monica's grandparents remained migrant farmworkers after moving to the United States.

Several women described a migration and settlement pattern in which Mexican migrant farmworkers eventually made a home in the United States. From permanent homes in the Imperial Valley, they continued to be migrant farmworkers, typically traveling to California's Central Valley to provide harvest-related labor in the summer and fall. The experience of Marjorie Salas, a mother of three and a teacher, provides an example of this pattern.

Marjorie's Mexican grandparents were migrant farmworkers, as were her parents. Her maternal grandmother had an extensive record of farm labor, beginning work in the fields as an eight-year-old child. Marjorie remembers her grandmother talking about carrying long bags to fill up with cotton and "how it would scrape their fingers." By the time Marjorie's mother was a child, her parents had left Mexico and settled in Brawley. From there, they followed the crops seasonally. Traveling north was hard on her mother as a "migrant student." The designation of "migrant student" is used to describe the children of farmworkers who migrate from school to school as their parents migrate from community to community to do field work. She was a very shy girl who had difficulty adapting to attending many different schools every year. She was afraid to talk in school, especially in school settings with many Portuguese students (also children of farmworkers), because, as Marjorie says, being around another culture was stressful. When she was not in school, she would sit in the camp alone all day while her parents worked in the fields. Marjorie described her mother's experience with sadness in her voice, clearly empathetic toward the child who had difficulty coping with the unsettled nature of migrant life and the loneliness she experienced along the way.

Christina Gilbert, a mother of two and the manager of a small retail store, provides another example of migrant farmworker grandparents who eventually settled in the Imperial Valley. Christina's grandfather was the first in her family to come to the United States as a migrant farm laborer. Christina's mother was born in Guadalajara, Mexico. Soon thereafter, the family moved to Mexicali, where they lived when they were not following the crops on the U.S. side of the border. Over the course of these cycles of labor migration, "they ended up stopping here [settling permanently in Brawley]." As Christina describes it, when her mother was thirteen or fourteen, her grandfather "immigrated her." Her parents live in Brawley, as do a number of other family members, including aunts, uncles, and cousins.

Elena Sanchez's family narrative is essentially a courtship story. Elena is a married mother of three who grew up in a farmworker family in Fresno, California. Both of her parents grew up in migrant farmworker families whose permanent homes were in Mexico. Her mother and father initially met as young teenagers at a dance for teen children of migrant workers in Fresno. Their families went their separate ways shortly thereafter, but a few years later, and again in a cycle of labor migration, both families returned to Fresno. Elena describes what happened: "My mom was packing figs when my dad bumped into her again. He thought he would never see her again. There was a packing company a few minutes from where my mom and my dad live now. That's where my mom was working and they had hired my dad as a fork lifter. And when he saw her, he said, 'I couldn't believe it was your mother.'" These teens, now seventeen years old, returned to Mexico with their respective families at the end of the migrant labor season but stayed in contact with each other. When they were twenty-one, they were married in Mexico. They soon returned to Fresno and began building a life in the United States. Both of them worked in agriculture-related jobs until their recent retirements.

Contemporary migration is complicated by the transnationalism and circular migration that characterize the experience of recent generations of migrants. Some second-generation Mexican Americans may actually have spent their childhood years growing up in Mexico (Foner and Kasinitz 2002, 271). A careful look at the biographies of Elena's parents reveals the complexity inherent both in describing the farmworker experience and in categorizing Mexican Americans by generational status, that is, as first generation or second generation. I use common criteria for attributing immigrant generation status. I consider the first generation to be composed of foreign-born individuals (the immigrant generation), the second generation to be composed of U.S.-born individuals with at least one foreign-born parent, and the third generation to be composed of U.S.-born individuals with two U.S-born parents (González 2002, 7). Both Elena's mother and father were born in California, one in Indio and the other in Merced. Both were born to Mexican migrant farmworker families who were in California working seasonally in U.S. agriculture. So, one would categorize these individuals as second generation Mexican Americans because they are U.S-born children of foreign-born parents. But, at the end of the harvest season, both families returned to Mexico. The parents of these infants were not immigrants. The question of generational status is more than merely methodologically interesting. Certain assumptions regarding common experiences by cohort, for example, that second-generation individuals will have attended school in the United States and will have achieved English language proficiency, may in some circumstances be unwarranted.

My purpose here is to recognize that the organization of migrant farm work sometimes turned conventional categories upside-down. A woman's pregnancy did not change the reality that for many Mexican households, migrant farm labor was determined to be the best option available for supporting one's family. When the crops were harvested, packed, and shipped, many families returned to Mexico with a new U.S.-born baby.

What is noteworthy is the frequency with which I encountered this situation. Many interviewees' parents were indeed U.S.-born children of migrant parents whose permanent home was in Mexico. It is also significant that these children relocated permanently in the United States. The pattern of eventual settlement is consistent with research showing that with the passage of time, there is a tendency for migrants to develop stronger ties to the host country and eventually settle permanently in that country (Massey and Liang 1989).

Several women related sad or bitter experiences in their parents' lives. The parents of Francesca Alvarez met and married in Mexico and came to the United States as a young farmworker couple. Francesca begins to cry as she tells me about the hard life her mother, Estella, had growing up in Mexico. Estella has only a first-grade education. She was the second oldest child and the only girl. Francesca explains that her grandmother wanted Estella to stay home and help her with the housework. Francesca's overarching childhood memory is that her farmworker parents were always working. A few years ago her father was hired at the Mesquite mine, a gold mine in Imperial County, and Estella got a job in a plastics factory. For both, these jobs represented a step up from farm labor and have provided them with a measure of economic stability.

Claudia Gomez's parents immigrated to the United States as ten- and eleven-year-old children in farmworker families. Claudia says her mother "had no education, really," but her father was very intelligent and wanted to graduate from high school. What happened, however, was that her father was a high school student and "he was going to graduate, but my grandfather made them leave school. He took all of his kids out of high school even if they were about to graduate and made them work. So they could get their house paid." Without a high school diploma, Claudia's father followed in his father's footsteps and became a farmworker, although he later got a job in construction. Claudia is very critical of her grandfather's parenting and draws a comparison to parenting decisions she might make. She says, "Like I need money and my son is twelve years old—I'm going to send him to sell newspapers or mow somebody's lawn? No way. Their job is to go to school and that's what I tell them. The only job you have right now is to go to school."

Rosa Navarra, who works in border security, tells the story of her father's parents. For some years, this family, migrant Mexican farmworkers with nine children, had no fixed address. She says, "They didn't have a home. They were like the gypsies. They were always moving. They had a vehicle . . . and my dad says that sometimes his dad had to go and sell it just to feed [his children]. Neither my father nor any of his brothers or sisters ever went to school. They always had to work in order for them to support the whole family." Rosa describes a family experiencing deprivation and living a marginal existence, showering outside or "looking for some water, somewhere." Her father was a U.S. citizen, born in Texas while the family worked in agriculture there.

Cynthia Mateo is a mother of one who worked the service desk at a retail store in Calexico. She related the experiences of her mother's family, who came from Mexico to do field work. Her grandfather did agricultural work and also worked in the copper mines; her grandmother "did cotton." She focuses on the positive aspects of her mother's childhood experience, saying, "My mom told me stories about the cotton fields—they were all high and the kids used to get lost in them. The stories she would tell me! She was the youngest."

I continue with immigrant stories, but those that follow are a bit different than what has gone before. The previous stories followed from the immigration decisions of the grandparents of the Imperial County women. The next stories follow from the immigration decisions of their parents. The parents of many of the Imperial County women came to the United States as teens or young adults. These individuals had, at least to some extent, initiated their own farmworker experience in the United States. The recentness of the immigrant experience shaped the consciousness and experience of these participants and, in many cases, made their stories more personal.

Esther Valdez has six children and works as a cashier at Walmart. Esther was born in the United States to a thirteen-year-old mother and a fifteen-year-old father. Both of these young people crossed the U.S.-Mexico border to be farmworkers. The first family member of Esther's family to come to the United States was her paternal grandfather, who came as a bracero and served as a cook at a migrant labor camp in Arizona. When Esther's father, Hector, turned thirteen, he joined his father at the bracero camp. On one of Hector's return trips from Mexico he brought his young girlfriend, Consuela, with him. Consuela soon became pregnant. Esther is sympathetic about her mother's circumstances. She says, "She didn't even know she was pregnant until she was six months pregnant. Because nobody taught her about birth control and how she was going to get pregnant. Those things that my grandmother was supposed to say were never told; they were a secret." At that time sex and reproduction were taboo subjects and were seldom discussed. The attitude was, "Hide it. There was something shameful [about sex] at those times." Hector and Consuela continued in farm work from their teenage years to when they were about fifty. Their farm labor–related disabilities have made it impossible for them to continue working.

Erica Martinez has a clerical job with the county and has three children. Her father, Sergio, first came to the United States as a farm laborer at age fifteen, when he accompanied all the men in his family who together left their village in central Mexico to cross the border for agricultural work. Sometime later, his entire family moved to Mexicali. From Mexicali, they continued their cycles of labor migration, working in U.S. agriculture. In Mexicali, Sergio met and married Erica's mother, Guadalupe. Soon thereafter, the couple moved across the border to Calexico, and continued to work in farm labor from the U.S. side of the border.

Several women described a gendered pattern of immigration in which men initiated the couple's or family's migration by going ahead to the United States and finding employment and housing for the family. For example, Celia Roberts's parents came to the United States as young married adults. Her father initially came alone and found a job maintaining the farm equipment of a large Imperial Valley grower. Once he had secured employment, his wife joined him and began doing field labor, picking tomatoes, cantaloupe, and lettuce. In a slight variation on this scenario, Angelica Perez related that her father began coming to the United States for seasonal farm work as a young teen. Her parents married in Mexico and a couple of children were born there while her father continued his cycles of labor migration. Then her mother and the children came to live in the

United States, where additional children were born. As Angelica says, "He came first, and then he brought her in."

The women I interviewed did not generally say whether their immigrant parents or grandparents had legally immigrated to the United States. They typically described their family immigration experience as straightforward and apparently free of trouble with immigration authorities. The experience of Ana Ramirez was different. Ana spoke at length about the details of her family's immigration because they had affected her so deeply. For many years her parents had lived in Mexicali and her father, Julian, crossed the border daily to work in a feed-lot in Holtville. At some point, Julian, his wife, Maria, and their two children established their home in Brawley. A few years later, it came to the attention of immigration authorities that Julian was working and living in the United States legally, but Maria and their Mexico-born children were in the country illegally. To resolve the issue, Maria and the children were required to return to Mexico while Julian stayed in the United States and initiated the immigration process for his wife and children. Ana explains, "They said, 'You can't live in the U.S. and do the [immigration] process.'" So Maria, now pregnant with her fifth child, returned to Mexicali with all of the children, including U.S.-born Ana. Ana describes this as a "fearful" time for her mother and a "traumatic" time for the children. Her mother, pregnant and alone with four children, was afraid. Ana describes the experience of living in a small house with no furniture in Mexicali. She says, "That's when we really [said with great emphasis] struggled." A year later, with immigration matters resolved, the family settled permanently in Brawley.

Priscilla Ortega, a vocational education instructor for the county and mother of two, told an immigration story centered on women's decisions to become farm labor migrants. At age sixteen, Priscilla's mother, along with her three sisters, began coming to the United States to work in seasonal agriculture. They returned to Mexico to live with their mother between seasons. All four sisters are now married and live in the United States. As the vignettes highlighted in this chapter show, and others would confirm, migrant teens or young adults frequently found their future husbands or wives in the fields and migrant camps where they temporarily worked and lived.

Growing Up in a Farmworker Household

Most women drew from their own experiences when discussing farm labor. Two-thirds of research participants grew up in farmworker households. Most of these women did not, however, grow up following the crops, as did many of their own parents. That is, they did not live in migrant farmworker households in which the entire family traveled for parents' field work. What explains this change? Typically the work of farmworker fathers was organized in one of two ways. Either men had moved into year-round jobs with local growers, or they did seasonal farmwork locally from around December through March, then did migrant work during the summer and early fall. In the first case, farmworker fathers benefited from an increase in year-round, full-time jobs in California agriculture; these jobs were almost always held by men. In the second case, men followed the crops while mothers remained home with children. Most mothers did farm work, but they did only local, seasonal work and were also able to draw modest unemployment benefits the rest of the year. A few women worked the grapes in Indio, but they commuted daily to this work. Other reasons for the change were child labor laws that kept children out of the fields and strong views that the migrant experience was detrimental to children's education and social development. The result of this change is that these children had much more settled lives than did the previous generation of farmworkers' children. The movement of families out of the follow-the-crop migrant workforce represented an important and positive change in children's lives; however, in some cases fathers were absent for extended periods of time.

The fathers of both Patricia Ochoa and Julie Peña owned their own trucks and hauled hay and sometimes cotton; this work is seasonal, with approximately three months of unemployment annually even if the driver is willing to follow the crops. Patricia Ochoa, at age forty-nine, was the oldest woman I interviewed. She was the mother of five and working in food service when we met. She was a child as the bracero period was ending and described her childhood years as "hard times." At this point, her mother was supplementing her father's irregular earnings from hauling hay by making homemade lunches to sell to the braceros. Patricia says, "She'd get up in the wee hours of the morning. Back then, the Mexican women made tortillas from scratch, you know. They'd stop by and they'd pick up a lunch, pay for it and go on their way. She had regular customers, but she would always make a few extra lunches because through word of mouth, she would have additional people stop by. Regardless of how many lunches she made, she would run out."

Several women grew up in Imperial County with parents who generally did local field work. Denise Ortiz, a married mother of one who is presently unemployed, is one of them. Denise's parents, Victor and Isabel, were farmworkers who usually worked locally. She says, "They picked the lettuce, tomatoes, the grapes, broccoli, asparagus. My mom used to go in and package, like lettuce, like salads. Yeah, for sure, my mom did the onions. Sorting them and stuff." All of these crops, with the exception of grapes, were harvested locally. Vans or buses would transport them and other farmworkers to Coachella, an hour away in Riverside County, to pick grapes, but they would return home at night. Denise and her siblings would stay with their aunts or their grandmother would stay with them while the parents worked. The downside of not traveling with the crops is extended periods of unemployment. Isabel continues in farm work. She is one of the "regulars" for a company that harvests onions. She sorts onions in a packing

Figure 6. A truckload of lettuce, ready for processing (*Credit:* Johno Wells)

shed in Calipatria, ten miles north of Brawley. In recent years, financial circumstances pushed her into following the crops. Denise says, "And usually, for the past five years, they would go up north to Lancaster during the summer. For the onions too. She would follow the company. But not no more. The person she lives with, now he has a full-time job all year-round. So she's going to stay home [and only work the onions locally]."

The farmworker mothers of the women I interviewed frequently worked with their husbands in farm labor or, in some cases, remained in it after men left it for other work. Theresa Romero's mother has a long work history in farm labor. She is currently a seasonal worker for the carrot crop. She earns minimum wage working in a local packing shed, usually from January through May. Theresa's father left farm labor for construction and then took the civil service exam, which resulted in his moving into a federal job. He has one of the better jobs among research participants' parents. Theresa's mother remains in farm work, in part because she speaks no English. In fact, Theresa has never heard her say a word of English. Her seasonal employment provides an adequate supplementary income to her husband's stable earnings.

Migrant farmworker fathers were sometimes absent for extended periods of time. Erica Martinez grew up in a household in which her father, Sergio, was away from home for a majority of the year as he followed the crops. The crops he worked were lettuce, tomatoes, corn, broccoli, and okra. The children remained at home with their mother in Calexico. Erica explains, "He was here probably from November, or maybe early December, up until March and the rest of the time he was gone. In early March, already he was gone." I asked Erica if Sergio was ever able to get a job with one of the local growers who keep workers on the job full-time and year-round. She responded, "No. Only with the companies that were 'come and go, come and go, come and go.'"

While most women did not grow up with the migrant farmworker experience, a few did. Miranda Flores, age forty-three, is one of fifteen children born to migrant farmworker parents who after several years of itinerant farm work, settled into a permanent home in Brawley. The birthplaces of several of the elder children—Texas, Arizona, and California's Central Valley—reflect the family's path of travel in seeking agricultural employment. The younger children in the family were born in Imperial County. The family continued to be migrant farmworkers in the summers. Miranda Flores says of her experience, "When we got out of school—as Mexicans, I don't know if we still do that so much—but, when I was growing up, our parents would take us to Bakersfield to help work in the seasonal, which is in the peaches and the oranges. And we sent money back for the rent and what have you. We lived in a government camp, you know."

The most extensive experience with cycles of labor migration involved Lucia Hernandez. Her parents had a home in Brawley but spent less than half the year there. The family's regular pattern was to travel from Brawley to Visalia in the summer to pick various fruits, then to Oxnard in the fall to pick tomatoes, to Oceanside in the winter to pick more tomatoes, and finally back to Brawley in the spring to work the broccoli and cauliflower. Lucia was a migrant student. She attended several schools throughout the year, starting school in Oxnard, then attending another in Oceanside, and finishing the school year in Brawley. She attended summer school in Visalia. Agricultural work has defined this family's life. Lucia's parents worked as farm laborers until they were no longer able to work. Lucia herself has farm labor experience, and her husband Romano has worked in a variety farm labor positions.

Women's Early Experience in Farm Labor

Some women's first job experiences were as farmworkers. Sometimes they joined their parents in this work. Carmen Silva is now a clerical worker for the county, but as a teen she regularly worked in farm labor. Carmen's parents have always been agricultural workers. Beginning at age fifteen, she joined them in the fields in Brawley whenever her school schedule permitted. She explains that she needed to be fifteen to get a work permit for doing field labor.

Two women grew up in farmworker families in Fresno County, California. Rosa Navarra talks about working in the fields from a very young age. She reminisces, "We were kids; we were about in kindergarten or first grade. I guess you could call it work because we would pick grapes and we would bring in the paper [used to pack grapes]. Our dad or mom would say, 'Go over there and get me so and so paper.' And we're little; we can only carry so much. But we would help. And my mom didn't really want to leave us alone, you know. So she would take us." Over the course of their school years, she and her siblings helped their parents in the fields. She says, "I don't know if it was legal back then, but we would go. Of course, we would never miss school." She describes picking walnuts, chilies, onions, garlic, pruning and picking grapes, and working the tomatoes.

Elena Sanchez's teenage years were defined by farm labor. She began by working with her mother cooking at a migrant labor camp that housed two hundred men. She explains:

> I was fourteen years old. My mom told me one day, she goes, "You're old enough to understand what hard work is. And I need you to get up at 2:00 in the morning to help me cook for the workers." We cooked for them—breakfast, lunch and dinner. They had to leave at 5:15 to start work at 6:00. I got up at 2:00 and helped make breakfast and lunch and then went to school. I would come home by 3:30. [My mother] would be cooking dinner by then. She would give me a couple of hours to do my homework at the kitchen table. And as soon as my homework is done, I'm back to work with her.

From age fifteen to age nineteen, Elena was a farmworker on the large ranch where her father was a manager. She says, "Every season, whatever it was, I was there. I was doing whatever they tossed my way." She eventually managed her own crew of migrant farmworkers. As a crew leader who was both young and a woman, Elena was doubly challenged. Her crews were made up of both men and women, but she had an easier time supervising the women. She says, "My communication with them was easier. Me and them, we both did the same work. We looked at each other equally. Men, there were some that wouldn't work because I was a female: 'You don't belong here, you belong at home,' that sort of thing." Eventually, the difficult gender dynamics on the crew would be resolved, although that sometimes meant that men who would not listen to her were fired. Elena explains, "After a while, my crew got really tight. We respected each other. We helped each other. . . . I had my routine. Get up at 4:00 in the morning, get my water ready, get my truck warmed up. Make sure I have my crew together— who was sick, who was not sick. I was lenient when they didn't have money to go to the doctor. 'Hey, you guys are sick. If you guys are sick, fine. If you have a hangover, you're in trouble.'"

Miranda Flores describes working as a day laborer in agriculture to earn money for clothing and other necessities. For her, earning her own money and having the opportunity to spend it on personal items for herself was a source of pride. It provided her with a small measure of personal autonomy. She says, "I came from a fifteen-kid family. I was going to junior high—seventh, eighth grade. At that time—they don't have it now—I used to come and would pick up the buses by La Providenca, you know, the big supermarket right here. We would get paid the same day. I think it was twenty-six dollars, but they give us twenty-three dollars, because they keep the three dollars for gas. So here I was, proud, coming home with twenty-three dollars for me to buy myself something to wear that night if my parents let me go out, you know."

PERSPECTIVES ON FARM WORK

Women's general perspective is that farm labor is the work of last resort. People who do farm labor cannot—for whatever reason—get a nonfarm job. Lack of English proficiency and low educational attainment are the most frequent explanations research participants gave for an individual's employment in farm labor. Farm labor is recognized as being hard on family life, physically debilitating, and providing inadequate compensation.[4]

Christina Gilbert provides an example from her own family experience. When she was ten years old, her father became legally blind and could no longer work. She says, "When my dad got sick we went through some years where, wow, we didn't have food or clothes. It was really hard. And then my mom went to work. Because she didn't speak English, she couldn't get a job. Not even in a kitchen, nothing. So she went back to work in the grapes, in the fields. She used to have to travel to Indio every day. They would get up at three in the morning." This work was especially difficult for her mother, Lola, because she went back to it at age fifty. Although it was very hard on her physically, she stayed with farm labor until she was sixty-eight. Christina says that her mother, a Mexican immigrant, still does not speak English, but she understands it. Christina does not believe her mother ever went to school. When Lola was seven, her mother died; her father remarried, had another child, and then the second wife died, leaving a six-month-old baby. This left Lola to take care of her younger sisters and a six-month-old half-sister. Christina says, "You know, it sounds unbelievable, but in Mexico, it happened all the time."

Denise Ortiz recognizes that thirty years of farm labor have taken a toll on her mother's health. Early on, there were no physical problems. But now, looking at her mother—just forty-nine years old—she says, "But now, I see my mom, that her hands hurt. And she has weakness—I think, I tell her, it's probably arthritis. And then she has something going on with her feet. Corns—so much water, junk. Other than that, kind of healthy, but she's a little bit overweight. And she needs to lose the weight. This year she just worked the onion shed which is up in Calipat [Calipatria]—like the sorting thing."

Esther Valdez, like Christina, explains her parents' thirty-five years in farm labor by saying that neither Hector nor Consuela had any education at all, and neither speaks English. She says, "My parents weren't welfare people. Both of them were hard workers. Both of them have bad backs from the bending, the bending, and the bending. And the picking up because they have to carry what they have to work with." Her parents also have severe arthritis, neck injuries, and problems with their knees and feet. Esther describes how the labor process in working the grapes contributed to the injuries they have today: "When they were working in grapes, the ground is very loose because they need the moisture for the grapes. But then they have to carry those boxes [of picked grapes], from way on the end all the way to the edge [where the truck is located]. They don't have to pack it, but they have to carry it. And they're like little mules. Back and forth. And picking up and putting down. And picking up and putting down. Picking up and putting down. That hurts their backs and necks." Esther demonstrates for me the position farmworkers take when they are picking grapes and shows me the place where her parents' neck pain is located. Now in their early fifties, Hector and Consuela are no longer able to work.

Erica Martinez makes the point that her father's extended absences following the crops for most of the year were difficult for everyone in the household. Her mother was largely responsible for raising the children alone. Many years of field work have taken a toll on Sergio's body and have cut short his work life. Erica says, "The lettuce is a back-killer. He struggled for two or three years to get on SSI. His back was bad; his knees were bad; his feet were bad. He's only been getting it for about two years. He was born in 1949, so he is fifty-six now."

One of the most frequently stated negative aspects of farm work is low wages. Most farmworkers earned $6.75 an hour, California's minimum wage at the time of this research. Experienced field workers earned no more than inexperienced ones. Family members of experienced agricultural workers deeply resent the flat structure of compensation for this work. Among farmworkers, the best jobs were seen to be those working as year-round, full-time regular employees for a grower. These workers earned between $7.00 an hour and $8.00 an hour; some employers provided health benefits (for workers, but not for their families). Among farmworkers, an $8.00 an hour job driving a tractor for a farmer is perceived to be a good job, with steadier employment, higher pay, and less physically demanding work than most farm labor jobs. These workers still do not earn enough to adequately support their families; some do have access to overtime, although this is not generally paid at time-and-a-half. The economic circumstances of seasonal farmworkers are more precarious because of the irregular and uncertain nature of the work.

Julie Peña's father used to own a truck for hauling hay. It was what the men in his family did. Her uncles and her dad grew up hauling hay, and her brother had his own hay hauling business for a while. Her father is now a hay loader, working to load the trucks of a larger operator. While hay hauling may appear to be an attractive entrepreneurial niche in agriculture, Julie sees its limitations:

At one point my husband said, "I'm going to drive a truck [and haul hay]." I said, "No you're not." It is seasonal. It slows down and that's when you say, "I've got to do some other things on the side." It is a hard way to earn a living and what are the results, as you get older? I see that on my uncles now. I see that, that they are so hard working, and as they get older, you know, for whatever reason, their health or whatever, who is going to pay for all this stuff, you know what I mean? In the long run this work is not that profitable. It might be good in the time being, but in the long run, no. Not unless you are working for a good company and he [the boss] is providing the benefits for you and what not.

Research participants perceive that farmworkers from Mexico keep wages for local workers low. Many point out that the location of the county on the Mexican border allows day laborers from Mexicali to work on this side of the border and spend their earnings on "the other side." They believe that $6.75 an hour can support a comfortable standard of living in Mexico. The daily minimum wage in Mexico at the time of this research was equivalent to $4.29 U.S. (California Center for Border and Regional Economic Studies 2005).

Monica Rodriguez's account of the circumstances of her father-in-law, a Mexican immigrant who came to the United States thirty years ago, captures perceptions of the most problematic characteristics of farm labor. She says:

He's been working in the fields this entire time, say thirty years. And he only gets paid seven dollars an hour. And he has no education. I just think, he was out there in the summer, at 120 degrees, and never complained about it. Never put up a fight, nothing, because he knew he needed to take care of his family. But he's been there thirty years with that shovel and he still gets paid seven dollars an hour. And that's because the minimum wage has gone up, not that he worked his way up from a lower wage. He has no health care. No health insurance. When he is too old to work, I just wonder what he's going to do. He doesn't have any retirement.

In short, Monica and others conclude that farm labor is a physically grueling, dead-end job that will leave you, after thirty years of employment, broken-down physically and financially insecure.

These women know too much about the undesirable working conditions and the physical effects of farm labor to be sentimental about it. At the same time, they respect the individuals, like Monica's father-in-law, who are willing to do this work to support their families. Gloria Espinosa is a twenty-four-year-old mother of a three-year-old son who did not grow up in a farmworker household but interacted with many field workers in her job in a grocery store that primarily served farmworkers. She refers to the perspective of her mother, a Mexican immigrant, in talking about farmworkers:

I'm not into all that political stuff about illegal immigration. All I know is that these people come here to work. They're not here to commit any crimes, but, sure there's always the bad people in every group. But they're here to work. They're not here to disturb anybody. If only people could understand how much it means to them to be here. It's kind of like when you're a kid and you see Disneyland. That's what the United States is to them. Exactly. The only reason I know is because I've heard my mom [say this]. Coming to the United States is like a fantasy to them. I don't know. It makes me happy that we are such hard-working people, but it makes me sad. . . . They don't get the respect. But, you know what, in the end, you don't do it for respect. You do it to feed your family. So, that's all that matters.

Esther Valdez is well aware that the low wage structure of agricultural work means that farm laborers struggle to provide the basic necessities of life, with little discretionary spending. Esther shared with me her dream to enable farm-worker families to do something that is generally outside their grasp—have a vacation. Esther becomes emotional and cries as she explains:

I still have in my head a dream. I want to buy a piece of property and I want to build homes. And I want them in front of the ocean. And, places where people can go and have a vacation. And look at how beautiful the ocean is and the fresh air and just be with their family. And by the fireplace and watch TV and roast hot dogs or marshmallows, or something. A place that would be affordable for vacations where they can go. There for people like us who work all year. Like my father and my mother, my father has his back broken, his arm broken, he's overweight. My mother, her feet hurt, her back hurts. And she's never had vacation.

Several women made the point of the physically demanding nature of farm work when they spoke of either their own or another family member's brief venture into farm labor. In general, these women were unprepared for the strenuous nature of the work and difficult working conditions in the fields. In retrospect, they find some humor in the situation. Beatrice Padilla is a bookkeeper for a seasonal labor contractor. Fifteen years ago, she had taken a job in the fields. She laughs as she tells me, "After one month in the fields, 'Forget it,' I said. I worked one month, that's it. Oh my God, never again. At that time, I cannot speak English as much."[5] Marta Lujan also laughs as she tells me about her parents' work. Her father did agricultural work and then moved into construction; her mother was a stay-at-home mom who "one time, she started working in the fields doing the carrots. She didn't last two days!"

Picking tomatoes for one day brought Eva Vallejo, now age forty-three and a mother of three, to a defining moment about her own life's path. Her parents did farm work early on but moved into other work. Her older brother would some-times do field work during his school breaks. On one occasion when Eva was fifteen, he took her with him to pick tomatoes for a day. She says of that day, "To me that was the biggest thing. I thought, 'This is it. This is my life change. I know I'm *never* [her emphasis] gonna do this kind of work.' And that's all it took was one trip out there." As an adult, she has had clerical and secretarial employment.

Returning now to the California Commission on the Status of Women study on women farmworkers, I note that women of a previous generation shared my interviewees' antipathy for farm work. When asked to identify the best characteristics of farm work, nearly half of the women in the 1978 Imperial County sample said, "Nothing." They understood, however, that they experienced barriers to leaving farm work behind. They believed the major obstacles they experienced to changing occupations were, first, their lack of education, and, second, their lack of proficiency in English. Many had little education, and very few of the women could read or write in English. In both Imperial and Fresno counties, women were confined to the lowest-status and lowest-paying tasks in farm labor. A survey of growers found that employers perceived women to be unable to do more physically demanding work that was higher skilled and higher paid (Barton 1978).

This chapter has considered the farmworker origins of the women participating in this research. Family experience with farm work was communicated through women's accounts of their own childhood experience and the stories they heard from their parents and grandparents. Women express great admiration for parents and grandparents who left Mexico for a better life in the United States. Most had very limited education and knew little or no English. They respect the people who labored in the fields, but they do not idealize the work. In assessing the employment options for themselves, their partners, and their children, all would likely conclude, "Anything but field work!"

CHAPTER 3

LIFE IN A BORDER COMMUNITY

The questions I asked about work and family frequently brought my research participants to talk about the border. The economic struggles experienced by most presented real challenges to supporting their families adequately. Many attributed the difficulty of finding stable jobs at decent wages to the community's location at the border. They also believed that major indicators of community well-being such as education, health care, and public safety were related to proximity to the border. This chapter explores the impact of the border on the individuals and families living in the Imperial Valley. It also captures for readers unaccustomed to the social environment of the borderlands a sense of the unique challenges and opportunities experienced by those living near the U.S.-Mexico border.

These women draw what are certainly appropriate conclusions when they observe their lives to be shaped by the border. While a border may be defined simply as a physical and political boundary between two countries, the social and political relations associated with the border are complex (Hansen and Mattingly 2006, 5). Border scholars typically conceptualize the border as a region (rather than a boundary) that includes both sides of the physical border. This conceptualization captures the dynamic nature of the border and the interrelationship between communities and people on both sides. By this view, the concept of symbiosis or interdependence that transcends national boundaries is the key to understanding border regions (Martínez 1998).

The U.S.-Mexico border is a two-thousand-mile boundary with settlement concentrated in several twin cities, from San Diego–Tijuana on one side to Brownsville-Matamoros on the other. These twin cities, with the exception of San Diego–Tijuana, are patterned in a similar way, with the Mexico cities larger than their U.S. twins. Further, the U.S. border cities are relatively less prosperous than other U.S. cities, while Mexico border cities are relatively more prosperous than other cities in Mexico. On the U.S. side of the border, Latinos are a majority of the population in all border cities except San Diego (Hansen and Mattingly 2006, 5).

In the Imperial County borderlands, Calexico, California, and Mexicali, Baja California, are the twin cities. Calexico had a population of 35,273 in 2005, while Mexicali's population was 653,046. Mexicali is located in the municipality of Mexicali, the Mexican *municipio* or county across the border from Imperial County. Mexicali is the state of Baja California's capital city (Noriega-Verdugo 2004). The Mexican populace is increasingly concentrated in border cities, a trend that reflects the operation of global processes that impact the populations of cities like Mexicali and residents across the border in Imperial County as well.

Mexicali's growth is associated in part with its ongoing position as a gateway for Mexicans seeking agricultural employment in California. Mexicali currently serves as home to a large segment of the Imperial Valley's agricultural work force. Mexicali residents make up most of the fifteen to eighteen thousand seasonal farm workers who harvest the crops in the Imperial Valley every year. These workers generally cross the border daily in anticipation of being hired as day laborers by farm labor contractors. Prospective workers congregate at the border at 4:00 or 5:00 a.m. and board buses that bring them to the fields in Brawley, Holtville, and elsewhere, and return them to the border at the end of the work-day (Martin 2009, 63, 147). Other individuals cross the border daily to work for Imperial Valley growers and agricultural services businesses on a semiregular basis in jobs unrelated to harvest. The majority of these migrant farm workers are men, because although paid farm labor typically involved the entire family in rural Mexico, women may find other opportunities in this urban setting.

Border control policies have also served to swell the population of Mexican border cities, including Mexicali, because U.S. authorities have routinely deported to the Mexican side of the border unauthorized individuals whose home villages were in central and southern Mexico. So, for example, detainees from Oaxaca may be "repatriated" to Mexicali, perhaps fifteen hundred miles from home.[1] Many of these people have remained in the border cities, never returning to Mexico's interior (Lorey 1999).

Another explanation for population growth in border cities like Mexicali is Mexico's Border Industrialization Program (BIP). This program provided economic incentives for foreign corporations to build factories called maquiladoras in Mexico's northern border zone. These export assembly plants enabled foreign companies to reduce labor costs and encouraged Mexicans, especially women, to relocate to the border region for employment (Quintero 2005). The growth of the maquiladora sector and its continued importance in U.S.-Mexico border regions provides one of the clearest examples of the transborder economic integration that characterizes globalization.

Figure 7. Labor contractor bus leaving Brawley, transporting farmworkers back to the border at Calexico at the end of their workday (*Credit:* Johno Wells)

AUTHORIZED BORDER CROSSINGS

Imperial County is a site of substantial documented border crossing. Its two official ports of entry are known as Calexico and Calexico East. The border crossing in the town of Calexico is the main entry point for pedestrians and personal vehicles. Calexico East is the commercial entry point for this area. The scale of transborder activity is obvious from the numbers. In 2005, when my primary fieldwork was done, pedestrian entries totaled 4,481,014, while 11,846,703 individuals entered the United States in personal vehicles (U.S. Department of Transportation 2009).[2] The sheer volume of border crossings raises the question of why so many of these occur. What explains 16 million annual crossings into a sparsely settled, agriculture-oriented county with a total population of less than 150,000? The answers to this question illustrate the interdependence of cross-border communities in general and the Mexicali-Imperial region in particular.

The Imperial County women frequently referred to the impact of the border on their family lives. They described the principal reasons for border crossing, both their own crossings and those of others on both sides of the border, as employment, shopping, education, medical treatment, and family visits. Prior to sharing women's knowledge, perspectives, and experiences related to local transborder activities, I consider the immigration regulations that make them possible.

In turning to border-related actions and interactions, it is relevant to note Carlos Vélez-Ibáñez's observation that the separation of people from north and south of the border has been "one-sided: the north trying to keep out the south, whereas from the south there was little or no perception of excluding those from the north" (1996, 4). This being the case, it is unsurprising that there are a number of rules and regulations that restrict the admission of Mexican residents to the United States and limit their stays. At the same time, there are special regulations that enable Mexican nationals living near the border to be deeply involved in the immediate U.S. border region.

Mexican citizens may enter the United States with a passport and valid visa or a Border Crossing Card (BCC). The BCC is especially relevant to understanding the transborder relations of the Imperial-Mexicali region. Also known as a laser visa or a local passport, it permits frequent border crossings for Mexican individuals who live in border areas and meet certain requirements. This card allows Mexican nationals to stay in the United States for up to thirty days if they remain within twenty-five miles of the border (seventy-five miles in Arizona).[3] The Border Crossing Card permits entry for personal business or pleasure, but does not permit entry for employment in the U.S. (U.S. Department of State 2010a).

Embedded in the credit card–size BCC is a machine-readable biometric identifier that is checked with every border crossing. Individuals seeking a BCC are required to provide employment-related information and indicate the reason for frequent border crossings. An important criterion to qualify for this card is the ability to "demonstrate that they have ties to Mexico that would compel them to return after a temporary stay in the United States" (U.S. Department of State 2010b).[4] Because financial stability and employment in Mexico are viewed as important indicators of intent to return to Mexico, the applications of many individuals are not approved (Bean et al. 1994). Many Border Crossing Card holders cross the border daily or sometimes more than once a day, accounting for a considerable segment of border crossings.

Another group of border crossers are Mexican residents who are legal permanent residents of the United States. In the Imperial-Mexicali border area, the largest group of these individuals are Mexican agricultural workers who became legal U.S. immigrants with the Special Agricultural Worker (SAW) program that was part of the Immigration Reform and Control Act (IRCA) of 1986 (see chapter 1). For various reasons, many of these chose to return to Mexico to live and to commute daily or weekly to jobs on U.S. farms. These workers, sometimes referred to as "green card commuters," have the freedom to cross the border at will (Martin 2009, 66).

Dynamics of the Border Region

Kimberly Collins, director of the California Center for Border and Regional Economic Studies, said in a conversation in 2005 about the dynamic interconnectedness of the Imperial-Mexicali border region, "Everyone gets what they want from the border." Her point was that everyone who lives at the border does so for a reason and benefits from it in some way. The border impinges on the lives of all border region residents, in ways that are positive and negative. But overall, they find compelling (and varied) reasons to live near the border.

In the course of this research I learned much about the impact of Mexican transborder activity on the lives of research participants and their communities in the Imperial Valley. I learned somewhat less about the border crossings of the Imperial County women and their families into Mexico. This follows from the emphasis of this research on the work and family lives of these women and their perspectives on the local community. The interconnectedness of the border region is illumined here by data from a number of sources, including women's experiences and observations. The transborder connections explored are those related to shopping, medical services, education, and family visits. Cross-border transactions related to employment will be examined in chapter 5. For now, suffice it to say that a consistent theme of women's narratives was the negative economic effects experienced by community residents when workers from "the other side" took local jobs.

Shopping

One of the main opportunities that proximity to the border provides is the ability to access goods and services from "the other side." Transborder shopping is a regular feature of U.S.-Mexico border regions. Mexicans shop in the United States for reasons related to quality, availability, and price. Martínez refers to these individuals as "binational consumers" (1998, 77). Mexican shoppers seek higher quality products, many of which are less available in Mexico, including food, clothing, and other consumer goods. U.S. prices are lower than prices in Mexico for some products, especially highly-tariffed imports (Martínez 1998).

U.S. retailers benefit tremendously by locating near the border. The success of many Imperial Valley retail businesses depends on Mexican shoppers. Shoppers from Mexico do most of their shopping in three commercial areas. The first is downtown Calexico. Pedestrian border crossers generally shop in downtown Calexico, where stores are densely packed into a half-dozen city blocks just north of the border crossing. The scale of these commercial establishments varies widely, from larger enterprises such as Sam Ellis, a locally owned department store, and JCPenney, to medium-size independent groceries and variety stores, to a multitude of small, crowded shops selling an assortment of cheap imported goods. Here most customers are Mexicans and business is transacted in Spanish. This section of Calexico has a very Mexican feel. Americans with little experience at the border might well assume they were in Mexico rather than the United States. Signs in grocery stores advertise "pollo" and food shops promote "tortas" and "menudo." Receipts for purchases may even be printed in Spanish. Downtown Calexico offers a broader variety of commercial services than do the other shopping areas. These include insurance brokers, legal firms (specializing in immigration law), and currency exchange.

Two miles north of the border is the second main commercial area that draws transborder shoppers. Shopping here requires a vehicle. This area, just off Highway 111, the main road between Calexico and Brawley, has a Walmart as its central feature. Other retailers are a mix of well-known American companies such as Toys R Us and Radio Shack as well as local establishments.

The third main shopping destination is Imperial Valley Mall, a gleaming new regional mall located nine miles north of the international border. A local Chamber of Commerce official explained the presence of this facility to me: "The IV Mall was built because of Mexico—for shoppers from Mexico. No way can the county support this mall."[5] This indoor mall opened in 2005, offering customers air-conditioned comfort and access to eighty stores. Most significantly, the mall provides a very typical American shopping experience, with major U.S. retailers such as Dillard's, Macy's, Sears, JCPenney, Victoria's Secret, and the Disney Store represented. Nothing in the mix of retailers suggests that the mall is anywhere near the Mexican border. Most Mexican shoppers drive to this mall in privately owned vehicles, but taxis are also frequently seen dropping off people who have presumably crossed the border on foot.

Shoppers from Mexico provide strong support for Imperial County businesses. A survey of the cross-border shopping activity of Mexicali households found that the top three products purchased in the United States are clothing, footwear, and chicken. Other items frequently purchased are appliances, auto parts, and other foods. Four in ten Mexicali residents spend more than fifty dollars when they visit the United States (CCBRES 2003). The widespread presence of license plates from Mexican states in store parking lots provides evidence of the importance of these shoppers. In my best effort to assess the percentage of cars with Mexico license plates in the Walmart parking lot on an ordinary, mid-week afternoon, I found almost half of cars to be from Mexico.[6]

The high volume of cross-border shopping markedly shapes employment possibilities in the Valley. In recent years, retail trade has been the business sector with the most job openings. Retail jobs typically pay low wages and offer part-time hours. They do not, in general, provide the full-time, year-round jobs that most of my research participants needed to support their families adequately. When discussing job options in the Valley, however, most women were very positive about the increasing number of jobs resulting from expansion of the retail sector. Many women were enthusiastic about the new Imperial Valley Mall, both because it brought hundreds of new jobs to the Valley and because it meant they no longer needed to drive to San Diego or Palm Desert to shop at a large department store. In fact, none of the women I interviewed worked at the new mall, although Natalie Torres, a young, unemployed single mother, was excited abut her upcoming interview at the Lane Bryant store.

Most of the women found retail jobs to be unsuitable for a number of reasons. First, none of them had the experience needed for a retail management position.

They understood this meant the mall jobs they were likely to get were part-time retail sales jobs with nonstandard shift hours that were incompatible with their family responsibilities. As Jennifer Castillo, a thirty-five-year-old mother of three says, "If they would give me morning hours, yes, but not evening hours. Because of my kids. But there's no way that that would ever happen. They need people for evenings and weekends. Evenings—it would be, what until 9:00 or something? And then weekends, and weekends—well, I mean—my kids have games and stuff." Some women thought they did not fit the profile of desirable employee characteristics sought by mall employers. Lucia Hernandez, age forty, said, "The mall has been good, but it really just helps the younger crowd. Older people have a more difficult time getting a job there. When I was attending a program for CalWorks, one of the ladies [staff] said that if the women wanted to get a job there, they needed to be pretty and perky."

Second, the presence of so many Spanish-speaking visitors resulted in many jobs requiring bilingual skills. One might assume that if the lack of bilingual skills presents an obstacle to the employment of Latinos, job seekers are likely to be deficient in English. In fact, it was lack of competence in Spanish that disqualified some women from particular jobs in this border region. The labor market experience of some women was dissonant with assumptions about the integration of immigrants into U.S. society. Many immigrants or their children decide not to pass on their native language to the next generation because "becoming American" has always required giving up the past. Historically, a badge of assimilation has been becoming English monolingual (Portes and Schauffler 1996). An underlying expectation is that economic rewards accrue to those who assimilate culturally. The Imperial County women negotiate the inconsistencies of the assimilation message in an international space. Here being "too Americanized" may mean not getting a job.

Every woman who participated in this research was fluent in English; however, not everyone was fluent in Spanish. Several third-generation women were not. For example, Helen Estrada is a twenty-eight-year-old mother of four whose Texas-born parents did not speak Spanish in their home. She has been looking conscientiously for a job, without success. She says, "I know if I did know two languages, I would automatically get a job. Actually, I was rejected twice because I didn't speak Spanish—I wasn't bilingual. Which is understandable, you know. They want somebody who can communicate with more customers."

The Walmart in Calexico is the clearest example of an employer whose hiring practices seem oriented toward appealing to Mexican shoppers. Here facility in Spanish is more important than English competence and job applicants with Mexican cultural traits seem to be favored over Mexican Americans who are more assimilated to American culture. Marta Lujan describes her experience applying for a job at Walmart in Calexico: "I went to pick up an application. I am speaking English, right? The person I am talking to is answering me in Spanish.

I think they wanted somebody that was totally Mexican and that maybe just spoke a little bit of English, but their main language was Spanish." She later had an interview at this Walmart. "They ask me questions in Spanish and I answer them back in Spanish." Marta did not get the job and concludes, "I think I was too Americanized. I don't know."

Cynthia Mateo worked for a while at this Walmart. She describes her bilingual language skills in this way: "I speak good English. My Spanish is good when I need to speak it, but I feel more comfortable speaking in English. And I would speak to my coworkers in English and they would respond to me in Spanish and I understood." Cynthia had a poor relationship with her more culturally Mexican coworkers and told how they had "bad-mouthed" her with the supervisor. In reflecting on this experience, she says, "I wasn't Mexican enough to work there. And it's funny because when I go to apply for other jobs, I have to show that I know English. That's not hard for me. But I thought, now I know how those people felt when they're discriminated on the other end. And it's like, oh my God, I'm not Mexican enough for this job. And it's like, it's a Walmart, okay, you know. But Walmart can be a very excellent job, because you can work up in that job too. But not Mexican enough for Walmart in Calexico!"

Monica Rodriguez makes the point that this close-to-the-border store is actually less interested in a bilingual staff than in a Spanish-speaking staff. She says, "Walmart in Calexico—you'll be lucky if you find somebody who speaks in English. I went to the Calexico Walmart once and I was looking for some crates. But I couldn't think of the word in Spanish. Crate—just a regular crate to file papers. I asked and asked and asked and they had no idea what I was talking about. So I had to leave. I had to go to El Centro and find somebody who could actually know what a crate was. That was my most frustrating time at Walmart."

In concluding this subject, I consider briefly transborder shopping among research participants and their families. Dallen Timothy points out that the shopping activities of U.S. residents are more leisure-oriented than those of Mexican shoppers who purposefully buy household necessities and consumer goods that will enhance their lives at home in Mexico. The shopping activities of Americans in Mexico are more likely to revolve around tourism and entertainment (2005, 58). Timothy's analysis refers to Americans of all racial or ethnic groups. Oscar Martínez looks specifically at cross-border shopping by Mexican Americans. He concludes that they are attracted to bargains in Mexico and cross the border for a considerable amount of shopping and recreation. They buy products including food, shoes, and clothing and access services at barber shops, hair salons, and tailor shops. They are also drawn to restaurants, bars, movie theaters and other establishments for weekend entertainment (1998, 107).

My study was not designed to examine how research participants and their families spent their leisure time. I do not know if these Imperial Valley families went to restaurants and theaters in Mexicali on the weekends. I do know that long wait times at the international border for reentry into the United States discouraged people from discretionary crossings. As I will discuss later, the most frequently mentioned reason the women I interviewed crossed the border was to visit family on the other side. Many, without family on the other side, saw no reason to go to Mexico, whether for shopping or some other purpose. Natalie Torres, for example, in referring to her family, said, "Yes, everybody's in the U.S. Don't even cross the border. No need." This finding is consistent with Ellen Hansen's observation that many border-area residents seldom or never cross to the other side (2006, 37).

At the same time, some women were transnational consumers. A few mentioned going to Mexico for "cheap haircuts" and manicures. Others mentioned that one could save money by buying some low-cost goods in Mexico, although they may not themselves do so. Julie Peña says, "I know a lot of people do buy a lot of things over there across the border because it's cheaper over there also. Which is fine. I won't go there myself unless my husband is driving."

Health Care and Medical Services

Border-region residents also cross the international boundary to access health care and medical services. In general, the transborder exchange occurring here is that Mexico residents gain access to higher-quality health care in the United States, while U.S. residents gain access to lower-cost health care and medical services in Mexico.

The movement of people from a developing nation to a developed nation for high-quality medical care raises complicated issues. One of the community leaders I interviewed in Brawley told me that many women from Mexico come to Brawley to give birth in the local hospital, Pioneers Memorial. This subject is sensitive because these women typically do not pay for the medical care they receive. There is considerable local resentment regarding this situation because providing this care depletes local community resources. The official I spoke with explained that the hospital tries to get grants from the State of California to offset some of the extraordinary costs associated with its location as a border-region hospital, but there is limited assistance available. The women I interviewed pointed to the closing of the hospital in Calexico as evidence of the stress on the medical system caused by border crossers. That hospital had provided a substantial amount of care to Mexican border crossers; as a result, it could not control costs, was not financially viable, and ultimately closed. They worry that they too could lose their local hospital. Both Pioneers Memorial Hospital in Brawley and El Centro Regional Medical Center accept Mexican patients who are at risk if they fail to receive medical care. This is consistent with their legal responsibility to provide emergency care to all, regardless of ability to pay. The policy includes providing childbirth services to pregnant women whose labor has advanced beyond the initial stages. Individuals who are not at risk are not provided care.

A Mexican woman might also be motivated to give birth at one of the Imperial Valley hospitals because the child would be born a United States citizen. None of the women in my sample or the community professionals I interviewed expressed resentment related to citizenship. Rather, their entire concern revolved around the depletion of this community's limited financial resources.

A principal reason for border crossings from the United States to Mexico is accessing lower-cost health care and pharmaceuticals. Many U.S. citizens, especially retirees, buy their medications and receive medical, dental, and optical care in Mexico at prices far lower than in the United States. For many retirees, this represents an economic strategy that permits them to stretch their fixed incomes. Pharmacies, dental offices, and medical practices are conveniently concentrated at major crossings in nearly all Mexican border communities (Timothy 2005, 60). Although many of the retirees who winter in Imperial County cross the border for medical services, few of the women I studied reported accessing health care "on the other side." This may be substantially explained by the low-income status of these women and the eligibility of children in nearly two-thirds of families for health coverage through California's public health care programs, Medi-Cal and Healthy Families. Crossing the border for dental care in Mexicali was more common than crossing for health care.

Accessing lower cost health care and medical services in Mexico is not exclusively an individual or family-level strategy; it is also an institutional strategy. The deep interconnectedness of the Imperial-Mexicali border region comes into view in examining employee benefits provided by Imperial County for county employees. The county offers two main choices for health-care coverage for employees. One option is a conventional Blue Shield of California medical plan offering a number of options based on varying co-pays and deductibles. The other option is a county-funded plan that uses health-care providers in Mexicali. Posted on the Imperial County website is the list of Mexicali medical providers and a flyer providing information about the shuttle available to transport insured individuals from the U.S. border to a twenty-four-hour clinic in Mexicali (Imperial County 2008). This clinic provides pharmacy, laboratory, x-ray, and other services.

Erica Martinez is a single mother of three who works for the county and chose the Mexicali-based plan. This plan is very attractive to her because it requires no annual or other deductibles and no co-pays. Erica says, "It pays 100 percent for me and my girls." She is very satisfied with the medical care provided in Mexico. The main impediment she encounters is border-related traffic delays. If she has midday appointments, she drives to them with little difficulty. "But," she says, "if I wait until after work, I am crossing with everyone who was over here working on this side." This means she encounters considerable traffic and experiences a slow crossing as she joins Mexican commuters returning home to Mexicali. The more serious problem she encounters, however, is long delays in crossing back into the United States. A two-hour wait to cross from Mexicali to Calexico is especially difficult if she is traveling with a sick child. Erica also has employer-provided Mexico-based dental and optical coverage. Her Mexico network dental providers include oral surgeons, endodontists, orthodontists, and pedodontists, in addition to general dentists.

Marjorie Salas is an elementary teacher whose dentist is in Mexicali, but her medical doctor is in Brawley. Nonetheless, she says, "Sometimes going to Mexicali to see the doctor is the easiest thing for us." She explains that it can be very difficult to get an appointment with their local primary care provider, but they can get an appointment with her parents-in-law's doctors in Mexicali. She concludes, "We can go there because they know us." They pay for these appointments, but the cost is not prohibitive.

Education

Observations at the pedestrian border crossing at First Street in Calexico reveal that a significant number of Mexican children cross the international border daily for school. A few blocks east of the border crossing, in clear view of the fenced barricade that separates Mexico and the United States, is the Calexico Mission School, a four-hundred-student private school associated with the Seventh Day Adventist Church (Calexico Mission School 2010). The school uniforms—all children in burgundy or white shirts, boys in dark trousers and girls in plaid skirts—easily identify students from this school. Approximately 85 percent of students in this K–12 school are from Mexicali; they cross the border daily from Mexico to the United States and back again (Steffen 2009). In mid-afternoon, dozens of students, some walking alone, some clustered in small groups, in some cases older students minding younger ones, can be seen approaching the border crossing. Also in evidence are women, some surely mothers, but also other women, perhaps grandmothers, aunts, or neighbors, who approach the border crossing with one or more younger children in tow. In addition, some parents cross the border by car and pick up their children in the school parking lot.

The situation of the Calexico Mission School and its students differs from the common observation of border scholars that a typical feature of life at the border is the movement of students from Mexico across the border to attend public schools in the U.S. (Martínez 1998; Vélez-Ibáñez 1996). Ellen Hansen's (2006) analysis of the border crossing activities of women in the border twin towns of Douglas, Arizona, and Agua Prieta, Sonora, found that while the most common reason for women's border crossing was shopping, many also crossed regularly to transport their children to and from school in Douglas.

In fact, I also observed a few junior high and high school–age youths wearing T-shirts and sweatshirts with logos from Calexico public schools and crossing the border from Calexico to Mexicali in the mid-afternoon. I assumed these teens were students returning to Mexicali after a day at school in Calexico. When I asked my community sources how it is that students from Mexico attend U.S. public schools, the universal response was that most of these families have a relative in Calexico. Border-crossing students are enrolled in the school as a member of the household of extended family members in the United States. Schools require proof of residency, but "proof" may misrepresent realities. As a result, classes in Calexico public schools are, as one woman said, "overpopulated," meaning large class sizes and crowded classrooms are the norm. Local public schools are less convenient to the international border than is the mission school. Some parents walk an elementary or middle school child across and border and put her or him in a taxi to be dropped off at a city school. After school, that child is either picked up by a taxi and brought to the border or a parent drives across the border and picks up the child at school.

The presence of nonresident students from Mexico in Imperial County public schools is a contentious issue in the community. Many believe the schools do not do enough to verify residence. Some rant on this subject in blogs and letters to the editor of the *Imperial Valley Press*, but cooler heads tend to make two points. The first is that the addition of students from Mexico increases the percentage of English language learners in classrooms, thereby increasing the daunting challenges already faced by classroom teachers. Second, Imperial County children are already some of the most disadvantaged in the state of California. Increasing student numbers functions to exacerbate existing inequalities.

Some Mexican American families living in Calexico enroll their children in private schools in Mexicali, illustrating the truly dynamic nature of border activity. Erica Martinez reported that her brother's family did this for several years. Another woman who lived in Calexico and did not meet the criteria for inclusion in my research sample told me that her younger brother was a student at a private school in Mexico. In fact, her mother sometimes made three round trips across the border per day—one drop-off trip to school in Mexicali, one pick-up trip home from school, and sometimes a trip back to school for extracurricular activities. These parents perceive the Calexico public schools to be substandard, but they cannot afford U.S. private schools. Mexican private schools represent a viable alternative because they provide a private school experience that is reasonably priced by U.S. standards.

Family Visits

The most frequently mentioned purpose for crossing the border was visiting relatives in Mexicali. It is significant to note here that a large majority of the Imperial County women no longer have close relatives in Mexico.[7] When I asked research participants where their family currently lives, only five women mentioned a grandparent, parent, or sibling living in Mexico, and all of these lived in Mexicali. Over the course of the interview, some women also referred to aunts, uncles, and cousins in Mexico; married women also mentioned visiting members of their husbands' family in Mexico.

Some women told me about visiting Mexico for family celebrations. Gloria Espinoza, for example, describes visiting her mother's family in Mexicali for parties, reunions, and birthdays. Their visits are special, she says, "Because my mom's family is really into music. One of them has his own mariachi [band]. They come to the United States and make a lot of money here. There's ten of them [in the band] and they make four hundred dollars an hour. So we like going because there's a lot of music."

Others mention visits to socialize with cousins or visit aunts, uncles, or elderly grandparents. Sometimes misadventures are associated with these border crossings, as was the case for Marina Mendez, when, three months prior to the interview, her car was stolen during a visit to her grandparents in Mexicali. Daniela Rosales told me about the time her mother's purse was stolen during a visit to family members in Mexicali; this was a serious matter because her mother was not permitted to cross back into the United States without identifying documents.

Antonia Alivar is a married mother of three whose international border crossings are a story of transnational caregiving. The story is a bit complicated. Antonia was born in the United States, but her parents later returned to live in Mexicali. She had been working in a factory in Beaumont, California, for several years when her mother in Mexicali became ill. Antonia's family then moved back to Brawley; from here she crossed the border regularly to care for her mother. Her mother died a year ago and now Antonia is concerned that her father is having a difficult time adjusting to the loss of his wife. She goes to Mexicali when she can to assist her father. As she says, "He does not have papers to come to the U.S." By this, Antonia means that her father cannot get a Border Crossing Card or visa for entering the United States. The likely explanation is that he cannot demonstrate he has ties predicting he will return to Mexico after visiting the United States.

Unauthorized Border Crossings

The women I interviewed did not talk very much about their community as a major site for border surveillance and enforcement. Neither did they suggest their community was inundated by illegal immigrants. They believed, however, that the two biggest problems in their community were jobs and drugs. Both were associated with the border, but in somewhat different ways.

It is unsurprising that in this county with the highest rate of unemployment in California and with many of the women I interviewed unemployed and looking for work, the first concern is jobs. Women did think Mexican citizens were taking "their" jobs, but the people taking them were not the Mexicans from southern states like Chiapas and Oaxaca who crossed the border illegally in the desert with coyote guides or swam across the All-American Canal. Rather, they were concerned about Mexicali residents who crossed the border legally in the morning, worked in the Imperial Valley (whether or not they were authorized to work), and returned to Mexicali at night to repeat the same routine the next day. The critical distinction here is that these transborder commuters were authorized to cross the border, but they may not be authorized to work. Research by Frank Bean and his colleagues (1994) on the legal status of Mexican commuter workers at the El Paso/Juarez border found that one-third of this group entered the United States legally with a BCC, but then worked illegally. In their typology of Mexican border crossers, they refer to this group as legal crossers/illegal workers. The subject of how the border shaped employment opportunities will be developed in chapter 5, where I examine the local job market.

The second most serious concern of the women I interviewed was drugs. For them, drugs were a border issue. The women were very aware of the illegal movement of large quantities of illicit drugs from Mexico into the county. They believed drug traffic raised the crime rate, contributed to a high rate of drug use in Brawley and throughout the Valley, and created a rampant presence of drugs in the community. Drugs were both a public issue and, for some, a matter of personal tragedy.

Imperial County as a Site of Border Enforcement

Introducing the subject of border enforcement adds complexity to our analysis. This chapter initially framed the construction of the border as a dynamically interconnected region. Conceptualizing the border in this way may raises questions about the heavy policing of the boundary between partner regions in an integrated social system that transcends national boundaries. These are contradictory impulses. The United States has since the early to mid-1990s adopted policies that increasingly construct the border to be a heavily guarded barrier between nations, while at the same time promoting the creation of a permeable, dynamic border region.

Historically speaking, U.S.-Mexico border enforcement is relatively new.[8] The Border Patrol was established in 1924 to control both the Mexican and Canadian borders. The international boundaries were divided into "sectors," with border control operations instituted in each sector. With the establishment of the El Centro Sector in 1924, Imperial County has played an important role in border control since the very beginning. The El Centro Sector covers an area of more than 23,400 square miles. Its agents patrol more than 70 miles of the United States–Mexico international border. Sector operations are conducted through four stations. In 2005, El Centro's apprehensions numbered 55,722 (Becker and Bennion 2008). The Imperial Valley is further involved in border security as the location of one of eight U.S. government-owned detention centers operated by the Office of Detention and Removal, a division of U.S. Immigration and Customs Enforcement (ICE). This facility, the El Centro Service Processing Center (SPC), is a detention center for adult males facing deportation or waiting for a decision on their immigration cases (U.S. Immigration and Customs Enforcement 2012).

Figure 8. A conversation across the border fence in Calexico (*Credit:* Johno Wells)

One of the strategies mentioned on the El Centro Sector website for accomplishing its mission is a highly visible deployment of agents. By all observations, this strategy has been successful. Border agents are regularly seen patrolling the county's population centers by a number of different means, including patrols on foot or horseback, by bicycle or motorcycle, in a variety of motor vehicles, and in low-flying helicopters.[9] While the greatest concentration of border control agents is evident in Calexico, I saw border agents in all Imperial Valley cities and towns. Community professionals I interviewed tended to believe most Mexicans in Imperial County were there legally. Their general viewpoint is that people who have managed to cross illegally will quickly move further north, where less immigration enforcement occurs. As one individual noted, "You can't even get into the county now from San Diego if you are illegal with the new checkpoint on I-8." The new checkpoint on Interstate Highway 8 monitors the immigration status of individuals moving east and west. She referred to the fact that the two long-utilized Border Patrol traffic checkpoints on California Highways 86 and 111 in Imperial County monitor northbound traffic to prevent illegal entrants from leaving the border region. These traffic stops are positioned more than twenty-five miles north of the border, also serving to deter Mexicans with border crossing cards from leaving their travel zone limit of twenty-five miles from the border.

The El Centro Sector's most difficult challenges to border enforcement are not in the cities, however, but in the mostly uninhabited desert and mountainous areas of the county. Immigrant deaths due to exposure were rare on the southwestern border prior to 1994 but rose dramatically with a new immigration policy that rechanneled illegal crossings from urban areas like San Diego, to deserts such as the Imperial County border region. Operation Gatekeeper was the border control operation that situated Imperial County at the center of U.S border control efforts and brought new challenges for the community.[10] The federal response to soaring illegal border activity was a dramatic increase in funding for El Centro Sector operations and hundreds of additional border agents. Heat-related exposure became the leading cause of border crossing death by 1998 (U.S. Government Accountability Office 2006), and the El Centro Sector became the sector with the highest number of these deaths. Local communities were unprepared for the sheer numbers of undocumented immigrants streaming into the county. Both apprehensions and border crossing deaths rose precipitously. The costs associated with these immigrants (whether dead or alive) placed a heavy financial burden on this resource-poor rural county (Ellingwood 2004).

The strain on local institutions precipitated by the new federal strategy of border enforcement is especially clear upon consideration of the statutory responsibilities of coroners and community hospitals. The Imperial County Coroner's Office is legally responsible for determining the cause of death, identifying the body, and notifying the next of kin when an individual dies in the county. This includes, of course, migrants who die crossing the border. The coroner's office performs autopsies and works closely with the Mexican consulate in Calexico to establish identification. Bodies awaiting identification are stored at Frye Chapel and Mortuary in Brawley. Eventually, many of the dead are buried in the paupers' section of the Park Terrace Cemetery in Holtville. The burial expenses for individuals who have been identified are paid by their families or the Mexican government. Unidentified individuals are buried as John or Jane Doe, with the county covering the costs (LeDuff 2004). Expenditures related to border-crossing deaths have been a multimillion-dollar expense for this poor rural county.

Many who survive the border crossing require medical care. These people are usually brought to the El Centro Regional Medical Center, the hospital closest to the border, where they are most commonly treated for exposure or injuries sustained in crossing the border. The El Centro hospital provides charity care in the amount of $1.5 million annually for patients assumed to be foreign nationals (Berestein 2004b). The hospital provides emergency care as it is required by law to do, but in most cases, it is not reimbursed from federal border control funds. (The Calexico hospital mentioned earlier in this chapter closed in 1995.)

As unlikely as it may sound in the California desert, the second major risk endangering illegal border crossers in the El Centro Sector is death by drowning. An estimated 550 individuals, most of them undocumented immigrants, have drowned in the All-American Canal, an aqueduct that provides the entire water supply for Imperial Valley communities and irrigates its agriculture (CBS 2010; Spagat 2011).[11] From the surface, water in the canal appears deceptively quiet. In fact, the canal has a strong undercurrent. Immigrants who attempt to cross the canal on a raft or swim across it are frequently unprepared for the perilous conditions they encounter.

The Imperial County border is an increasingly barricaded one. Increased budgets have provided hundreds of additional border guards, steel fencing, high-intensity lighting, motion detector sensors, thermal imaging devices, and remote video cameras. In the post–September 11, 2001 era, an insecure Mexican border has been reframed as a threat to national security (Tirman 2006). In this context the American public has generally supported a heavy investment in border security. The Secure Fence Act of 2006 has also gone forward, providing $1.5 billion to provide additional fencing (a type of tactical infrastructure) and enhanced electronic surveillance (sometimes called virtual fencing). One of the stipulations of this law is a border fence from west of Calexico, California, to east of Douglas, Arizona, a total distance of approximately 360 miles (American Immigration Lawyers Association 2006).

In recent years the Tucson Sector has become the sector registering the most immigrant crossing deaths annually. This change is believed by many to be associated with a shift of the illegal immigrant stream further east from the now more heavily fortified Imperial County border to the less tightly guarded Tucson Sector border in Arizona. Over the course of the past decade, human smugglers have increasingly viewed the Arizona desert as the easiest route for guiding would-be immigrants across the U.S. border. By 2008, 45 percent of all apprehensions of illegal immigrants in the southwestern border area were in the Tucson Sector (U.S. Department of Homeland Security 2009).

I did not ask questions about current U.S. immigration policy or border politics, nor did the Imperial County women weigh in on the national conversation on these matters in any substantial sense. The concerns they raised were local and immediate. These women, second- and third-generation Mexican Americans and U.S. citizens, had next to no direct interaction with border enforcement personnel. Certainly, they experienced border control as part of the larger social context in which they lived. They endured traffic checkpoints like everyone else; Border Patrol circulated through their neighborhoods. But they did not seem to see the border control enterprise as something that related very directly to them. As far as I knew, they accepted the Border Patrol's presence and activities without analysis or critique. Their general sentiment seemed to be this: we live in a border community, so we need the Border Patrol to do its job. In fact, the common characteristic that allowed these women to be quite disengaged on this subject was the reality that all of them were U.S. citizens; the Border Patrol was a matter of concern for people who were undocumented. This made all the difference. The main point women made in talking about border control was that Border Patrol agents had some of the best jobs in the county.

Antonia Alivar was the only woman I interviewed who described an incident with the Border Patrol. Her family's desperate economic circumstances had placed them in a housing situation in proximity to undocumented immigrants. Antonia had lost her job and her unemployment had run out. Her husband had been ill and unable to work. This family of five rented a tiny two-bedroom mobile home without heat or air conditioning in a run-down mobile home park. I asked her if the park was safe and quiet. She says that it was, but told me about frequent visits of immigration agents to the park. She told me about an incident in which her husband was outside and came to the door of the trailer and asked her for his wallet. She opened the door and found two Border Patrol officers standing there. She reminds me that they are U.S. citizens, but it scares her when this happens. As she explains it, this park is home to many "illegals."

Drugs at the Border

Illegal drugs are a matter of serious concern in the Imperial Valley. The community's drug problem alarmed the women I interviewed. Everyone who discussed drugs viewed them as a border-related issue. They are aware that they live in a place that is known to be a principal corridor for the movement of drugs (heroin, methamphetamine, cocaine, and marijuana) from Mexico to destinations in the United States. Drugs are not a new issue in this community. Imperial County's reputation as a place with a high rate of heroin addiction goes back several decades. Brawley has had a reputation for having an especially serious drug problem. Methamphetamine use has now joined heroin as a serious problem in the county.

Drug trafficking is big business. Despite heavy surveillance at the border, massive quantities of illegal drugs are smuggled from Mexico into the United States every year. Both local newspaper stories and U.S. Border Control press releases show that the seizure of large quantities of drugs occurs regularly and represents a major success for law enforcement. In cases involving substantial quantities of drugs, the typical scenario is that the drugs had been smuggled from Mexico and were in transit out of the El Centro Sector when border agents interdicted them.

I elicited the Imperial County women's perceptions of the relationship between life in a border community and illegal drugs. In exploring the work and family lives of these women, I was interested in their perspectives on raising a family in Brawley. I asked questions including: What is good about Brawley as a place to raise children? What is difficult about it as a place to raise children? More than half of research participants identified illegal drugs as a significant community problem and expressed concern about raising their children in this environment. They believed drugs to be a problem that was getting worse and they closely connect the problem to the community's proximity to Mexico. Women were not ignorant of the presence of drugs in other locales. Many echoed Denise Ortiz's perspective: "I know it's everywhere, but you see it more here."

Ana Ramirez says, "I think we have a big drug trafficking problem. Crime is also bad, and it is all related to the drugs. The drug problem has gotten worse over the years." As Ana sees it, the big problem drugs in the Valley are metham-phetamine and heroin. She recognizes that the meth does not necessarily origi-nate in Mexico, but she says, "I know we have a lot of heroin. And that has to come from, you know, the border."

Miranda Flores has a complicated and tragic family story that is marked by drug addiction. She is one of fifteen children born to farmworker parents. Two of Miranda's brothers and one sister died from heroin addiction. Now one of her younger sisters has a serious drug problem and is unable to care for her daughter. Miranda currently has custody of this niece. She says, wearily, "When's the chain going to stop? When is it going to stop? This happens a lot here in the Valley because there's a lot of drugs here, especially because we are next to the border. There's so much drugs."

Stephanie Ruiz believes that drugs in the community have created a danger-ous environment for her five-year-old daughter. She says:

> You know, we live by the border. So there's a lot of drugs coming back and forth. And that's corruption. I don't want that around my daughter. It's every-where, you know, but this is where it comes from. It comes from Mexico, then it comes here, and then it goes up north. You look at the news and there's a lot of stuff happening here. And in Mexico. And it's just crazy. It scares me. And not so long ago they said there was a girl that was kidnapped and I think, you know, I can't even leave my daughter out. That's why I'm very overprotective. Like to be with her when she goes out because it is just scary. It's everywhere.

Stephanie connects drugs, crime, and the border. She tells me that when she moved into her current apartment, an upstairs unit, there was no room for her washing machine, so she put it out on the balcony by her sliding door. She says, incredulously, "So I had it there and somebody stole my big washer!" She explains the situation by repeating the sentiment she expressed earlier: "I don't like the drugs. You know, we live by the border. There's a lot of people around that are stealers, thieves."

Stephanie operates from a fairly generalized sense that the border, drugs, and crime create danger for her daughter. Other women express a particular concern that life in this border community means that, given the high rate of illegal drug use, children may be exposed to significant drug-related activity. Rosa Navarra pro-vides an example of this sensibility with an example from her son's soccer game:

> I'm a team mom, a soccer mom. And I really hope for and think that the Brawley Police Department should do more drive-alongs by the parks. Because my son two weeks ago and all of my soccer team, they all experience—actually from here to there [pointing to a wall six feet away]—seeing some people do drugs. They were doing pipe, crack, and all that other stuff. And the boys are like, "Wow." But since I'm in law enforcement, they [her sons] know about everything already. About the guns, everything. But not all the kids are aware of that.

On a similar note, Francesca Alvarez graduated from Brawley High School, left for Phoenix, and now, at age twenty-one, has returned to Brawley with her fiancé and baby. She too is alarmed to see drugs being used openly. She says, "We've been noticing that there's a lot of drug addicts here. We live close to the fields and in the afternoon we go walking; and we see this guy shooting up in the canal. There were drugs here before, but it's gotten worse."

This discussion has centered on women's perspectives about drug use in the community but has not considered how drugs have impacted their own lives. In undertaking this research, I understood that the use and abuse of drugs was a matter of concern in Imperial County. What I did not anticipate was how many of the women I interviewed had family lives marked by illegal drug use. Many disjunctures in their personal lives were explained by drugs. The impact of drug use on the family experience of research participants will be noted in several places in ensuing chapters.

This chapter captures a fundamental paradox at the Imperial-Mexicali border. On the one hand, U.S. citizens and Mexican citizens with the requisite documents cross the border to engage in various economic and social activities. Mexicans cross to the United States to shop at Dillard's. Americans cross to Mexico for prescriptions. Mexican children cross to attend the Calexico Mission School. Mexican Americans cross to visit relatives. And on it goes. In addition, some cross-border activity reveals connections between Imperial Valley communities and Mexicali that go beyond the decisions and preferences of individuals. For example, marching bands from Mexicali high schools participate in the annual Cattle Call Parade, a major community event in Brawley. And some women told me they crossed the border when their children had soccer games in Mexicali.

At the same time, the U.S. government spends billions of dollars on fencing, technology, and personnel to limit the access of some Mexican citizens to the U.S. side of the border. The "war on drugs" is fought in large measure at the border. The paradox at the Imperial-Mexicali border is the same one that characterizes the entire U.S.-Mexico border. This examination of life on the border reveals contradictory impulses toward what Peter Andreas called "a borderless economy and a barricaded border." The present situation is that the border is "more blurred and more sharply demarcated" than in the past (2003, 4). It is ironic that the North American Free Trade Agreement (NAFTA), which facilitated the cross-border movement of goods and services between the United States and Mexico, was instituted in 1994, the same year that Operation Gatekeeper, the program resulting in massive increases in funding for border enforcement, was implemented.

The concepts of "border as regional social and economic system" and "border as physical boundary" pull us in different directions. Yet taken together, they capture the dynamic border-based tension between impulses toward integration and differentiation (Bean et al. 1994, 6; Lowenthal and Burgess 1993). This tension predicts that public policy–related discussions of border issues are likely to be contentious. Individuals who mostly see the border as a geographic boundary "tend to highlight divergences in state interests and the need for policies that protect these," while individuals who mostly see the border as an interconnected region "tend to highlight convergences in state interests and the need for policies that foster further integration" (Bean et al. 1994, 6).

CHAPTER 4

NEGOTIATING WORK
AND FAMILY

Negotiating work and family is a central concern for most women with children in U.S. society. Women are increasingly mothers and workers. How do the mothers in this study experience their work and family roles and responsibilities? Having explored the personal context—farmworker origins—and the community context—life in a border community—I now turn to this question of how these second- and third-generation Mexican American women manage their work and family lives. The limitations of the local labor market surely shape their work–family interface. Because Imperial County has high unemployment and too few stable, full-time jobs, the work-related activities of many women and their partners take the form of looking for jobs rather than actually working a job.

This chapter examines the viewpoints, decisions, and experiences related to the construction of the women's work and family lives. It focuses on four main subjects: women's decisions whether to work, child care–related issues, the negotiation of work and the extended family, and gender and family life. This line of inquiry connects us with two important and interrelated themes in the literature about Mexican American families: assumptions about family traditionality and familism. Both of these are related to the question of the continuing significance of Mexican culture in the lives of these women. I did not initially intend to analyze these data in reference to continuities and discontinuities with Mexican culture. I do not think the organization of Mexican-origin families can be explained as a culture artifact. But I found that research participants themselves frequently invoked Mexican cultural norms and values in explaining their thinking or behavior in work and family matters.[1] I am honoring their words in analyzing how culture and structure shape their family lives.

Because extended family connections are central in explaining how many women manage their work and family lives, it is relevant to introduce the concept of familism here. In doing so, I draw upon Baca Zinn and Wells (2000). Familism is an orientation toward and obligation to the family. It represents a collectivist rather than an individualistic stance toward life, with group solidarity taking precedence over the preferences of individuals. Familism is generally viewed as a defining characteristic of Mexican American family life, although the empirical evidence for it has been mixed, due in part to a number of different ways of operationalizing the concept. Ramírez and Árce (1981) clarified the meaning of this term by conceptualizing familism as made up of four dimensions: demographic, structural, normative, and behavioral. Each of these dimensions can be measured and analyzed independently of the others. Demographic familism refers to characteristics such as fertility patterns and family size; structural familism considers the prevalence of extended family households; normative familism is an attitudinal component that centers on values related to family unity and solidarity; behavioral familism focuses on the interaction between family and kin networks.

An important conversation in the literature relates to the persistence of familism in second-, third-, and later generations of Mexican Americans. It is abundantly clear that familism serves the immigrant generation well. Family networks facilitate immigration and settlement. Relying on kin is an important survival strategy for immigrants. The extended family system serves as an important resource for newcomers in a foreign and sometimes hostile environment. Familistic behavior has also been found among second- and third-generation Mexican Americans of all social classes. The extended family system has long served poor and working-class households of all racial and ethnic groups as a means of circulating scarce resources to network members in their time of need (Baca Zinn and Wells 2000; Sarkisian, Gerena, and Gerstel 2006; Stack 1974). In addition, research also finds that second- and third-generation Mexican Americans who have acculturated and experienced upward mobility continue to place great value on extended family relationships (Vélez-Ibáñez 1996).

WOMEN'S LABOR FORCE PARTICIPATION

The contemporary trend with the greatest impact on family life in the United States has been women's increased labor force participation. It is increasingly likely that women—single or married, with or without children—will be employed. The most important factor explaining the rise in women's employment is the shift from a manufacturing economy to a service economy. This macrostructural transformation produced more of the service jobs that women typically fill, while reducing the manufacturing jobs that men typically fill. Men's lower earnings have resulted in the decline of the "family wage," that is, earnings sufficient to support a family on the wages of one worker. A substantial majority of U.S. families now depend on women's earnings to make ends meet (Baca Zinn, Eitzen, and Wells 2011).

Hispanic women historically have been the group of U.S. women with lowest labor force participation. In recent years, Hispanic women's labor force participation has risen sharply, but remains lower than women in other racial or ethnic groups. Of particular note, Latinas with children are significantly less likely to be employed than are other U.S. women.[2] The two principal explanations for somewhat lower labor force participation for Mexican American women have been family traditionality and generational status. The field of family studies originally approached the subject of the Mexican American family from a deficit perspective that viewed these families as mired in a traditional culture that would prove counterproductive to joining the social and economic mainstream of the United States. Thus, lower rates of women's labor force participation were attributed to persistent Mexican cultural norms and an unwillingness to adopt more contemporary family patterns (Baca Zinn and Wells 2000, 253).

Newer research and analyses provide a different picture. New immigrants are initially expected to be strongly influenced by the norms and values of their country of origin. But the process of settlement changes things, frequently altering family dynamics and reorganizing gender expectations about work and family roles as family members adapt to opportunities and constraints in their new environment (see, for example, González-Lopez 2005; Hondagneu-Sotelo 1994; Kibria 1993).

In fact, Mexican American women's labor force participation is closely tied to their generational status. Immigrant women have lower educational attainment and higher fertility than do second- and third-generation women (Duncan, Hotz, and Trejo 2006; Dye 2005). Both of these variables are associated with lower labor force participation. Therefore, it is unsurprising to find that immigrant women are much less likely to be in the labor force. An analysis of labor force participation among U.S. women ages twenty-five to fifty-nine by Duncan and his colleagues finds employment patterns of U.S.-born Mexican Americans (76 percent in labor force) to resemble closely those for white (80 percent) and African American (78 percent) women.

As to the interplay of structure and culture in this matter, Glick (2010) points to a significant development in the literature on immigrant families. She notes that scholarship is shifting from an emphasis on explaining generational differences in family processes as the result of changing cultural values or attitudes. Increasingly, researchers take structural conditions into account because they not only shape opportunities but may also serve to "alter attitudinal orientations" related to particular family behaviors (2010, 500). Thus, higher rates of labor force participation for second- and third-generation Mexican American women may reflect not so much an accommodation to U.S. cultural norms as a realistic appraisal of the structural realities of the U.S. economy in general, and their own local labor market settings in particular.

WHETHER TO WORK

None of the women I interviewed believe it inappropriate for mothers of young children to work. Their farmworker origins predict that they will be well acquainted with the necessity of women's labor force participation for the maintenance of families. Most of the families represented in the research have been involved in agricultural work for several generations. Women who grew up in the context of agricultural employment are aware of the exploitatively low wage structure in agriculture that has historically required the work of men, women, and children to provide earnings at a subsistence level (Dill 1988). Indeed, most of the research participants' mothers have picked grapes, packed onions and carrots, sorted lettuce, or other done other types of farm labor to provide for their families.

Most of these daughters and granddaughters of farmworkers do not perceive that they have the option of not working. The circumstances of their lives have simply not brought them to a place where their income may be viewed as supplementary or as not absolutely necessary. Here women's perspectives vary by marital status. The six never-married mothers say that it is precisely because they are single parents that they must work. Natalie Torres, mother of one-year-old Samantha, says, "I knew I had to work. Because I'm a single mother. And we all want good things for our kids, so we need to work." Daniela Rosales, the twenty-two-year-old mother of eighteen-month-old Justin, says matter-of-factly, "I need to work for my baby."

Single mothers seek employment because they are committed to taking financial responsibility for their children. They also work, or seek work, because it is a condition for receiving public assistance. The program providing public assistance for needy families in the United States is a welfare-to-work program called Temporary Assistance for Needy Families (TANF). California's version of this program is California Work Opportunity and Responsibility to Kids (CalWORKs). Women receiving benefits through CalWORKs were required to spend thirty-two hours per week in welfare-to-work activities such as applying for jobs to receive cash aid.

Women's labor provides more than mere survival. These women know that their work provides a higher standard of living and sets a positive example for their children. Stephanie Ruiz says, "I think of going to work as bettering me and my daughter. It's more money, more things for her. But other than that, of course, I don't ever want nothing to happen when I'm at work. That's the only thing I think about—What if? That's why I have a phone if anything happens. I always have my daughter on my mind. Always. I'm really protective over her—who picks her up, things like that. But other than that, I would prefer to be working because it's going to better her. I can get her more things."

Gloria Espinoza, age twenty-four, acknowledges that working when you have a baby is difficult, but suggests it is beneficial to her two-year-old son. She says,

"You have that attachment to your baby. At the same time, you know that you need to feed your kid, you know, and clothe him, and everything. But I've always been a very independent person. I can't say I'm not emotionally attached to my son; I've just been very independent. He needs to be independent too. He needs to see his mom working." Young, never-married mothers, even those with little labor force experience, are committed to working "so I can buy things for a better life for my child."

Twelve women are separated, divorced, or widowed mothers. Some of these women had an opportunity to be out of the labor force when their children were very young but do not have that option now. It is often a change in marital status or the anticipation of that change that brings them back into the labor force or requires them to find a better job. Erica Martinez was out of the labor force when her three daughters were young. She says, "When I was with my husband, he pretty much took care of things [financially], but then he got to be lacking. I can say right now that he is an alcoholic and I pretty much swear he is into drugs as well. So he began lacking in that sense. That is when I started to work. I started seeing things falling down and I said [to myself], 'I better start getting on track because if anything happens, you're going to need to keep up with the kids.' Because I knew he wasn't going to be responsible for them anyway."

Erica's supposition that her husband would opt out of financial responsibility for his children proved to be correct. This former farmworker now works with Mexican car dismantlers who import auto parts from salvaged vehicles on the U.S. side of the border for use in the Mexican market. His income is not reported in California, so he is able to evade paying child support. Erica fully supports the children with her clerical job as a county employee.

Beatrice Padilla's work experience has been closely related to her marital status. She has been married, divorced, remarried, and now is widowed. Her periods of regular employment have been when she was a divorced mother of three and then when her second husband died. Without Mr. Padilla's good salary as a county employee, she has taken a seasonal job, working every January through June as a bookkeeper for a local farm labor contractor.

Some women in this category are in the midst of difficult family transitions. These women are typically struggling to find work or are working in a part-time, low-wage job that does not allow them to support their children adequately. They are typically looking for a better job, not looking to get out of the work force. Angelica Perez, age twenty-five, is in this situation. She is pregnant with her fourth child and separated from her farmworker husband. She has been employed by the county as a part-time home health aide for three years, working approximately twenty hours a week. The job pays minimum wage and provides no benefits. Despite her pregnancy, she is now looking for a full-time job at higher pay because she knows that if she is to be principally responsible for the support of her children, she will need to earn more.

The economic circumstances of the twenty women with partners, fifteen married women and the five cohabiting women, were shaped both by men's labor market credentials and the structure of the local economy. Half of these women were married to or partnered with men who had not completed high school. These men generally had few employment options other than farm work, or, if they were lucky, construction work. Both jobs are unstable and provide less than year-round employment. The most commonly reported wage for farm work was minimum wage.

Among women whose husbands had better jobs, there were still house payments to make, high utility bills to pay, and the costs of raising children. These women believe they need to work at least part-time.

In most cases, women's wages were vital to sustaining families. When I asked whether they had considered staying home with their children when they were small, most women indicated that this was not an option, for reasons that were quite obvious to them. So, for example, Antonia Alivar says, "I do not like to leave my babies to work, but I need to work because I need clothes for my babies, and food." Consuela Reyes says, "No. Because I think I would give them a better life if I work. My kids need things." Priscilla Ortega says flatly, "No. Because I needed to work. We needed the income."

The crucial difference between the employment credentials of women participating in this research and those of their husbands and partners is educational attainment. Women who are better educated than their male counterparts have been able to move into white-collar service-sector employment much more readily. The experience of research participants is typical of a gendered occupational pattern found for second- and third-generation Mexican Americans; that is, the movement out of blue-collar and into white-collar occupations has proceeded more rapidly for women than men (González 2002, 115). In my research, women have found niches of service employment in fields in which women tend to be overrepresented: in social services, education, child care, and as nursing assistants.

Women's work sometimes provided the stable base that families relied on, while men's more contingent employment was far more open to question. The example of Carmen Silva is instructive here. Carmen and Miguel have a stable, twenty-year cohabiting relationship. Miguel, age thirty-eight, is a farm laborer who works fairly continuously every year from November to June; he has done this work since he was eighteen years old and has never been paid more than minimum wage. Carmen, Miguel, and their three daughters are dependent on Carmen's earnings as a clerical worker with the county. Her job pays $25,000 annually and provides health insurance for her, sick pay, paid vacation, and a pension plan.

Denise Ortiz's earnings are essential to the achievement of her family's goals. Denise is a capable twenty-eight-year-old mother of a ten-year-old son and has worked in human resources, earning $30,000 to $33,000 annually in the past several years. She has been the dominant earner in the family for much of that time but was recently laid off. Denise never considered not working. She says, "I like to work and I like my money. And if I don't have enough money, then I can never get what I want. And what we need. We need the money and, you know, want to have a home. You know, want to travel. I want to have another child. But [long pause], not at this time. Some day. When I can afford it and when I'm really settled—like I say, 'Okay, I'm going to stay here in this town.' And supposing nothing can happen, you know, let me go again. Secure somewhere." Denise's recent job loss has left her worried about the family's financial situation and disappointed in the realization that her hopes and dreams are deferred further into the future.

Lucia Hernandez, a remarried mother of four, explains that she had no choice but to work as a young mother. She says, "I needed to work because my first husband was awful [laughs]. He didn't work at all!" Lucia had to provide for her entire family, the two older children and her ex-husband.

Sometimes women's transitions into formal employment were precipitated by the workplace injury of a partner. Esther Valdez's world was turned upside-down when her husband Alberto, a farmworker, sustained a serious back injury on the job. At the time, she was a stay-at-home mom making extra money baking cakes and cupcakes. She explains, "Actually when I had to be home with my children, I did cupcakes and cakes to sell. Alberto would go out there and park the car and the kids would go out and sell the cupcakes. The kids and myself were always the bakers and the kids were the ones selling. They just knocked on doors and asked. We gave them for twenty-five cents a cupcake and the cakes, we sold 'em for three dollars. And we did pretty good actually. We made like seventy dollars a day." When the doctor told Esther that Alberto might be permanently paralyzed, she determined that she would need to support the family. She got a job working 3:00 a.m. to 10:00 a.m. in a doughnut shop and then would go to another job as a home health aide for the county, working 10:00 a.m. to 2:00 p.m. Later in the day she would go to Imperial Valley College for training to become a Certified Nursing Assistant (CNA). Alberto eventually recovered, but by then Esther was firmly committed to continued labor force participation.

Esther has now made a strategic decision to work at Walmart because it is the best way she knows to get health insurance for her family. She earns $8.70 an hour and pays $100 per month for coverage for her family of eight.[3] Esther is also thinking ahead to their retirement and is buying Walmart stock with part of her earnings. She explains, "I heard that maybe we wouldn't have Social Security when my time came around. So, I'm thinking about that."

What women would like to do and what they actually do in the labor force sometimes differ based on the degree of support they receive from their partners. Claudia and Manuel Gomez have five children. Claudia wanted to work, but would not put her children in day care. She orchestrated a split-shift parenting schedule in which she was home during the day and worked when her husband was home in the evening. She found that her husband could not or would not keep up his side of the bargain. She says, "After hearing all that banging and all that noise all day at his job [on the construction site], he wanted it quiet at night, but he had to take care of the children. So we went through a lot. I had to leave my job as well for that, because he couldn't deal with it." Marina Mendez would like to work more than she currently does, but she and her partner Ramon disagree on this matter. She would need to put their eighteen-month-old son in day care, but Ramon does not want her to do this. He wants her to wait a year or so until the boy can attend preschool. Marina is not pushing the issue for now and continues in part-time work.

Working Mothers and Child Care

Mothers who join the workforce typically must address the necessity of child care. The organization of child care in the United States requires parents, largely unassisted, to buy the care they need in the marketplace (Helburn and Bergman 2002, 2). Working parents, especially working-class and poor parents, frequently struggle to find accessible, quality care they can afford. Finding or not finding the right child care may determine whether a mother is able to work or may impose limitations on her work hours. Many parents anguish as they negotiate the trade-offs between the cost and quality of their child care options. Child care represents the largest work-related expense for most working mothers. Some rural communities have an insufficient supply of child care, limiting employment options for women who need to work.

One of the surprising findings of my research is that child care presents little difficulty for the Imperial County women. These women are embedded in family and community support networks that provide access to reliable and affordable child care. Most women have either government-subsidized child care or a family member who provides child care. Only one mother had a child in a private center with unsubsidized, nonfamily care. Among families needing child care, approximately two-thirds have care provided entirely or mostly by family members.

Mexican American women (and other women of color) are more likely to use family-provided care than are white women (Lamphere, Zavella, and Gonzales 1993; Uttal 1999). This tendency has been explained in various ways; it may represent a cultural preference for kin-care, the proximity and availability of kin, or an opportunity to minimize the cost of child care (Uttal 1999). Uttal's interviews with Mexican American mothers using kin-based care found them to be embedded in extended-family networks providing socioeconomic support. The interrelationship of extended families around the provision of care for children is an example of familism. Behavioral and structural dimensions of familism come into view in the care provided children in family members' homes or by kin sharing housing in extended family households.

CalWORKs provides significant funding for child care to enable welfare recipients to look for work. Low-earning families are also eligible for subsidized child care assistance. Care is provided either free of charge or on a sliding scale depending on income. The women I interviewed who were eligible for the subsidized care programs and used them were happy with the care their children received. For example, Angelica Perez works evening hours as a home health aide. She brings her three children to a licensed home-based care center that is open in the evenings. She says of the setting, "It's really nice." Some women brought their children to county-supported child care centers. Another group of women, six mothers, report what they think to be the best of all child care options for low-income mothers. They participate in a program in which parents are able to choose the individual who is paid to provide child care. In these cases, three mothers, two friends, and an aunt provide care. As Stephanie Ruiz says, "My child care provider is my best friend. She's very good with my daughter, so I have no problem with that. She gets paid when I go and complete the thirty-two hours. She gets paid through the CalWORKs." She refers to the time she must spend weekly in welfare-to work activities to be eligible for cash aid and child care (California Department of Social Services 2007).

A few women are suspicious about child care provided by strangers. For example, Francesca Alvarez says she prefers care provided by family or friends because her son "is little and he doesn't talk. He can't tell me if someone is hitting him." When Sylvia Moreno's children were young, her concerns about day care kept her out of the labor force. She explains, "I did want to go to work, but with everything that happens, you know, you see stuff about the day cares or whatever. My kids were too small to tell me if someone was doing something [abuse], you know."

Some express a perspective similar to that of Claudia Gomez, who says, "I don't want to leave my children with no one." It is worthy of mention here that Claudia has a large extended family in the area, but they are not particularly close. The presence of family in the community does not necessarily mean that a mother will ask family members to provide care or that they will agree to do so if asked. But the determination not to use day care does not necessarily keep these women out of the workforce. Instead, they may use split-shift parenting and other arrangements with family and friends. Margarita Campos, a divorced mother of three who is currently unemployed, says, "If I would find a nice day care that I would trust, I qualify for the program where the county pays that day care for you—for low income." Because she has not found this, she has developed a complex arrangement with friends who work different shifts to fill in the care gaps when she works.

A large majority of women interviewed rely on family members to care for their children while they work. The most frequently named family members were mothers, followed by sisters or sisters-in-law and fathers. In some cases, women have a somewhat complicated web of care, but care provision is anchored within the family. For example, Priscilla Ortega pays a nonfamily person to pick up her son at school and bring him to her sister's home; the sister is paid to provide after-school care.

Marjorie Salas expressed an idea I did not hear from anyone else. She said, "That's the thing with Mexican families, you don't take them [your children] to a day care. You take them to your family." Some years ago as a single mother of two young children, she used both family care and a community day care center out of necessity. Now she pays her sister-in-law, a stay-at-home mom, to care for her third child. Marjorie is ambivalent about this arrangement. She is happy Robby is in family care but is concerned that he is sitting in front of the TV all day and as a result he is not developing the oral skills he should have by now. She notes that her two older children did go to day care and they did not experience speech delays.

Reliance on family for child care is especially prevalent in extended-family households. In this case, care is seamless, with both child and caretaker remaining in their home setting. Mothers are especially grateful for this arrangement. In some cases older (and infirm) parents have moved in with an adult child; these grandparents provide child care. Ana Ramirez, a teacher who is a single mother, lives with her parents, elderly people of limited means, and assumes responsibility for most of the bills. At the same time, they provide important assistance. Her father drives her son to and from school every day. She says, "I am very blessed that he can do that." She appreciates that her parents are always home, so her son is never alone. In some cases a woman, her husband, and children have lived for many years with his or her parents in an extended-family household.

Sometimes, unmarried mothers and their children have continued to live with her parents. Theresa Romero and her younger sister have always lived at home. When Theresa became pregnant, she and her parents strategized to determine an occupational path that would enable her to support the child adequately. They developed an elaborate plan that would require Theresa's parents to take considerable, if not principal, responsibility for the care of her infant daughter, Crystal, while she trained for and then began a career as a border control agent. This career would enable Theresa to provide the financially stable life she desired for Crystal. She describes the plan:

> I was going to be located with the Tucson [Arizona] sector. And even that was going to be very hard for me, but my parents have always supported me. They're like, "We'll keep the baby. You go over there and you do what you have to do. We'll drive up to Yuma on your days off so you can see her and your mom will drive up and stay with you." Everything had been all planned out. It

was just—I could not go through with it. I can't be away from home that long. I went to the Border Patrol and I took the test, did the background [check], went to the academy and lasted two weeks. I couldn't bear to be without my daughter. I was in Georgia.

Theresa has instead begun a career as an optical technician. Her mother, a seasonal farmworker, has cared for her granddaughter since infancy. When she goes to work packing carrots, they pay a neighbor to care for Crystal.

Extended household arrangements well accommodate employment situations in which women work nonstandard hours. While the 24/7 economy provides goods and services at convenient times for customers, the challenge of finding appropriate child care for the night shift or weekends often creates additional stress for low-income mothers (Bianchi and Milkie 2010). In Theresa's case, when she is scheduled to work on Saturdays, she has no serious concerns because she is able to work out arrangements for Crystal's care with three other adults in the household.

Several families had transnational child care strategies, that is, child care arrangements that required the crossing of the U.S.-Mexico border. So, for example, when a family has working parents and school-age children, a relative might come up from Mexicali during school breaks to care for the children. Or, if the relative does not have a Border Crossing Card that allows for frequent border crossings, the children might visit relatives in Mexico for school breaks. In one better-off family, a caregiver from Mexico was hired to come up for the workweek. Celia Roberts, a thirty-five-year-old mother of two sons and a daughter, worked as an assistant in a medical office and her husband worked for a plumbing and heating company. Celia explains that Yolanda, the care provider, was picked up at the border on Sunday evening and returned to the border on Friday evening after work. She was paid one hundred dollars per week for her work. I asked Celia if they had an extra bedroom for the woman to use. She answered, "No," that Yolanda slept on the sofa in the living room. She explained that the Mexican woman had low expectations for accommodations. Celia said, "A lot of people will do that, you know. They come here and they are satisfied with very little wage. One hundred dollars a week will go quite far over there, so she was very satisfied." Her perspective on the earnings differential between the United States and Mexico is quite accurate. In 2005 the minimum wage per *day* in Mexico was $4.29 in U.S. dollars (computed on the basis of 11 pesos per dollar exchange rate in 2005).

Antonia Avilar has had a friend come up from Mexicali to provide care for her three children. Because Antonia's family of five lives in a small two-bedroom trailer, the friend stays with a cousin in Brawley. Antonia pays her fifty dollars a week. When she has worked overtime, she pays more, up to eighty dollars per week.

Both Erica Martinez and Margarita Campos have elaborate child care strategies that include a transnational component. Erica explains that she has no real worries about the provision of care for her daughters. She says, "I live with my mother, [so] she helps me out with my girls. If she is sick or what not, my neighbors—we've been there for quite some time—they pretty much help out. And, if that doesn't work out, I have a lot of family members across the border and they will come over to my house. So child care hasn't been much of an issue. At one point I had to pay relatives [from Mexicali] to take care of my girls when my mother was very ill. One or two days is not a problem, but week after week, I need to pay."

Margarita's plan for child care when she is working relies on friends and her fifteen-year-old son to care for the two younger children. In the summers, either her mother from Mexicali comes up to provide child care or her children go down to Mexicali to their grandmother's home. Transnational child care strategies once again reveal the U.S.-Mexico border area to be a dynamic region of social and economic interdependence.

Roschelle (1997) found evidence for the decline of familism among Mexican Americans and other U.S. minorities. In her quantitative analysis, the provision and receipt of child care assistance were the central measures of women's involvement in familistic behavior. Roschelle suggested the deteriorating economic position of racial-ethnics in U.S. society may have rendered minority families unable to participate in networks of exchange because they lack the resources to do so. My qualitative study of Mexican American women in one of the most disadvantaged places in the United States finds something quite different. Here the provision of child care by extended family members serves as a vital resource that enables families with young children to survive economically in a context of high poverty and broad underemployment.

The work and family literature clearly shows that a deficit of care characterizes the experience of many U.S. working families as employed parents struggle to construct networks of care for their children (Nelson 2000, Hansen 2004). Hansen (2004) considers the "asking rules" that guide parents' willingness to ask for help from family and friends.[4] She finds network transactions to be guided by rules of reciprocity, which assume that receiving support creates future obligation. Thus families stretched to the limit may be isolated from the support they desperately need by their inability to reciprocate. Again, my research shows something quite different. The familism that is an aspect of the culture of the Mexican American families I studied includes clear expectations about caregiving across generations. These expectations were shared by both caregivers and care recipients in kin networks. But I did not find evidence of keeping score or negotiating paybacks. Family networks functioned as a major resource for promoting positive outcomes among extended kin. In many cases, the support for caregiving was facilitated by coresidence.

Nearly all of these mothers of young children had access to either publicly subsidized child care services or family-provided care. Most had little or no out-of-pocket expenditures for child care. This does not mean working mothers were spared from the challenges of integrating work and family, only that child care difficulties did not stand in the way of their labor force participation. For many, the piece that was missing in the work–family interface was a job.

NEGOTIATING WORK AND THE EXTENDED FAMILY

Evidence of familism among this sample has already been seen in the presence of extended family households and the reliance on kin networks for child care. I found familism in two additional and unexpected circumstances as well. First, the employment outlook in the county is grim. One of the strategies several families eventually used in coping with a flat local job market was moving to a place where extended family members already lived and testing their economic fortunes there. They cut the risks and costs of relocation by moving into the households of these extended family members. Women reported that their families lived with relatives for long periods of time, up to several years. Women reported, for example, moving in with a sister-in-law's family in Las Vegas, a mother-in-law in Banning, California, and a partner's sister in Phoenix.

Antonia Avilar, her husband Luis, and their three children lived in Banning for a total of four years. They moved in with Luis's mother and shared her small home. The work they had in Banning, while low-wage work, was full-time and stable; it was better work than they could find in Imperial County. In Banning, Antonia worked in a plastics factory while her husband worked in maintenance for an apartment complex. Since returning to Brawley, Antonia has worked on-call in a nursing home and as a part-time cook in a restaurant; she is currently unemployed. Luis developed cancer and has been unable to work.

Denise and Raul Ortiz and their son Michael lived for three years in Las Vegas with Raul's sister, her husband, and their children. This move enabled Raul to break out of agricultural employment, which he had not been able to accomplish in Brawley. He got a job in a gas station and was later promoted to assistant manager. Denise gained valuable experience working in a medical office.

Women were matter-of-fact in describing these moves. Moving in with relatives seemed to be understood as a customary pattern of extended family relations. In explaining her family's move to Las Vegas, Denise Ortiz says, "My husband's sister lives in Las Vegas, so we had a place to stay." She did not amplify further. The private nuclear family—consisting of a married couple and their dependent child living in a separate household—has long been idealized in U.S. society. But the likelihood of living in a nuclear-family household correlates with social class. Working-class and poor families, with insecure resources from unstable jobs, have more difficulty achieving this ideal. For families in higher social classes, the assumption that your family might move into the nuclear family household of a sibling for an extended period of time might be unimaginable.

The structural underpinnings of a family's decision to seek employment in a better labor market where extended family members already reside are obvious. The cultural component is seen here in the unquestioned expectation and obligation to share housing within the extended family network. Coresidence did not necessarily represent a transitional measure, but was sometimes continued well after newcomers found jobs.

Second, I encountered what I term the "call to come home." Several women told me how they, their partners, and children had left the Imperial Valley for economic reasons and then were drawn back by the pull of extended family circumstances. Many times couples left steady jobs in better local labor markets to return home to the Valley. The Avilars, for example, moved back to Brawley when Antonia's mother in Mexicali became seriously ill. The circumstances for Francesca Alvarez and her partner, Tony, are similar; this young couple was living in Phoenix, where Tony worked in construction and Francesca worked in a furniture store. Her mother became ill and they came back so Francesca could care for her mother. Now neither of them can find local employment and they live with her family. After living in Phoenix, a major metropolitan area with a high number and wide variety of available jobs, the couple is rather stunned to find how difficult it is to find even a bad job in the Imperial Valley.

In another instance, Julie and Roberto Peña had lived in Las Vegas for four years and were faring well. Then, five years ago, Roberto's parents asked them to move back to the Valley so Roberto could help his aging father with his car-repair business. This family, including four children, lives with Roberto's parents. Julie reports that her husband is paid only $7.50 an hour, but they receive free rent. Julie was initially somewhat reluctant to move in with her in-laws. She says, "I told Roberto, 'Okay, we're only going to live with them for a little bit.' Because I've always had my own place. And to live with someone underneath their roof, their house, their rules, their whatever, you know, that was kind of hard. Five years—okay, it's time to move." The children are now very attached to their grandparents. Julie appreciates all they have done for her family, but now concludes, "I need to have my own family and my own home." She hopes they will be moving out soon.

Denise and Raul Ortiz moved back to Brawley and into his parents' household when Raul's mother was diagnosed with a serious illness. On the subject of leaving her job in Las Vegas, Denise says, "I really liked it there too, but we had to move back to the Valley." They stayed in the parents' household for a total of three years and later moved to Palm Desert to accommodate the good job Denise found there. Unfortunately, both Denise and Raul had just been laid off from their jobs in Palm Desert when Raul's mother died. Now they have moved back to Brawley again and back into his father's house. Denise frames the move in terms of Mexican culture. She explains that as the youngest child, Raul is expected to watch over his father. She says, "And my husband is the baby [of the family], so it's like we are there to kind of watch over him so he won't be alone." Denise presents the situation ironically, "Either way, we would have ended up coming back." The familistic assumptions of Mexican culture predicted their return under one of two scenarios. First, without jobs, Raul's parents would have taken them back into their household without question. And second, as it turned out, cultural expectations about adult children's responsibilities for their parents' well-being required them to move back.

The narratives of these Mexican American women reveal the continuing significance of the extended family system in the construction and maintenance of family life. In some cases, familistic behaviors may be described as cultural adaptations that enable network members to cope with structural disadvantage. The cultural aspect is apparent in the very high value these individuals place on their family relationships. The actions that proceeded from strong family ties in several cases were these: when parents were in need, adult children sometimes quit their jobs, packed up their household belongings, moved back to Brawley, and usually moved in with the parents. Furthermore, they moved to a place where it was very difficult to find employment. This is not a recipe for economic success. But let us look deeper. As a structural matter, we must locate these extended family relations in their social class context. All of the families involved in these kin relations are working class or poor. As such they live close to the economic edge. Their employment is not very secure and their wages have not created a stable economic foundation for family life. It is in this structural context that working-class and poor families rely on their kin. They value highly their family relationships to be sure, but given their disadvantaged economic position they have little recourse other than to depend on them for assistance when life is difficult. Let us also note that none of the adult children who heeded the "call to come home" owned their own homes or left jobs with $50,000 salaries and generous pension plans. Middle-class families with resources at this level might equally value their families but demonstrate it differently. For the Imperial County women, family is experienced as both a resource and a responsibility. For people of limited means, reliance on the extended family proves to be a rational way of spreading out responsibility for care and economic support of families across generations.

GENDER AND FAMILY LIFE

In this section I consider the organization of gender in the families of women participating in the research. The family is a gendered institution, that is to say, gender is deeply embedded in the practices and policies that organize family life (Acker 1992). I am interested in what women told me about the gendered experiences of their family lives, especially as they relate to labor force participation and the care and nurture of children. Patterns of gender relations are created and sustained in particular social and spatial contexts. The fact that the

Imperial County women live in spatial proximity to Mexico and were raised by parents who were immigrants or children of immigrants suggests some continuity with Mexican cultural ideals and practices. At the same time, we know that the processes of immigration and settlement tend to shift gender relations in a less patriarchal direction for the immigrant generation (Hondagneu-Sotelo 1994). Over the course of the interviews, some women, but by no means all, did invoke Mexican culture in explaining their actions or the events of their lives. In most instances, women mention Mexican cultural norms in contesting them. Most often their comments related to Mexican culture referenced assumptions about a sharply divided gender system in which women's role as mother was primary, men dominated in family decision making, and marriage was permanent.[5]

There is no singular scholarly formulation of what traditional Mexican cultural ideals regarding the family would amount to, but women invoked Mexican culture in ways that are consistent with scholarly understandings of this subject. For our purposes, Adelaida Del Castillo's characterization of gender-based cultural ideals for family life in Mexico is useful. She writes, "According to the traditional ideal, men have authority over women, the husband has authority over his wife as does the brother over his sister; and while the older have authority over the younger, the father remains the ultimate authority over the household and family matters." Men's primary role is to provide for their families economically, while women fulfill their primary social roles in being wives and mothers (Del Castillo 1996, 212, 217). This traditional ideal posits a gender system that is fundamentally patriarchal, with men dominant and women subordinate. Other tenets of the family gender system are the understandings that couples marry young, that premarital pregnancy results in marriage, and that marriage is permanent (Schneider and Silverman 2010).

Cultural ideals may in fact be quite inconsistent with the ways people can and actually do organize their family lives. Ideal representations—in this case about Mexican families—create an assumption that all families in a particular setting will be organized in the same way. In fact, the uneven access of all groups to social privileges and opportunities predicts a diversity of family forms and structures. Further, cultural ideals are resistant to revision, despite changed circumstances. As global processes of social and economic change have transformed Mexico, the societal underpinnings supporting the traditional family ideal have weakened. This means the traditional formulation of the Mexican family describes contemporary families in Mexico less and less. For example, dramatically higher labor force participation for women, more female-headed households, later marriage, and smaller families have accompanied massive social change in Mexico in recent decades.

Although the women I interviewed believe it is appropriate for mothers to work, some experienced considerable pressure to stay out of the workforce. This proscription was frequently framed in terms of Mexican culture. The explicit or implicit rationale for rejecting women's labor force participation was that women "belonged" in the domestic realm, while men "belonged" in the work force.

Marjorie Salas's parents-in-law are opposed to her working. She relates an exchange she had had with them the day prior to our interview:

> Yesterday my in-laws were saying, "You married him, now you are supposed to stay home no matter what your husband provides." But that's not possible. We can't afford it. You see it goes back to Mexican values—that women are supposed to stay home. My mother-in-law said, "Well, didn't your mother teach you this, that women are supposed to stay home and watch the children and make sure to have dinner [ready]?" I said, "Oh no, no, no! My mother did not teach me that. My mother taught me that I needed to provide for myself in case I was on my own." And so that was our discussion yesterday [laughs].

Marjorie knows from her own family experience that women cannot just plan to be homemakers. When her mother married, she did have every expectation of a permanent marriage. Marjorie says, "With my mother, you know, it's, 'You're married and now you're with that person for the rest of your life until death do you part,' and she would always say that. And he turned out not to be a very good person, so he left when I was four and my mother had to start working. And so, she worked her entire life."

Miranda Flores has had reason to rethink assumptions about both women's labor force participation and the permanence of marriage. Three months before the interview, after twenty-seven years of marriage, her farmworker husband Lorenzo left town with his latest paycheck and the family car. Miranda married Lorenzo when she became pregnant at age sixteen. Until her son was born, she attended Teen Mothers, an educational program for pregnant teens. She quit after his birth. The fact that Lorenzo had not permitted her to work now affects her ability to provide for herself. Miranda explains how a young woman might interpret this prohibition as love and care, but in the end, not working may create dependence and susceptibility to poverty. She says:

> You see this happens: He says, "I don't want you working." Oh, all I hear is, "He loves me. He doesn't want me to work." They make you think, "Oh my God, you're so special." What an idiot. I could have been doing something over here or at least finishing school. Instead of having kids early. You're home taking care of the kid, your baby. Your husband goes to work. It's like a picket fence type of thing in your mind. 'Cause you're young. Look at me now. I tell my kids—don't do the same thing I did. And if you do get married—like my son—let your wife work. Because it's not going to be fair for her to lose out—if something happens. Same thing for my daughter. Don't get married. You're too young. Don't even think about it. You know what I mean? Because there is too much in this world right now.

Miranda says that the idea in Mexican culture that you stay with your marriage, no matter what happens, is still out there, but "those are the old ways. Now, it's like, the smart girls, they see what they got to do. And that's when they boot the guy out the door. But we're like the old way—I was doing the traditional Brawley. But now it's too late." Miranda explains, in part, why she did not contest Lorenzo's decision that she should not work. The assumption that husbands have the final say in family decision making is a deeply ingrained supposition in a patriarchal gender system (Amato et al. 2007).

The same theme—self-recrimination in the aftermath of conceding to patriarchal authority—also figures importantly in Christina Gilbert's life. She, like Miranda, now regrets her willingness to yield decision making to her former husband. Christina described to me the sharp decline in her family's economic situation when they moved from Las Vegas, where they both had good jobs, back to Brawley. She says, "In Las Vegas, we had everything, everything. It was no big deal to have six to ten thousand dollars in the bank account at a time. It was no big deal. We had a five-bedroom house, three baths, three-car garage, and a big, huge yard. We had everything, but he wanted to come back to work in a family business. So, stupid me, the typical Mexican wife [laughs], I was like, 'Okay, if that's what you want. As long as you are happy.'" I asked Christina if she thought most Mexican-origin women would react as she had done. She responded, "It depends how you were raised. It just depends how you were raised. Because some women that I know would say, 'Hell, no. I am not leaving.' But I was raised, my sister was raised, and my brother was raised that we, as far as the women—my sister and I—do whatever our husbands say. If he wants to leave, then we leave. If he wants to stay, then we stay. His decision is what goes." Christina says she thinks that increasingly, more Mexican-origin women hold the "Hell, no. I am not leaving" rather than the "If he wants to leave, then we leave" perspective. She thinks this reflects the fact that Mexican American women are becoming more independent and assertive.

Christina explains her understanding of men's and women's appropriate roles in decision making as reflecting how she was raised. Interestingly, however, she also says, "Even though in my mom's household, she made all the decisions." She explains that her father could have "put his foot down and said, 'Lupe (her mother), I don't think so. It's not going to go that way.' But he never did." In Christina's family of origin experience, prescriptions for men's dominance and women's subordination are located more in ideology than practice. It appears that children were taught traditional gender norms by parents who did not visibly practice them. Christina and her husband Kevin were recently divorced. She now lives in subsidized housing and has a part-time job. She ruminates about her current situation and says, "Why did I even leave Vegas?" With respect to gender ideology, there may be discrepancies between what people say and what they do. Research since the 1980s finds that Mexican American couples who espouse patriarchal gender ideology may nonetheless engage in egalitarian decision making (Baca Zinn 1980; Ybarra 1982).

Sylvia Moreno told me that her marital status is "common law," and that she has been with the father of her three children for thirteen years. She initially explains her status in this way: "I don't want to get married. I don't have anything against it, but I don't think it's for me. I feel like if something happens between us, I don't want to have to deal with no paperwork. My kids know their dad." Later in the interview, Sylvia expressed strong ideas about women's need to establish economic independence. In this way, women can avoid being overly-dependent on men, which she believes can lead to partner abuse. She says:

> If you have your own money, you basically have control over your own life. You don't have to ask him for money, like if he was your father. I work. I have my money. I get to do what I want to with it, just as long as the bills are paid and my kids are fine. I think men are intimidated [by this type of thinking]. But that's why they work too. So they can make their own money. As long as you meet each other half way with the bills, and don't complain about it—because bills do have to get paid. I like to make my own money. That's why half of these women are always getting battered, beat up. Because men are so used to, you know, they say, "She doesn't listen to me." So they turn about and beat the crap out of them. No. There's no need for that.

Sylvia believes that marriage creates a paternalistic relationship between women and men that leaves women vulnerable and, perhaps, physically endangered. In rejecting marriage, she affirms that she will be both financially independent and equally responsible for the support of her children. Sylvia's views do, in fact, capture two robust findings in the gender and family literature. First, research over several decades shows that Latinas enhance their status in their families though employment. Second, working wives are less likely to be victims of partner abuse than are wives who are out of the labor force (See, for example, Baca Zinn 1980; Gelles and Strauss 1988).

Although U.S. men's weekly hours of housework and child care have increased over several decades, women continue to be disproportionately responsible for domestic work (Sayer et al. 2005). Many of the Imperial County women expect their husbands to be more involved in parenting than is actually the case. While women want partners to help with the children, some men assume their responsibility to the family ends at breadwinning. It has been difficult for Christina Gilbert to work because she could not depend on her husband's assistance with the children. During several years of their marriage, Christina and her husband Kevin lived with her parents in Brawley. When this was the case, Kevin expected Christina's mother to care for the children in Christina's absence. "All he would have to do is work. He could leave and come back and leave and come back. It's my fault also because I let him be that way." When they lived in Las Vegas, the couple tried to work staggered shifts to minimize the children's time in daycare and save money. Cristina explains, "He would get home by 5:00 and take care of the kids until I got home. It was hard for him. He wasn't used to it. My son hated his high chair. His dad would leave him in it a lot."

Eva Vallejo has tried for many years to get her husband Tomas more involved in parenting their children. Tomas' contributions to family life are consistent with the separate spheres model for gender roles prevalent in the U.S. in the nineteenth and most of the twentieth centuries. This model prescribed bread-winning as men's responsibility and home and family as women's responsi-bility. Eva is very frustrated by her husband's behavior. She explains, "I truly believe that no matter how much I would like for my husband to get involved in all the aspects of everything, his whole deal is—work, and then come home and eat. And he's getting better at it, but it's like, 'I'm sorry. I'm gonna hit my fifties here pretty soon and it's taken you all this time to get, to get to this point that, yeah, you gotta get more involved. Our kids are here just for a short time and then they're out of the house. And you know, you gotta get involved.' The separate spheres model was undermined by the major social and economic transformations that brought women into the U.S. labor force in the final decades of the twentieth century. This massive entry of women into the work-force may be described as a change of revolutionary proportions. The Vallejos provide an excellent example of what Arlie Hochschild (1989) has called "the stalled revolution." This couple has moved well beyond separate spheres in that Eva has for many years had a full-time job; at the same time, Tomas has not made a corresponding move into greater family involvement. The couple now shares breadwinning, but Tomas continues to expect that Eva will nurture the children and attend to their needs.

Sometimes mothers negotiate their parenting responsibilities in light of what they describe as their partners' deficits in this area. Julie Peña expresses the need to be hyper-attentive to her children's well-being because she cannot fully depend on her husband. She says,

> It is hard to work or go to school when you have family responsibilities. Okay, I'll take an example. Yesterday, I was at work and my husband gets into what he's doing; he's really into it. So he forgot to pick up my daughter from school. So she's out there. She's only in first grade. So she's only six years old. Well she's out there for a long time. She's out there for about an hour. And that totally scared her, you know. And I thought, Oh my gosh, you know. Here I am look-ing for a full-time job, but I'm kind of scared in a way, you know. I need to make sure my kids are safe!

Julie raced to school to pick up her daughter Amber. When she arrived, Amber was waiting alone, with no adults in sight. She concludes, "I know from the finances that I need a full-time job, but my kids! I've got to think about that."

Mothers as Primary Parents

The experience of women, whatever their race or ethnicity, in negotiating work and family is undoubtedly shaped by conventional thinking about the organization of gender in the family. Two of the central cultural assumptions continuing to shape family life are these: first, children are principally the responsibility of mothers; and second, mothers should immerse themselves in the care and nurture of their children. These assumptions have consequences in the day-to-day lives of women who are parents, predicting exhaustion and guilt for working mothers and supporting fathers' nonparticipation in the lives of their children (Garey 1999, 193).

For the women I interviewed, the role of mother held central importance in their lives. Their greatest concern was the well-being of their children. In examining their perspectives on work, mothers recognized that providing a decent standard of living for their children required their labor force participation. The role of worker was important to them, but it was largely important instrumentally as a means by which they took responsibility for their children. Thus, providing for their children was an extension of their role as mother. In examining their perspectives on parenting, these working women did not promote a gender division of labor in which their husbands and partners co-parented the children, that is, shared parenting equally. Instead, women view themselves as the primary parent. They do believe fathers have an obligation to be involved in their children's lives. They also want men to lend a hand in the everyday necessities of family life. But men are mostly viewed as helpers. When parents work different shifts, women expect fathers to be competent and attentive parents in their absence. When mothers experience overload, they would like their partners to assist them so their load is manageable. Most women believe their partners are not doing enough to help, and want them to do more. But ultimately, mothers intend to remain fundamentally responsible for raising the children. Women's intensive involvement in parenting provides them with authority in matters related to their children's well-being that they are reluctant to concede or even to share with their partners.

The Imperial County women frequently assert the primacy of women's role as mothers. Women work out of necessity, but at the same time believe it makes it more difficult for them to fulfill their unique responsibilities as mothers. Elena Sanchez expresses this concern, "You are the only one who can give the caring and the punishing to your children. It's very, very hard when you have to depend on someone else to make them go the right way and not the wrong way. You don't know what's going on with your kids because you are working, but it will always be on your mind. Okay, are my kids getting treated right? Are my kids eating? Are my kids changed, because I have a son in diapers? The last think I need is for him to get rashes."

Many working mothers experience the tension of working the double-day. Their responsibilities for work and family produce overload and leave them stressed and over-extended.[6] In response to my question of whether she found it hard to work, Sylvia Moreno says:

> Yes, it's hard [said emphatically]. It's really hard [laughs]. It's hard because you have to deal with work and after work you come home and deal with the kids and their homework and the bills and the food and the problems and . . . [said rhythmically]. And then you have to go to work and deal with stuff there, the problems there, the stress there. There's days where I think, Oh my gosh, I think I'm going to have a nervous breakdown. But no, you just count to ten [laughs]. It's always constant. Always doing something. If it's not at work, it's work at home. You never rest. Being a mother and working, you're always basically working—except when you sleep.

Marjorie Salas wakes up earlier than her husband because she has to get everything and everyone ready for the day. She rises at 5:00 or 5:30, depending on how busy her upcoming day will be. Marjorie's three children range in age from two to thirteen and are involved in different things, so it is hard to find the time to do everything. "It is just very difficult." She is the one who plays with the kids and feels the need and obligation to devote a lot of time to them. She says her husband does not feel that obligation; his priority is work. Both Marjorie and her husband are teachers. While her husband prioritizes work over family, Marjorie must juggle the demands of both. A busy family does not allow her to shirk the time-intensive demands of her job. She says, "You know, going home after school, I still have to grade papers. My Saturdays and my Sundays, I come to my classroom. So my kids are like, 'Mom, when are you going to give us time?'"[7]

Like Marjorie, other women fear that women's double day means that children are not getting the time they need with their mothers. Eva Vallejo, who struggles to get her husband more involved in the lives of their children, is uncomfortable with the compromises mothers must make to be both workers and parents. She says, "I think it is difficult trying to be a good mother while working. It is possible to find child care and find a way to pay for it, but there are still time issues. You don't have the time to spend with your children that you would like."

Esther Valdez articulates in stark terms the dilemmas she and other working-class women encounter in negotiating work and families. Esther believes that working is actually detrimental to the children, but she has no real alternative. She explains, "Children need a lot of taking care of. And, um, I have to make a choice between providing—not good, but just enough for everything—to have food, bills paid, and just a little bit of nice clothes on them. It takes away the time I need for them. And actually the love, the conversations, the listening, the homework. I'm too tired to be with them with the homework. I feel, really honestly, if I didn't have to go to work, I would be able to have my children get a better education."

Elena Sanchez described a circumstance in which the financial gains her family would experience by her working did not offset the compromise it necessitated in the fulfillment of her role as mother. Elena preferred not to work when her children were very small. She usually waited until they were walking. But two years ago when her youngest was three months old, she took a job "working the seasonal." She explains:

> It was just for a month or so packing chilies. There you have to be fast—you couldn't be slow. You had to stick those chilies in the packages. It was the first time I had to depend on someone I didn't know to take care of my newborn. And it really hit me after four weeks, when I stayed home for the weekend because it was Christmas, so they gave us the weekend off. My son didn't know me. The way I brought him home, and how I slept him, and how I fed him—was very different from how Natasha [the care provider] was doing it. And when Natasha did it he was comfortable because he got used to it. So when I got home and took care of him, he was fussy. I quit that Sunday night. I called and said, "I can't come back."

Ultimately, for Elena, the compromise she made, trading off time with her infant son for income the family needed, was not sustainable. She decided that her primary responsibility as the nurturing mother of an infant superseded her responsibility as co-provider.

The concerns these working mothers have about not spending sufficient time with their children are consistent with research on the work-family interface. Work-family conflict negatively affects the psychological and physical well-being of women more than men. Evidence suggests that continuing cultural scripts assuming maternal devotion and holding women ultimately responsible for a successful family life create pressures that take a toll on working women's lives (Bianchi and Milkie 2010, 713).

Empowered by Motherhood

Many women have been empowered by motherhood. They have been principal caregivers and decision-makers in the lives of their children. They have gained moral authority through the heavy investment of their time in the care and provision for their children. Some now assert their right and responsibility to make difficult decisions about the future of marriage or partner relationships. The guiding principle in making decisions about staying with or breaking up with partners is the long-term best interest of the children.

Substance abuse is the most common reason for women's decisions to divorce or separate from their husbands. Given the rampant substance abuse in the Valley, everyone is aware of the capacity of drugs and alcohol to ruin the lives of promising young people. Erica Martinez has long been separated from her husband and the father of her three girls. She believed his alcohol abuse created an inappropriate environment for the children. For Monica Rodriguez, it is her husband's involvement in drugs that led her to initiate divorce. She is determined to keep her sons away from drugs.

If Erica Martinez and Monica Rodriguez exited their marriages because of their partners' substance abuse, Miranda Flores presents an interesting counterpoint. Miranda stayed with Lorenzo, in part, because he did not use drugs. Drug abuse was endemic among members of Miranda's large family of origin. She says, "I've seen sisters hurting because they had husbands who used drugs. And getting robbed [by their own husbands]. And on top of that my brothers had wives that they were taking from. So that's why I stuck with my husband. Because he worked and he didn't use [drugs]. And I don't want to go up against his will because I don't want to lose him and then I might end up with something like that." In Miranda's case, she stayed in a difficult marriage because she thought she and her children would be better off with their father than they might be with someone else who just might bring drugs into the home. Miranda was disempowered by Lorenzo's decision that she could not work. As an economically dependent woman with children, she perceived that her only real options were to be supported by one man or another.

Patricia Ochoa says very explicitly that her husband Joe's disregard for their children's financial stability has resulted in their permanent separation. When Joe lost his job, Patricia opened a family daycare to provide for the family. As Joe's alcoholism created increasing family turmoil, Patricia and the children left the home. She understood that Joe had difficulty coping with the loss of the breadwinner role. She explains his behavior by saying, "Him being a Hispanic and the machismo and all of this, you know, it, it took its toll. I understand that. It took its toll. He felt that I was supporting him." Joe then took steps that resulted in the loss of her daycare license. This was a defining moment for Patricia. She says, "I didn't know if it [the separation] was just temporary or what. Well, because of his actions—that made our separation permanent. If he didn't care, this is the way I looked at him, if he didn't care enough for his children, he took away from his children, he took away their means of, their financial means, you know, the daycare, which is what we had. And if he didn't care about that, then what is that telling me? It's not—if it was just me—that's totally different. But he took away from his own children, and what is that? So he made it permanent."

Claudia Gomez is becoming increasingly dissatisfied with what she views as her husband's inadequate contribution to the family. She has difficulty coping with his unwillingness to share the cooking and cleaning at home. He had a disabling workplace accident that left him unable to work. She says, "It's frustrating! You can only handle so much. And I can't send him off to work. My husband is thirty-one. How is a young man, young guy, supposed to just sit on his butt at the house and not do nothing?" Claudia wonders what it would be like to be on her own, but for now, evaluates that option in terms of its effect on her children. She speculates, "And if you leave them [your husband], it affects the kids in different ways. They've all got different personalities. I've got five little personalities on my hands." For now, Claudia has decided to stay in the relationship. Crucial in her decision-making process has been her best judgment as to what is best for her children.

The decisions of these women to divorce or separate from their husbands and fathers of their children (or to consider it seriously) may seem incongruous in view of traditional Mexican cultural norms that emphasize men's authority, women's passivity, and marital permanence. Let me note again that traditional norms may be principally cultural ideals that, first, may be weakening; and second, may not necessarily be embodied in practice. Second- and third-generation Mexican Americans are negotiating both Mexican culture (to the degree it is perpetuated in their families and community) and also, and more immediately, the realities of their lives in U.S. society. The family ideal in the U.S. has been the nuclear family, a married, heterosexual couple household with a breadwinning father and a full-time wife and mother. This cultural ideal has declined dramatically in practice, with less than ten percent of U.S. households embodying that ideal form (Baca Zinn et al. 2011).

Power relations in nuclear families are patriarchal. Men's authority derives principally from the economic resources they bring into the family. Kandiyoti uses the term "patriarchal bargain" to refer to "the existence of set rules and scripts regulating gender relations, to which both genders accommodate and acquiesce, yet which may nonetheless be contested, redefined, and renegotiated" (1988, 286). Barrie Thorne writes that in the patriarchal bargain of the traditional nuclear family, women exchange their domestic services and subordination for men's economic support and protection (1992, 8). This bargain was based on structural conditions that largely no longer exist today. The traditional nuclear family bargain has been undermined by the macrostructural transformation (discussed earlier in the chapter) that drew women into the workforce while also destabilizing men's employment. Social structural shifts that altered patterns of work for women and men have also reshaped relations of gender and power in families. A consistent finding in the gender literature is that women's earnings translate into influence in the relationship (See for example, Amato et al. 2007; Greenstein 2000). Women's employment also means they are less dependent on the earnings of men. The old patriarchal bargain has broken down because working women can, in the postindustrial economy, be largely self-sufficient.

The fact that women can support themselves and their children, even at a marginal level, gives women a degree of self-determination they could not have when they were relegated solely to the domestic sphere. What happens then if women believe men's presence in the household presents a risk to their children? What happens if men are no longer good providers and then are unable or unwilling to take on other responsibilities in the family? Erica, Monica, and Patricia made decisions to separate from husbands who were a negative influence on the children. The men were also unreliable providers. The women were able to provide for their children by their own earnings (although Patricia did require some transitional public assistance). A generation or two ago, women—with fewer economic resources—might have decided to endure a detrimental domestic situation so children would have a roof over their heads.

Recent urban-based research also finds substance abuse to precipitate women's decisions to break up with the fathers of their children. Edin and Kefalas (2005) studied a racially and ethnically diverse sample of poor mothers and their families in the most economically depressed neighborhoods of Philadelphia. These urban mothers (mostly never-married) are in many respects quite different from my more economically diverse sample of Mexican American women (mostly married, divorced, and separated) in a rural setting. But important similarities are these: first, mothers view their relationships with their children as primary, taking precedence over partner relationships; second, a major factor leading to the break down of the partner relationships is their partners' drug and alcohol abuse; and third, both groups of women express concern that the continuation of these relationships puts their children at risk.

This chapter has explored the work-family interface for these second- and third-generation Mexican American women. First, I find the Imperial County women to be committed to labor force participation. Given family history and local labor market context, this is hardly surprising. Growing up in farm worker households, which most did, meant that most women had a model of a mother who worked. Given men's meager earnings, families also depended on women's work for survival. The situation today is that the structure of the Imperial Valley's local labor market still does not provide many "family wage" jobs for Mexican-origin men.

Second, nearly all women had workable, low-cost (or no cost) child care arrangements. All women with jobs had either family-provided or government-subsidized child care. Some paid a small contribution to the cost of public care and in a few instances, paid family members to provide care. Cost and availability concerns did not deter labor force participation.

Third, extended family networks provide opportunities and responsibilities related to the work-family nexus. Kin networks may facilitate work opportunities in other locales, but they also required children to leave jobs in other places to provide care and assistance for kin in Brawley.

Fourth, women frequently contested patriarchal assumptions or blamed themselves for their earlier concessions to male dominance in areas related to family decision-making and employment. Women resisted men's perceived "right" to leave the childrearing to mothers. But women also identified strongly with their role as mothers. Motherhood is often viewed as exacerbating existing gender inequalities by increasing women's dependence because mothers frequently reduce their labor force participation and husbands increase theirs while women focus on the work of child care. The situation looks different, however, when husbands have personal difficulties and marginal earnings. Women are empowered as primary parents and also as primary providers to break their relationships with these men.

Familism is sometimes viewed as part of the "cultural baggage" of traditional values and behaviors that contribute to the social and economic marginalization of Mexican Americans. My research does not support that view. Extended family networks function principally to help people "get ahead" rather than hold them back. Familism proves to be a resource that helps women cope with the structural realities that require their labor force participation in this low-wage, rural setting. Family-based assistance in the form of child care provision supports and promotes women's employment, an outcome that is surely inconsistent with traditional gender norms. A majority of women rely on family members for child care. The family care that enables women to work is structural familism. Cultural familism is seen in mothers' strong preference for family care.

While this chapter finds considerable familism, it uncovers little inclination toward traditional family patterns. Both of these reflect structural realities. First, familism, as manifested in the extended family system, is a mechanism that enables one of the most disadvantaged groups in U.S. society—Mexican Americans—to cope with poverty and racial-ethnic discrimination. Second, the disadvantaged position of Mexican Americans in this society also predicts that their family arrangements will be flexible and adaptive as they respond to the fluidity that accompanies an insecure resource base.

CHAPTER 5

THE LEGACY OF
FARM LABOR

The Imperial County farmworkers' daughters and granddaughters want to leave farm work behind. For them, the essence of upward mobility is exiting farm labor and all that it means. But they live in a place where upward mobility is difficult. While they ultimately want more than merely moving into nonfarm employment, for most, this is the first hurdle. This chapter considers the extent to which the legacy of farm labor continues to shape the adult lives of these women.

In tracing the significance of farm labor in the lives of the Imperial County women, I have already examined their farmworker origins. In chapter 2, women told stories about farm work as it related to the childhood experience of their parents or the immigration experience of parents or grandparents; they talked about their own childhood experience growing up in farmworker households; they also offered their current perspectives on employment in farm labor. Women understand that farm labor brought their families to the United States. They respect the commitment and perseverance of family members who labored in the fields but want better working conditions and greater economic stability than this work afforded their parents and grandparents.

The ability of women who express a strong desire to leave farm work behind to actually do so depends on the availability of other jobs in the community and their access to these jobs. These women worked or sought work out of economic necessity and encountered few obstacles to child care. They were willing and eager workers who encountered structural barriers to employment. The extent to which women are able to create lives outside the bounds of farm labor depends on contextual features of the community in which they live. The Imperial Valley clearly presents serious obstacles to moving up and out of farm labor and its influence. This chapter finds that characteristics of the place they live—a

Hispanic-majority, agriculture-oriented area at the U.S.-Mexico border—present significant barriers to escaping the daily impact of farm work on their lives.

Getting Ahead in Imperial County

In this section I ask how space or place promotes or retards the ability of these daughters and granddaughters of farmworkers to leave farm work behind. Framing the issue in reference to spatial inequality is useful in addressing the structural dynamics of a high-poverty area such Imperial County. In general, high poverty areas are best explained by long-term, complex social and economic factors rather than personal troubles such as disability or temporary layoffs (Beale 2004). Therefore, understanding barriers to upward mobility requires the consideration of the particular opportunities and constraints of various locales. Analysis in terms of spatial inequality has explanatory power because "[i]t examines how and why markers of stratification, such as economic well-being and access to resources as well as other inequalities related to race/ethnicity, class, gender, age, and other statuses, vary and intersect across territories" (Lobao, Hooks, and Tickamyer 2007, 3). In short, it helps us understand the structure of inequality in particular places.

The Imperial County women want to do more than merely secure a nonagricultural job. They also want to build an economically stable life for their families. They and their partners experience several obstacles to accomplishing the twin goals of exiting farm work and enhancing economic well-being. The most consistent complaints are that the local job market is both limited and very competitive. Common sentiments are that "there are no jobs" and "everyone is competing for the same jobs." Given the high rate of unemployment in the county, these perceptions about the local economy are not surprising. A large number of unemployed individuals are indeed competing for a limited number of jobs. But the level of underemployment is a matter of even greater concern. The underemployed include the unemployed, the working poor, discouraged workers (who have given up looking for work), and involuntary part-time workers (Jensen et al. 1999). Underemployment is pervasive in Imperial County. The people I encountered looking for jobs were competing not just with the unemployed but also with a large group of underemployed individuals looking for better jobs that would allow them to stabilize their economic situations.

An ample literature captures the disadvantages of rural labor markets.[1] In brief, rural areas have more than their share of low-paying, part-time, and temporary jobs. When rural residents survey local employment opportunities, they typically find a limited range of options. The inability of rural residents to find adequate employment reflects both the structure of rural labor markets and patterns of remuneration. Rural labor markets lack diversification, with employment tending to be concentrated at the low end of the service sector in retail trade and personal/consumer services; these jobs tend to be low-wage, low-skill jobs with limited career ladders (Wells 2002). Urban labor markets have more differentiated occupational hierarchies with a wider range of options, including more high-pay, high-skill jobs (Gibbs 2002, 52). The better service-sector jobs, those in professional and business services, constitute a higher proportion of jobs in urban areas (McLaughlin and Coleman-Jensen 2008). Rural areas also have lower pay scales than urban areas. This means that when a rural worker has the same qualifications and works the same job as an urban worker, the rural worker is likely to be paid lower wages (Jensen, McLaughlin, and Slack 2003, 126). Women's employment has risen with the expansion of the service sector and openings in gender-typed jobs usually held by women. While women hold a larger share of jobs in rural areas than in the past, these labor markets lack the stable, well-paying jobs that women need (Tickamyer and Henderson 2003).

Some women do attribute the difficulty of finding a decent job to living in a small town in an agricultural area. In Brawley, the good jobs that people want are few in number, so competition for these jobs is fierce. At the time I interviewed Francesca Alvarez, she had an interview scheduled for a job in bookkeeping at a local supermarket. The job pays nine dollars an hour, which she thinks is too little for the job, but she is getting desperate for work and will take "anything." She says, "It is so hard in a small community because there is so much competition. So little jobs and so many people, you know, looking for a job." Part of the problem in finding a job in Brawley is said to be that there are even fewer jobs in the small towns in the vicinity of Brawley. Residents of towns such as Holtville and Westmorland compete for jobs in Brawley, while many Brawley residents, in turn, look for jobs in El Centro, the largest city in the county, where there are more opportunities than in Brawley.

Living in an agriculture-dependent county that is reliant on the field labor of a Mexican-origin workforce predicts heavy competition for jobs. Angelica Perez makes an astute observation when she says, "I think everyone in farm work would like a better job." Chapter One introduced the image of "farm labor's revolving door" to capture this reality. The point is that immigrants, mostly rural Mexicans, enter the United States to fill a farm labor void. But then, because seasonal farm work is physically difficult, low paying, and unstable, they hope to move out of seasonal farm work as soon as possible (Taylor, Martin, and Fix 1997). Thus, in communities with substantial farmworker populations, we can expect a large number of job seekers. The labor market characteristics of agriculture-dependent areas predict, however, that nonfarm jobs will be hard to secure. The Imperial County women are competing for jobs not only with each other but also with Mexican immigrant farmworkers, many of whom are now permanent residents or U.S. citizens.

The story of Juanita Lopez, a forty-eight-year-old farmworker, provides an example of the work lives of farm laborers in the Valley and why many are trying to leave this work. Juanita is one of several immigrant women I interviewed over the course of this research who are not part of the daughters and granddaughters of farmworkers sample. Because they were not U.S.-born, they did not meet the criteria for inclusion in the sample.[2] Juanita is a Mexican immigrant looking to move up and out of farm work. She has twenty-four years of experience in farm work; her husband has twenty-eight years. It is becoming more and more difficult for Juanita and her husband to get work in the Valley. She attributes this to the fact that they are getting older. Juanita says, "My age makes it difficult for me to be hired. The supervisors are looking for people who are younger. They give the work to people who come from Mexico. They don't have papers, but they get the jobs. So people who live here do not have work. It is difficult. Right now in the county, the work is slow. Right now, no mucho trabajo."

The typical annual pattern of employment for the Lopezes is to get as much work as possible in the lettuce season, which is November to March. This usually amounts to three months of work because they are not continuously employed. Juanita explains, "They say, 'Stop.' and 'I'll call you later.'" In April they pick and clean onions; they may also pack corn for a couple of weeks. Then they pack grapes in Coachella, sixty miles to the north in May, June, and the first week of July. There is typically no work between July and November. All of the jobs pay minimum wage. I asked Juanita if her husband was ever able to get a year-round job with any of the Brawley growers. Her answer is no, that the growers pick just a few workers to continue at the end of the season. She explains, "They say, 'You, and you, and you.' They give me just a few weeks and then stop the work. For my husband also."

Juanita knows that her limited English proficiency may be an obstacle to getting a nonfarm job. She aspires to find a job at a market where she can speak mainly Spanish. She explains, "Cashier is work that is work all year." Juanita studied English for two semesters in adult education, but as for her husband, "Nada." Without English, she assumes he will continue in farm work. As she says, "It is hard."

Strong competition for jobs is one of the main challenges faced by the women participating in this research and their partners. Sylvia Moreno's partner, Ruben, is trying to move out of farm labor. He currently works in processing hay, but he is always looking for a better job. Sylvia says that Ruben will go anywhere there is good pay. He will just be happy if he is supporting his family. He usually goes into the One Stop and finds out about jobs online and then goes in to fill out an application. "But," Sylvia says, "when he does that, he's up against so many people because this town is in need of jobs really bad. This whole Valley is. So he's like, 'I'm up against all these people.'"

Women with limited labor market credentials, usually in the form of education or recent work experience, had in some cases been looking for a job for a very long time. Stephanie Ruiz is a twenty-six-year-old high school graduate who is long-term unemployed. She would like a job as a housekeeper, cashier, or stocker. She had two interviews in the past six months. The great disappointment of her extended and thus far unsuccessful job search is that the job she almost got in hotel housekeeping did not work out. She says, "I did have a job. They were going to give it to me at the Super 8 Motel in Westmorland, a very nice motel. It's clean. They have a Jacuzzi. But I didn't have a dependable car so they didn't give it to me." Extending the palm of her hand, she continues, "I had it right there!" For Stephanie, securing a job is an elusive goal that seems nearly impossible.

Patricia Ochoa eventually got a job in food service but was astonished to find how difficult it was to secure employment. She says, "I thought I had experience and you know, with my background [family home day care] and knowing how to do this and that and whatever, but no, it's everybody—there's one job opening and a million people applying for that job. And it's hard, it's very hard."

Individuals with low education attainment encounter the most difficulty in finding jobs. But an associate's or bachelor's degrees does not necessarily provide access to a job in your chosen field. Rosa Navarra makes the point that a degree, in her case an associate's degree, is helpful in getting a job, but it is still a challenge. "You're not competing with those people [from the other side], but it's still hard because you're in the Valley. But you have a better chance. That's just the way it is in the Valley. It's very competitive because we're so small." A very limited job market means that some well-educated people are working outside their fields. So, for example, Priscilla Ortega, with a B.A. degree in criminal justice, is teaching remedial math and reading for a company that provides services for the county's work readiness program for youth.

Julie Peña refers to the strong competition that exists for county jobs. She recently earned a B.A. in psychology but has not yet been able to move into the better job she hoped to get working in mental health for the county. She says, "Right now I want to broaden my choices as to employment. I know there is nothing at the county in behavior health right now. So that's why I am kind of jumping over to social services—trying to see if I can get in there. But, they have a test you gotta pass and everybody and their momma and daddy are trying to pass that test at the same time. There's a lot of people applying for the same positions. It's so competitive here."

On one level, the experiences articulated above are typical of those encountered by job seekers in other rural labor markets. Research consistently shows, however, that minorities experience considerable labor market disadvantage in rural areas. Historical analyses find that racial disadvantage is exacerbated in rural areas, that is to say, that rural minorities are further disadvantaged in comparison to their urban counterparts. Rural minorities have been found to be especially susceptible to underemployment (Slack and Jensen 2002).

Rural minorities are the poorest of the poor and those most isolated from opportunity structures in their communities. Rural Latinos, Native Americans, and African Americans generally live their lives far outside the American social and economic mainstream. Racial subordination in the United States has deep rural roots. Snipp contends that what rural minorities share is "the experience of living in close proximity to the historical remnants of the institutions explicitly created to conquer, oppress, and maintain their subordinate position in society" (1996, 127). For Mexican Americans in Imperial County this means continuing to live in the shadow of industrial agriculture, an institution that has prospered here by providing temporary, backbreaking employment at poverty-level wages to vulnerable Mexican immigrants.

Minority residents of rural communities with large minority populations experience substantial challenges to achieving economic well-being.[3] Greater minority concentration predicts higher levels of economic hardship for these residents. Research also finds the extent of racial inequality, a measure of comparative advantage or disadvantage, to be related to the percent of minorities in the population. When the representation of minorities in the population increases, disparities between the household incomes and poverty levels of white residents and those of minority residents also increase. Minorities tend to do better socioeconomically in counties with lower minority concentrations, while the white population tends to do better in counties with higher minority concentrations (Albrecht, Albrecht, and Murguia 2005).[4] The association between minority concentration and economic hardship is highly relevant to this study, given that three of four Imperial County residents are Hispanic. As the Mexican-origin population becomes increasingly dominant in the U.S.-Mexico border region, we cannot assume this demographic change has produced major opportunities for upward mobility. In fact, the opposite appears to be the case. Minority concentration in rural areas tends to signal isolation from the social and economic mainstream.

Several women believe that living at the border creates a nearly overwhelming obstacle to their getting ahead financially. They believe the border negatively impacts the local labor market by creating competition, producing low-quality jobs, and keeping wages low. Erica Martinez sets up the border dynamic succinctly:

> We work on this side and we are looking for a job on this side. We are competing with the people who come across the border. They are willing to come and work for $6.75 an hour. We are competing with people who work over here and then go back to Mexico. They come and go every day. So if they are paying them $6.75 an hour, they more than appreciate the money. What we get paid an hour is what they get paid in Mexico a day. So even if they work a part-time job—four hours a day at minimum wage—$6.75, they're in heaven. Because they go back to their lower cost of living.

Erica thinks this situation keeps local wages low and local unemployment rates high. Theresa Romero believes that the community's location near the border

Figure 9. Mexican workers crossing the border at Calexico, returning to Mexicali after a day of work in Imperial County (*Credit:* Johno Wells)

contributes to poor quality employment in the county. She says, "There's lots of part time jobs in the Valley. Nobody who was born and raised in the Valley wants a part-time job at $6.75 an hour. But someone will cross the border to do it. This keeps employers from needing to offer full time jobs with benefits."

These women are not misguided in drawing a connection between the border, jobs, and earnings. A substantial body of literature captures what is termed the "border earnings penalty" along the U.S.-Mexico border (see, for example, Dávila and Mora 2008; Mollick, Mora, and Dávila 2007; Smith and Newman 1977).[5] This research finds that workers who live in U.S. border counties earn less than their counterparts in other areas of the United States. A border earnings penalty has been found for each of three major groups living in the border region: Mexican immigrants, U.S.-born Mexican Americans, and U.S.-born non-Hispanic whites. Earnings differentials are not attributable to lower educational attainment along the border. Significant earning disparities persist despite what is actually higher educational attainment along the border for each of these groups, in comparison to their counterparts in the interior of the United States (Mollick, Mora, and Dávila 2007).[6]

Some women react with frustration to the lack of employment opportunities in the Imperial Valley. Sylvia Moreno thinks local people should be hired for local jobs. She says, "People from the other side come over and they take our jobs. And I'm like, okay, how do they expect us to get anywhere? But that's just how it's working out right here." Rosemary Correa is a thirty-year-old divorced mother of four who is currently enrolled at Imperial Valley College. She is advancing her education in the hope of landing a stable job. She has strong opinions on this subject and thinks the biggest problem with jobs is "[a] lot of them are taken by immigrants that come into our town [Brawley], and especially to El Centro and Calexico—that take our jobs as U.S. citizens. They get underpaid and they don't care. And then they go pay their cost of living over there. It is so cheap over there. And I can't stand it! Economically, you'll never get nowhere here. I get so upset sometimes!"

Some women were more sympathetic to the circumstances that might lead Mexican individuals to take a job in the United States. Francesca Alvarez says, "You know, I understand they come over here to progress. But at the same time, it's hard for people that live here. It's harder for us because we live here and companies take advantage of that. Instead of paying us eight dollars, they'll pay them six dollars."

In particular, the Imperial County women resent transborder commuters, the Mexicali residents who cross the border daily for jobs on the U.S. side, who "take our jobs." They believe that when people from "the other side" take local jobs, it keeps wages low for everyone. In fact, the literature generally supports their viewpoint. Smith and Newman, in their classic article on the border penalty for wages, find a clear relationship between the presence of what they call a "cheap" labor pool and depressed wages (1977, 58). Their argument is that significant disparities in wages and standards of living between the United States and Mexico precipitate a large flow of labor from Mexico to the United States. This migration leads to an excess supply of labor at the U.S. border and depressed labor market conditions in U.S. border communities (1977, 51).

While everyone experiences the border earnings gap, there is reason to believe that these Mexican American women and their partners experience greater earnings disparities than other groups in the locale. A majority of these daughters and granddaughters of farmworkers are low-skilled workers. The earnings of low-skilled workers at the U.S. border are more negatively affected by the presence of a Mexican workforce than are higher-skilled workers. The explanation is that low-skilled Mexican Americans and the Mexican immigrants are generally competing for the same jobs. It is important to note, however, that an earnings gap exists across many sectors of the economy. Mora, Dávila, and Mollick's (2008) research examined earnings in the manufacturing, construction, and retail or wholesale trade sectors of the economy in border counties and the U.S. interior. They found that U.S.-born Mexican Americans working in any of these sectors at the border experienced a greater earnings gap than did Mexican immigrants or Anglos.

LEAVING FARM WORK BEHIND

The women participating in this research were raised in the shadow of farm labor. I examine the degree to which women have exited farm work and its influence on their lives. First, I consider the employment of these women, taking into

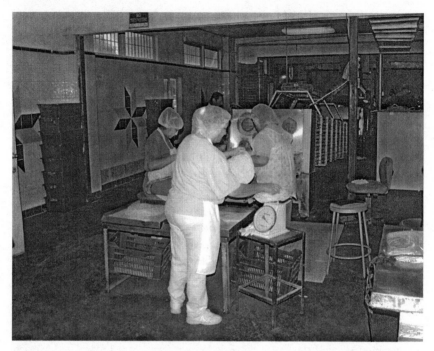

Figure 10. Women working in tortilla factory, Brawley (*Credit:* Johno Wells)

consideration their alternatives to farm labor in the community. Next, I consider the extent to which women remain connected to the harsh realities of farm labor through the employment of their partners. Finally, I explore the women's continuing connections to farm work through employment providing services to local farmworkers and their families.

Women's Employment

None of the women is currently a farm worker, but four did spend some years in this work and one woman is currently looking for a job in seasonal farm work. Carmen Silva's first job at age fifteen was as a farmworker. She says that her parents, who themselves were seasonal farmworkers all their lives, gave their children the clear message, "This is not what you want to do." But Carmen did farm labor off and on, juggling it between working at a local tortilla factory and McDonald's (all at minimum wage), until her oldest daughter was three years old. Since then she has done clerical work, first at the local hospital, and now for the county.

Esther and Antonio Valdez worked as a farmworker couple for several years after their marriage. Esther explains that first Antonio got a job driving a tractor and then she got a job "inspecting the bugs" at the same company. Esther describes her work in agricultural pest control: "I was checking the lettuce, checking for bugs. I drove around the whole Valley. We checked a lot of fields. I had to walk in the fields to see if we had pink worm or whatever was in the crops. And I would tell the boss what I found. Actually I became pretty good. He let me work by myself and he would take off. I did that for three years."

Rosa Navarra did field work into her mid-twenties. When her older son, Edward, was a toddler, she and Edward's father took him along with them into the fields. She says, "I did the seasonal work in the grapes when he was little. He wasn't even in school yet. He'd be playing in the rows and throwing dirt and everything. He was just a little baby. It was just for a little while—doing the seasonal." When her second son was born, she stopped working for a few years. In recent years she has been positioning herself for a job in border security. After working in security at the border crossing in Calexico and completing an associate's degree in administration of justice, she had just been hired for a job in border security at the regional detention center in El Centro. Rosa explains, "We're the ones that supervise the men and women that are not documented that Immigration brings in. They call the detention center 'el corral' in Spanish." This new job represents substantial upward mobility for Rosa.

After several years of field work, Elena Sanchez got a job in food service at the convention center in Fresno. Since then she has become a certified medical biller. After she got her first office job, she reflected on her decision to get a credential that would allow her to do clerical work instead of manual labor. She recalls, "It [the office] was a good atmosphere. I was thinking about my past, and thought about that I wasn't working out in the sun. I'm in an office and I'm not straining my muscles to carry stuff. I'm not crunched down—like in some positions, workers are required to be on their knees all day planting. It was something different I really enjoyed. I learned a lesson of life there [in the fields]—instead of making it harder for yourself, make it easier for yourself. So, I decided to make it easier."

Out of desperation, Miranda Flores is currently looking for work in farm labor. For Miranda, as for other women, farm labor is the work of last resort. She grew up in a large family that followed the crops seasonally. She stopped doing farm work when she got married at age sixteen. Miranda is now a displaced homemaker who has been out of the labor force for eighteen years. She says, "I went to look at Jack in the Box and all those places. Well, right now, they don't need anybody there." So, she hopes to do seasonal field work "just temporarily to get some income coming in."

Miranda attributes the difficulty she is having finding a job to the social networks operating in small towns. These make it more difficult for people without local connections to get a job. I mentioned to her that I had talked with several other women who were looking for jobs. She responded by saying, "Exactly. Right here in the Valley, it is very hectic. Very hectic. Because by the time I hear a job going on, somebody is there already. Say you know Jack in the Box is going to be needing somebody. And you tell your friends or relatives. By the time I go there—[I hear,] 'Sorry it's filled already.' And that's what's bad about the Valley.

Lots of people don't get jobs because they tell their friends—and the friends tell their friends—and it's a big hassle. There is so much competition for jobs here."

The employment of the Imperial County women is almost exclusively in the service sector, especially food service, health care, education, and clerical work. Several women worked in food service, some as servers in various restaurants, one as a cook at a Mexican restaurant, another as a shift manager at a pizzeria, and another as a cashier at Kentucky Fried Chicken. Several earned minimum wage working as home health aides, others worked as clerical workers for the county or the local hospital; one was a social worker. Other women were cashiers or retail clerks. As was mentioned above, one woman worked in border enforcement.

Nearly one-third of the women had, during their high school years, participated in a summer program that provided work experience for children of migrant farm workers. The federally funded Migrant and Seasonal Farmworker (MSFW) programs provided paid employment throughout the summer for participating high school students. Women now in their twenties and thirties usually referred to these summer jobs as their first paid employment. They worked as retail clerks, receptionists, library assistants, and day care workers. The purpose of the programs was to prepare children of migrant workers for nonagricultural employment by providing nonfarm work experience. The fact that none of the women who had these summer jobs ever worked in farm labor would seem to be a testimony to this program's local success.

The concept of employment hardship is useful in examining the labor market situation of Mexican-origin women (De Anda 2005). Employment hardship is a concept that encompasses joblessness, involuntary part-time work, and working poverty. It is relevant to my analysis because it captures both the quality and quantity of work. De Anda contends that much of the employment-related research underestimates the labor market disadvantage of Mexican American women because it relies on statistics that describe the earnings of full-time workers only. As a result, the economic difficulties experienced by workers who are involuntarily part-time are largely invisible. De Anda found that Mexican American women were more than twice as likely to experience employment hardship as were white women.[7]

The Imperial County women experience considerable employment hardship. Many are unemployed. Most of the jobs they are qualified for are part-time. Full-time, year-round jobs are very hard to find. Competition for jobs is fierce and wages are low. The challenge to finding adequate employment is revealed in the observation that women who have full-time jobs are employed almost exclusively in the government sector of services (as teachers, social service providers, border security personnel, and the like). Only Theresa Romero, an optical technician, has a full-time job with a private employer. This reality points to the limitations of the local labor market in this agriculture-reliant border county.

Husbands' and Partners' Employment

Many women have remained connected to the everyday realities of farm labor through the employment of their husbands or partners, many of whom are long-term farmworkers, former farmworkers, or temporary farmworkers. An ongoing relationship with farm work means that women continue to create their family lives on an insecure and inadequate resource base. The experiences of the Sylvia Moreno and Carmen Silva illustrate the challenge of supporting a family on farmworker's earnings.

Sylvia Moreno's partner, Ruben, has worked in agriculture and construction. Ruben's work for the past several years has been in farm labor, working at a hay-processing facility. He generally works between 28 and 36 hours per week, for $7.50 an hour. Because he earns more than minimum wage, many locals would say Ruben has a "good" job in agriculture. But his hours are not regular and his employment is not year-round. He is laid off approximately two months every year, usually in the spring, when rain interferes with cutting and processing hay. Sylvia says, "See, when that happens, that's when we have a really hard time. He gets unemployment for those weeks, but it doesn't help out that much." She is a shift supervisor at a local pizzeria, working between 30 and 45 hours per week, for $7.25 an hour.

Carmen Silva's partner Miguel, is a farmworker. He is a Mexican immigrant who works steadily for local growers every year from November to June. In the summer, his regular pattern has been to travel to Bakersfield to work in the onion fields. Last summer's experience was financially disastrous for them when heavy rains interfered with the work. "So he would work for maybe three days and then be off for four days because of the rain. So it wasn't worth the groceries and the money. We were spending more money than he was actually making." The plan for next year is that, for the first time, Miguel will not travel to Bakersfield for summer work. Carmen says that this situation puts a lot of pressure on her. Miguel has done field work for twenty years and has never been paid more than minimum wage. This family is reliant on Carmen's job with the county for financial stability and benefits.

Denise Ortiz and her husband, Raul, find themselves in an unanticipated relationship with farm work. The Ortizes thought they had left farm work behind. Raul has had nonfarm jobs for many years, but he is now back in farm labor as the work of last resort. Denise is very careful to construct this as a temporary situation. Raul was laid off from his job as an apartment manager, and as Denise says, "My husband was just desperate because the unemployment [compensation] was not good enough. It's like, 'I need more.' I go, 'Well, it's up to you, if you want to go out there.'" He now works alongside his father and brother doing irrigation work for a local farmer. "They are putting down sprinklers and piping. That's all I know. It's not one of his favorite things, but it is some money." Raul has not actually told Denise how much he is being paid per hour, but he is working more than eight hours a day and earning $350 to $400 per week. He likely earns around $8.00 an hour. Raul's father and brother have done farm work all their lives, but it had seemed that Raul had progressed beyond it. From the standpoints of both Denise and Raul, this is not the work he should be doing.

Other women with husbands in farm work are Lucia Hernandez, whose husband is a hired beekeeper, and Eva Vallejo, whose husband is a self-employed truck driver who hauls hay. Both Angelica Perez and Miranda Flores are recently separated from their farmworker husbands.

Seven additional research participants are married to or divorced from men who worked as farm laborers in the past. One cannot assume that men who moved out of farm work were upwardly mobile. Some have had extended periods of irregular employment or involvement in illegal activity.

The workforce experience of husbands and partners is not characterized by labor market success. It was difficult or impossible for these men to find good jobs. The most prevalent category for men's employment was farm labor, followed by construction. Most jobs in these categories did not provide year round employment. Other men were employed as auto mechanics, carpet installers, custodians, and commercial truck drivers. Only two men had jobs with public employers: one was a teacher and another a mail carrier. Several men were unemployed because of the seasonal nature of their work, disability, or illness. One man was in a residential rehabilitation program for substance abuse.

Low educational attainment characterizes this group of men. Half the husbands and partners do not have a high school diploma. Without a high school education, most men do not have work opportunities beyond field work; the few who worked for construction contractors considered themselves lucky. The limited range of occupational categories available in this rural county reflects both the realities of the local rural labor market and broad structural conditions. In today's postindustrial economy, educational credentials increasingly determine access to better jobs, in both rural and urban settings. Men without high school diplomas, whatever their race or ethnicity and in whatever spatial context, are effectively relegated to the economic margins. Only one of these men has a college degree.

Alex and Priscilla Ortega are a couple who have had a successful strategy for exiting farm labor. Priscilla has lived in Brawley all her life. Her parents were farmworkers, both of whom did local field work. Her father also did migrant field work in the summer "up north." Alex is the son of farmworkers; he has worked a total of ten years in agriculture. After five years in seasonal field work, he secured a job as a full-time fork lift driver for a hay company. This job paid just over minimum wage. Around three years ago, Alex moved out of farm labor. Priscilla explains the couple's strategy: "When I graduated from San Diego State, that's when he decided to go to school and get like a short type of training for a career. To better ourselves. That's when he went to truck-driving school." When they made this decision, their son Richard was four years old. Alex now works full-time driving a truck and sometimes has significant overtime.[8] He usually works 40 to 50 hours a week and has more than doubled his earnings. The couple has now bought a house, added another child, and looks forward to a bright future. With a university degree, Priscilla is poised for one of the good jobs in the county.

It is perhaps counterintuitive to find many women with partners who are employed in agriculture. One might expect that women who reject farm work for themselves and want their children to avoid it at all costs would not be interested in relationships with men who are farmworkers. But the situations in which women find themselves reflect the dynamics of race/ethnicity and social class in local marriage markets. Although interethnic relationships are on the rise, most individuals date and find a mate who shares the same race or ethnicity and social class background (Jepson and Jepson 2002). For Mexican American women in Imperial County, this means that many of their potential partners will be men in farm labor. None of the women I interviewed criticized her partner because of the work he did. Comments focused instead on the financial challenges attendant in supporting a family on farmworkers' earnings and of partners' efforts (mostly unsuccessful) to find other types of work.

Serving Farmworkers: Community Jobs and Family Care

Next I consider the extent to which women retain a connection to farm labor through their employment in jobs that provide services to farmworkers and their families. Taylor and his colleagues note that in rural areas with majority Hispanic populations, growers may well control the local economy, but the established Mexican American population may play a large role in the community's political and public institutions (1997, 45–46). Consistent with that observation, in Brawley and other Imperial County communities, Mexican Americans hold many, if not most, jobs in leadership positions as managers, directors, and administrators and in more rank-and-file positions in education, local government, and nongovernmental organizations. Specifically, among research participants, members of the established Mexican American population, those with appropriate English proficiency and educational or vocational credentials, are employed in positions that serve Mexican migrant farmworkers or immigrants and their children. In other cases, they provide services to retired or disabled community members.

Several women work in county offices that provide services for farmworkers and their families. Lisa Cabrillo, Erica Martinez, Carmen Silva, and Priscilla Ortega provide direct service or administrative support in county programs that, for example, verify and process unemployment claims, monitor program requirement compliance for TANF recipients, and support the job-search efforts of individuals seeking alternative employment.

Lisa Cabrillo, a granddaughter of farmworkers, is a social worker for Imperial County. Because she is bilingual she has what is called a "Spanish caseload."

Not surprisingly, immigrant farmworkers who know little or no English make up a large segment of the caseload for Spanish-proficient county workers. Lisa explains how this affects her work and the work of others by describing the difficulty of determining the eligibility of contract farmworkers for social assistance:

> Spanish caseload is very difficult to work because those clients tend to work a lot of seasonal jobs and you're working reports on a monthly basis with income changing, varying, a whole lot from month to month, season to season because of the fact that they're a lot of the times working with labor contractors. That makes a big difference. There's a lot more paperwork to deal with when you're having to work the reports because they get paid on a daily basis a lot of the times and you have to process check stub by check stub. Other people, like, let's say, the English only, they'll have a job at Von's, for example, where you get paid on a biweekly basis. You're only working with two check stubs. You process those check stubs, that's it. The other ones [Spanish-speaking farmworkers], on the contrary, they work for labor contractors. They're gonna send you about thirty check stubs from day to day.

Priscilla Ortega works for the Imperial Valley Regional Occupational Program (known locally as ROP), a program that provides training to enable individuals to acquire entry-level jobs. Priscilla, one of the five women with college degrees participating in the research, notes with some satisfaction that she now teaches remedial math, reading, and work readiness in the same ROP program in which she participated as a youth.

Other women work in school settings interacting with farmworkers' children on a daily basis. Ana Ramirez, Marjorie Salas, and Monica Rodriguez are teachers. Eva Vallejo is a school secretary. Julie Peña is currently an instructional aide, while Jenifer Castillo is an on-call aide with the school system. Until recently, Natalie Torres was a teacher's aide with United Families, a state-subsidized preschool program for children in low-income families. Theresa Romero worked for eight years in a migrant education program that provided developmental day care for migrant children.

Local public schools play an important role in the integration of immigrant children or U.S.-born children of new immigrants into American society. The role of teachers is central in this process. Imperial Valley schools have a high rate of English language learner (ELL) students. Nearly three in ten students in Brawley elementary schools are English learners (California Department of Education 2010). The three teachers who participated in this research spoke about how working with immigrant children, many of whom are children of farmworkers, and their families shapes their work lives.

Ana Ramirez is passionate about the needs of English language learner students. She is a "lead teacher" this year, meaning she has an additional role as a teacher in support of other classroom teachers with ELL students. She is very experienced in working with the "newcomers," so she assists other teachers in planning for ELL students and modifying curriculum to meet their needs. She explains, "Our school programs have just changed and now all teachers have English language learners. Before, all these students were grouped together. I had them all; all the [ELL students at this grade level] were with me. I had thirty-five students." Ana notes that she fought for the change, in part, based on her own experience as the daughter of Mexican immigrants. Ana was an English language learner in school. Sometimes her teachers did not know Spanish, so she had to manage in English. She says, "I learned it fast because either I survived [in the classroom] or I didn't." Ana is passionate in her belief that immigrant children should, with appropriate support, be educated along with "English-only kids" in English-language classrooms.

Marjorie Salas contends that the State of California's emphasis on standardized test results creates tremendous stress for teachers and their English language learner students. She says:

> I love to teach, but so many things have changed. With the testing the kids have to take, it's like you have to prepare them for the test. We have a lot of students that are English language learners and they really struggle. I was an English language learner. I struggled and I still do at times. It's not fair! And it's just so much stress. It's so much stress, and I've, I've been thinking of changing careers for that reason because I'm no longer as happy as I was. You know, I still love to teach. I love to work with kids, that's never going to change, but the stress on, on the type of work that I have, has made me want to change.

If Marjorie gives up her teaching career, it will be ironic indeed, given the adverse circumstances in which she struggled to achieve her goal of becoming a teacher. It was her mother's encouragement and her own determination to create a stable life that inspired her to both work full time and attend college as a young single mother. After nine years as a teacher, she is still paying off her educational loans.

Monica Rodriguez notes that the parents of many of her students are immigrant farmworkers who do not know English. This affects the teacher–parent relationship until parents figure out that she is bilingual. She says, "I know even in my own classroom, when parents peek in—they stop themselves because they don't think I speak Spanish. That's because I don't look like I speak Spanish. And they'll kind of look around to see if they see their child. And I'll walk over to them and ask them [in Spanish], 'Are you looking for somebody?' And then they do a big sigh, and say, 'Maestra, I didn't think you spoke Spanish.' It's just a big relief, you know." Teachers in the district are not required to be bilingual because English is the language of instruction. Marjorie Salas mentioned a situation just a couple of days before the interview in which a coworker was having a parent–teacher conference. Because the teacher spoke only English and the parent spoke only Spanish, Marjorie translated for them.

In a community with limited employment options, many women take jobs as part-time care providers for the In-Home Supportive Services (IHSS) program administered by the county. IHSS is intended to enable elderly or disabled individuals to remain in their own homes. These women provide personal and domestic services for Medicare or Medicaid recipients, a large proportion of whom are elderly or disabled farmworkers. Part of the legacy of farm work in this community is a high rate of disability resulting from either on-the-job injuries (trauma) or decades of body-punishing work in the fields. The Imperial County Department of Social Services reports that in September 2005, the local IHSS program had a caseload of more than 4,500, and approximately 3,500 service providers (Imperial County 2007). These 3,500 jobs represent an important source of employment (albeit part-time and low-wage) in this economically depressed community. Some care providers are Certified Nursing Assistants (CNAs).

Five farmworkers' daughters work in this program. Lucia Hernandez, Marina Mendez, and Esther Valdez are employed by the county to provide care for their own disabled farmworker parents through the program. Home health aides work a set number of "authorized hours" providing a set of "authorized services" based on a client-assessment by the county. On the high end of authorized work hours are Angelica Perez and Christina Gilbert with seventy-two to seventy-six hours per month. On the low end is Maria Mendez, who is authorized to provide nineteen hours of in-home care for her father and seventeen hours for her mother for a monthly total of thirty-six hours.[9] This work pays minimum wage and provides no benefits.[10]

Family Care Work

Finally, the continuing significance of farm work may be seen in women's relationships with their parents and sometimes parents-in-law. In many cases, women provide physical care or economic support for parents who are disabled and unable to work or are retired but lack the means to support themselves. The physically debilitating nature of farm work, the seasonal nature of the work, and the low-wage structure of compensation generally explain these situations. Ana Ramirez says of her father (a retired agricultural worker) and mother, "I am their pension plan." Other families have remained in Imperial Valley rather than seeking better jobs in other geographic locations because of their responsibilities to care for and support their parents.

Esther Valdez's farmworker parents, at the ages of fifty-two and fifty-four, are no longer able to work. As she provides care for her parents, Hector and Consuela, Esther relives her childhood experiences, thinking about the work that aged her parents prematurely and regretting that she was unable to help her parents avoid the disabling injuries that resulted from decades of farm labor. Esther says:

My parents were hurting when they were working. But my parents didn't know of anything—that they could even go to the doctor. It was ignorance. They didn't know about it. So they kept working. To them it was normal. And they never looked for therapy or anything like that. So, even now, they're in pain and they take walks or they take pills because they think that by walking it's going to go away. And maybe it will, you know. It's not as bad as if they just sat down. But yeah, they were in lack of an education. I really feel bad, and sometimes I feel guilty because I was ignorant too at the time. And wasn't able to help them as the older daughter. And right now, I think, "If I would have known, I would have told them." But I didn't know either.

I remind Esther that she was just a girl then and ask (rhetorically) how she could be expected to know about these things. In fact, this "older daughter" is just thirteen years younger than her mother and fifteen years younger than her father. Esther is very protective of her parents, and they rely on her to a considerable degree. Their reliance on her is explained at least in part by the fact that they do not speak any English.

Living in Imperial County presents challenges to these women's hopes for creating financially stable family lives outside of farm work. They live in a poor place, an agriculture-reliant county at the U.S.-Mexico border, that provides limited opportunities for upward mobility. Jobs openings are few and competition for all nonagricultural jobs is intense. Many jobs are part-time, minimum-wage jobs that provide only marginal employment. A large segment of the workforce is underemployed.

A superficial look at the women who participated in this research may suggest that they have indeed left farm work behind. After all, they no longer work in the fields as did their parents or grandparents. But a closer look at the realities of their family lives reveals something else. The husbands or partners of some women are farmworkers. Many have parents who continue in farm work. Others provide care for parents who are disabled or financial support for parents who cannot make ends meet. In addition, many women have jobs providing services to farmworkers and their families. The labor of these women—now in service to the farmworker community—keeps the issues and concerns of this group on their minds. Part of the legacy of farm work is poverty, physical injury or disability, and an uncertain future. These prove to be far more difficult to leave behind.

CHAPTER 6

SURVIVING NOW
AND BUILDING A
BETTER LIFE FOR LATER

This chapter considers the microlevel strategies used by the families represented in this research as they respond to macrolevel constraints and strive to achieve personal and family goals. The chapter has two major concerns. The first is to examine how these daughters and granddaughters of farmworkers (and their partners, if present) manage to provide the basic necessities of life for their families in a context in which it is difficult to do so. The second is to analyze what women say about upward mobility and the obstacles they encounter to achieving it. These subjects connect to two larger public issues: the impact of the structure of California agriculture on farm-dependent communities, and prospects for upward mobility among second- and third-generation Mexican Americans in the United States.

Rural areas present specific barriers to self-sufficiency and upward mobility. While rural areas have many problems in common, particular patterns of difficulties are associated with the type of economic activity that dominates the locale. As Tickamyer and her colleagues summarize succinctly, "Among these problems are severe deficits in resources, employment opportunities, infrastructure, social and human capital, leadership, and political influence at more central levels of government" (2002, 236). What is especially relevant for this analysis is that Imperial County is a farming-dependent county and the structure of its agricultural production is labor-intensive, requiring a large pool of flexible, low-wage labor.

A perhaps unforeseen consequence of the labor-intensive model of agriculture is the significant costs it creates for rural California communities (Taylor, Martin, and Fix 1997, 37). Because workers receive poverty-level wages, they are eligible for public benefits in their local communities. In paying low wages, growers pass along some of the costs of supporting these workers to federal, state, and county governments that partially underwrite, for example, the cost of their food and housing. The rural communities that bear these costs are arguably those least able to do so.

Another angle on the public costs associated with the current structure of farm labor comes into view when the hazards associated with the work are examined. Disability prematurely shortens the work lives of many farmworkers, who require public assistance at several junctures. First, Supplemental Security Income (SSI) is available to disabled farmworkers. Then, if the disabled worker needs assistance to remain at home, home health care is provided through the county's In-Home Supportive Services (IHSS) program. Frequently, the care providers are women with children, and because home health aides receive only minimum wage, caregivers qualify for government subsidized child care. The concerns of disabled farmworkers came into clear view in this research because many women had disabled farmworker parents and some women were home health aides providing assistance to disabled farmworkers.

My intent here is not to argue that communities should not be responsible for providing assistance for all needy members of the community. Rather, it is to point out that when agricultural interests contend that the current system is the best way to produce the inexpensive food that Americans expect, this nation must recognize that the total cost is actually considerably higher than what is portrayed. Both racial and economic inequality are firmly embedded in the structure of agriculture. Low wages, insecure employment, and physically debilitating work for Latino farmworkers create both tremendous profits for growers, who are predominately white, and significant costs to society.

"Supporting My Family Today"

The Imperial County women manage to support their families in the face of several challenges. Jobs are hard to find, and given the low-earning capacity of many jobs, having a job does not mean that you can adequately provide for your family. This chapter considers how the families actually manage to patch together their economic subsistence. Employment is the main strategy for economic survival. Nearly all women are in the labor force, but many are unemployed and looking for work. The competition for jobs is formidable. The jobs that are available are overwhelmingly part-time, low-wage, and seasonal. A majority of their families survive with the support of at least one public program. At the same time, this sample is economically diverse, with nearly one in three families earning forty thousand dollars or more annually.

When work is unavailable or provides inadequate support, families rely on a variety of other resources. To understand how the families of these women managed to survive economically, I asked them about their sources of family income, by which I mean sources generating cash that could be used to provide for the family's subsistence. I asked specifically about income from twelve potential sources, including wages, unemployment compensation, child support, CalWORKs cash aid, and Supplemental Security Income. I also asked about assistance from a variety of government and private programs providing non-cash assistance. These included Food Stamps, Medi-Cal, housing assistance, child care assistance, and home utility assistance. This information, in conjunction with women's accounts of giving and receiving support through their social networks, reveals how these families actually manage to make ends meet in this poor rural place.

I consider here how women and their partners provide the basic necessities for their families, including a roof over their heads, nutritious food, quality child care, and access to medical care. First to be considered is the provision of housing, generally a family's largest expense.

Providing Housing: Private and Public Strategies

The households represented in this research divide fairly evenly into three groups. One-third of households own their own homes or pay unsubsidized rent. This group of families has the highest-paying jobs, the most stable employment, and the most stable family arrangements. Another third live in government-subsidized rental housing. These families live in low-income housing provided by the Imperial Valley Housing Authority or have Section 8 housing. The families in this group are quite diverse, with single mothers, couples who have fallen on hard times and lost their family homes, and couples with stable relationships and stable employment, whose low earnings render them eligible for subsidized housing. The final third live in extended-family households in which other family members own the property or are responsible for the rent. It might be expected that these individuals were in the most fluid family and employment situations, but this is not necessarily the case: many extended-kin households are long-standing and do not reflect an "emergency housing" situation.

Many Imperial County women talked about their desire to own a home. For most, it was a hope for the future. Just seven families owned their own homes. Finding a low rate of home ownership is noteworthy, in part, because home ownership has long been much more accessible in the Imperial Valley than in many places in California. Home prices have historically been low in the Valley. An important offset to the low-wage structure of this agricultural area has been the availability of modest housing at modest prices.[1]

By the time I began my fieldwork in 2005, however, the situation had changed drastically. Large real estate developers had moved in with plans to build hundreds of new homes. Prices were escalating dramatically. The conventional wisdom held that the county's real estate boom was driven, in part, by market pressures from San Diego. Housing prices had risen so high in that major metropolitan area that, it was said, San Diegans were now expressing interest in living in El Centro, Imperial, or Brawley, and commuting to work in San Diego. Some even speculated about the possibility of commuter train service between El Centro and San Diego.[2]

Rising housing prices caused grave concern among the more economically stable families represented in my research. Those who currently rented or lived with relatives and hoped to buy eventually saw that they might be priced out of the housing market. Marta Lujan and her husband, ages thirty-seven and forty-five respectively, had purchased a house in Brawley six months prior to our interview. She said, "I was getting desperate because the houses were going up. I just wanted to get into a house because we had been renting for a long time. Yeah, it's exciting, but it's like depressing because you go in there and you see it needs so much work." Marta describes the house as a "very old home" that was in poor condition, but priced low. They bought the house for $140,000; she maintained that six months later the house was worth $220,000.[3]

All home owners, with one exception, were married couples with annual earnings of more than $50,000. The exception is Patricia Ochoa, separated from her husband, who despite much lower earnings managed to keep up the payments on her house, enabling her five children to remain in their family home.

Six families paid market-price rent for their housing.[4] In most instances, these families had annual family incomes of at least thirty thousand dollars, too high to be eligible for subsidized rent. In a couple of cases, low-income families paid market-value rents while they bided their time on waiting lists for subsidized rental housing.

Antonia Avilar, whose family lives in a small, substandard mobile home without heat or air conditioning, is discouraged by her inability to get into subsidized housing. This family of five is in desperate financial straits. Antonia cannot get the records needed for the county to process their application for cash aid.[5] The only public assistance the family currently receives is food stamps. Antonia applied for subsidized housing two years ago and was put on a waiting list. Now the housing authority says it has no record of the application. Antonia would like an easier application for housing help and welfare. She says, in frustration, "I would like someone to come to my home and see if I need help—not ask for papers."

The demand for Housing and Urban Development (HUD)–subsidized housing in the Imperial Valley was strong. The thirteen families living in subsidized housing have incomes ranging from just a few thousand dollars annually (receiving only welfare benefits) to approximately twenty-eight thousand dollars (a family of five).[6] The top choice for most families who qualify for housing assistance is the Section 8 program that subsidizes rents for families who live in units owned by participating private landlords. The obvious attraction of this program is that it is "tenant based" rather than "project based," permitting renters to decide on the type and location of housing for their family, for example, a single-family home in their preferred neighborhood (Turner and Kingsley 2008). This popular program has a perpetually long waiting list.

Less popular but nonetheless fully occupied is low-income housing owned and managed by the Imperial Valley Housing Authority. These units range from one to five bedrooms; the many-bedroom units reflect the large family size of some households needing housing assistance, especially in a prior generation. Some of the women in the study are reticent about living in the local housing projects. Some older projects have a reputation for being disorderly and perhaps even dangerous. Priscilla Ortega, for example, explains a shooting in the street outside her home by saying that she lives close to the projects. She assumes that gun violence spills out from the projects and onto her residential street. In recent years the county has added new low-income housing developments. Cynthia Mateo believes she and her daughter are very fortunate to have the opportunity to live in the new housing project in Brawley. It has amenities including dish-washers and built-in microwaves and is, she thinks, very "family friendly."

Twelve families live in extended family households in which other family members own the house or are responsible for the rent. A reasonable assumption might be that the most destitute families make up this subgroup, that is, that housing status serves as a proxy for economic status. The realities are much more complex. In the pages that follow, I describe these extended arrangements in detail, first, because extended family arrangements are thought to be a defining feature of Mexican American families; and second, to illustrate that coresidence meets many needs and serves a variety of purposes.

In some instances coresiding with family members did constitute "last option" or "only option" housing. Four unemployed single mothers lived with family members out of economic necessity. Two of these were young single mothers who were unemployed and lived with their parents but hoped they would soon get jobs and apartments of their own. The other two women had fallen on hard times. Miranda Flores, abandoned by her husband, now lives with her sister and brother-in-law. Cecilia Diaz is a thirty-seven-year-old mother of seven children whose circumstances have declined since her divorce five years earlier. She was born in Brawley, lived most of her adult life in San Diego, and then returned to Brawley after the divorce. Cecilia says, "I didn't have anywhere else to go. So I had to come back to Brawley because I had family here." In a series of painful events that followed, she lost her housing and, along with three of her daughters, moved into her disabled mother's small apartment. She temporarily "sent [her] other children back with their dad," but then lost custody of them. Because of further unraveling of her personal circumstances—her mother's car has broken down and they have no money to fix it, so they are now "on foot"—two of her three daughters have now also moved back in with their father in San Diego. Cecilia is desperate to find a job and secure suitable housing so she can get her children back.

Four two-parent families who moved away from Brawley but later returned for family-related reasons now live with parents or parents-in-law. Denise Ortiz, Julie Peña, and Elena Sanchez and their families live with their husbands' parents. Francesca Alvarez and her family live with her parents. The family circumstances precipitating the return to Brawley have already been discussed for all families except the Sanchezes. Elena and Raymond Sanchez lived briefly in Brawley, Ray's home town, after they were married; they then moved to Fresno, Elena's home town, and lived there several years. Both had good jobs in Fresno, but Ray quit his job over an unfortunate workplace misunderstanding. He then decided he wanted to move back to Brawley and to his family. This family of five lives with Ray's parents. Ray's previous job with a cement company in Fresno paid sixteen dollars an hour with full benefits. His new job in construction in Brawley pays seven dollars an hour without benefits. Elena continues to look for a job but is not committing to stay in Brawley longer than the current school year.

These four families moved back to Brawley for kinship-related reasons. Three returned to provide care or assistance for a parent, and the Sanchezes returned as a kind of homecoming for Ray. Two of these women either hope to or have used coresidence as an opportunity to fulfill educational goals. The willingness of Julie Peña's mother-in-law to help out with child care enabled Julie to finish her B.A. degree, something she probably would not have been able to do back in Las Vegas. Francesca Alvarez, though she returned from Phoenix to help care for her mother, how hopes her mother can "watch" her son while she completes her B.A. degree. Both instances illustrate the reciprocity that underlies the functioning of kin networks.

The final four women who live in extended family households in which others are primary householders—Erica Martinez, Ana Ramirez, Theresa Romero, and Monica Rodriguez—are single mothers who live with their parents. Their coresidence is not principally motivated by economic need. Each one could live independently in single-family households. In all cases, the most vital resource they receive from parents is practical assistance in meeting the competing demands of being both good parents and good workers. In fact, for both Erica Martinez and Ana Ramirez, economic assistance flows from daughter to parents. The money these women bring into their parents' households likely enables both sets of parents to remain in their homes. Erica and her parents split the mortgage payment and all bills; her parents, former farmworkers who are not yet retirement age, pay their share of the bills from their disability checks. Ana pays most of the bills because her parents spend much of her retired farmworker father's meager retirement income (Social Security benefits of eight hundred dollars monthly) on medical expenses. Both sets of parents, while not in the best of health, provide after-school care, transportation, and other practical day-to-day necessities for their grandchildren. For these households, the extended-family arrangement is mutually supportive.

Theresa Romero, age thirty-one, and her younger sister, Sandra, have always lived at home. Both could live independently if they chose but have not been so inclined. In fact, I first met Sandra, a university graduate with a responsible job in Brawley, who then introduced me to her sister, who met the criteria for participation in the research. Theresa explains the family's financial arrangements this way: "It's never been a matter—I've worked since I was eighteen—that we're all going to pool our incomes together. It's always been—I guess it's the way we were brought up—it's like we (she and her sister) say, 'We're going to pay this or that.' We take some of the expenses away from our father and mother from our own earnings." Theresa's daughter, Crystal, was born eighteen months earlier. Crystal's father is not involved in her life, but Theresa's family shares responsibility for her care and well-being.

Finally, Monica Rodriguez moved back into her parents' home with her two boys when she separated from her husband. With her teacher's salary, she certainly could afford her own home. In living with her parents, she is relying on them for emotional support in this difficult time of transition. She also depends on her mother to provide care and nurture for her boys. She says, "My mom is their second mom. She really is."

A total of fifteen families represented in this research live in extended-family households. I have described the circumstances of the twelve who live in homes in which other family members are responsible for paying the mortgage or the rent. In three other cases, women research participants are the householders of record and a parent or parents live with them. The mothers of both Beatrice Padilla and Lisa Cabrillo live in their households. Beatrice's mother has lived with her for thirteen years, present through many family structure transitions as Beatrice was married, divorced, remarried, and widowed. The Cabrillos are one of the highest-earning couples. Lisa and her husband earn more than $60,000 annually and own a home. Lisa's mother lives with them and is their child care provider.

Lucia Hernandez's parents live with her family of five. This reverses the prior situation in which Lucia and her family lived for many years with her parents, Ernesto and Delores Salazar. The Salazars are an immigrant farmworker couple who were able to buy a home but lost it to foreclosure a few years back when they were unable to find work for several months and missed some payments. Now the Hernandezes rent an apartment and the Salazars live with them. This household of seven struggles with poverty.

The high rate of household extension is a distinctive feature of this Imperial County sample. Three main conclusions may be drawn about how household extension functions for these families. First, extended-family households distribute resources across generations, from family members with more adequate or stable resources to family members with less adequate or stable resources. A reasonable assumption might be that resources are distributed from more economically secure parents to less economically secure adult children, mostly in their twenties and thirties. In many cases parents did indeed share resources with children and grandchildren. In addition, in several cases, resources were distributed from adult children to parents. These exchanges were, in many cases, part of the legacy of farm work. Working in the fields had taken a physical toll on some parents, leaving them in their fifties and unable to work. Other farmworkers had reached the statutory retirement age but lacked resources to live independently.

Second, household extension supports other familistic behaviors. Coresidence is just one of a number of ways that extended family networks provide assistance. Kin networks provide both instrumental support in the form of, for example, housing, transportation, and child care, and expressive support in the form of emotional assistance (Baca Zinn 1982). For economically self-reliant single mothers who lived with their parents, family extension relieved women of the overload frequently experienced by single mothers who "do it all" and provided a home for children with the daily presence of other loving adults who shared in their care.

Third, a structural analysis anticipates that the explanation for household extension is principally socioeconomic (Sarkisian, Gerena, and Gerstel 2006). This is generally but not always the case. Indeed, pervasive underemployment in the Imperial Valley has created a context in which many families lack resources to live as independent households. But household extension serves families with varied experiences. A significant segment of the population of the Imperial Valley is poor or near-poor. Given the limited quantity and poor quality of jobs, most individuals will not get the lucky break they hope for, that is, getting a full-time, year-round job with benefits. For physically debilitated farmworkers, it is too late for a break. In this environment, extended-family households are a positive adaptation that increases housing stability for all involved. In a few instances, however, extended family households are better explained by care and support than by economic interdependence. Here I find two main scenarios: parents in difficult circumstances who receive care and assistance from their adult children and single mothers who receive emotional support and practical assistance in child rearing from their parents.

Other Public Supports and Private Strategies

Given the labor market context of Imperial County, it is predictable and, in fact, the case that many families, both unemployed and working families, will qualify for public assistance in various forms. Families participate in public programs to provide food, school lunches, cash, child care, and health coverage for their children.

Fourteen of thirty-eight families participate in CalWORKS, California's version of the TANF welfare program. Their cash assistance grants range from $214 to $1,150 monthly. The program requires 32 to 35 hours of work-related activities weekly to receive benefits. The lives of Daniela Rosales and Consuela Reyes provide examples of approved work-related activities. Daniela is the twenty-two-year-old mother of an eighteen-month-old son. She is working on her GED and searching for a job. Consuela is the twenty-eight-year-old mother of one-year-old twins. She has been looking for a job for a couple of years. She is taking an Imperial Valley Regional Occupational Program (IVROP) class providing training for office occupations and applying for jobs. IVROP provides "work-readiness" programming for public assistance recipients deemed to need additional skills to achieve self-sufficiency. Consuela's job search is limited. She is looking for jobs in Brawley only, because she lacks transportation to get to El Centro or somewhere else. She explains that her family does not have a car, so she walks wherever she goes. As I went about my business in Brawley on a day-to-day basis, I regularly saw Consuela, a petite woman, always wearing white athletic shoes, pushing a large double-stroller in various areas of the town. I talked with her occasionally. At the end of my stay in Imperial County I encountered her again; she was excited to tell me that she had just secured a job with an insurance company.

Parents receiving cash assistance through CalWORKs are "sanctioned" if they do not complete their required hours. Sanctioned parents continue to receive cash aid for their children, but not for themselves. Rosa Navarra was sanctioned for continuing to attend college. She says, "The welfare system cut me off because I wanted to continue my education and they wouldn't let me. They thought I had enough education to get a job." She refers to the TANF provision that education is supported only to the extent that enables a client to get a job, not necessarily a well-paying job. Rosa resisted this provision, deciding to continue in school, have her benefits reduced by sanction, and then to rely on her family for the additional support she needed. She says, "I would get help from my brother, from my mom, moneywise."

The use of subsidized child care services was discussed in an earlier chapter. Eleven women receive this assistance. These mothers are both CalWORKs participants and lower-income employed women who meet eligibility requirements. Many families rely on food stamps and free or reduced school lunches to provide adequate nutrition for their families. Nearly half receive food stamps. School-age children in more than half of these households are eligible for free or reduced-price school lunches.

The area in which households in this sample are most reliant on public supports is health coverage. The children in twenty-three families have health coverage through California's public health care programs, Medi-Cal and Healthy Families. For most, the coverage is free. It is a tremendous relief for lower-income parents to know that their children's medical care will not be compromised by their inability to pay for it.

For the fifteen remaining families, health coverage is or is not provided for children for several different reasons. Four families provide insurance through a city, county, or federal job. Four other families have employment in the Brawley public schools. School employees make high individual contributions to their health plan. Each of the four women employed by the school system complain about the cost. Eva Vallejo describes the cost of health benefits as "outrageous," but her family needs it because her husband is self- employed. She pays $450 a month for family insurance and then hesitates to go to the doctor because the co-pay is an additional $20. Marjorie Salas makes a similar point. She says, "So when my husband says, 'Have you made an appointment to see the doctor?' It's like, 'No, because we don't have anything [for the co-pays].'"

Four families have a worker with a private sector job that offers family health coverage. Two families pay the required employee contribution for the coverage (Rosa Navarra and Esther Valdez); two others have declined the coverage. The two families declining coverage are the Ortegas and the Roberts. Priscilla Ortega's employer provides health insurance for her. Insurance is available for the children and her husband if she pays half of the additional premium. They have opted out of this coverage. Celia Roberts' husband's employer provides family health insurance, but the employee contribution to the policy is $1,500 annually. And then, there are deductibles and co-pays. Celia thought it would cost them a few thousand dollars per year for the coverage. They declined it, believing "it was a little higher than what our income could allow." Now the family is confronted with "huge" medical bills. First, the bills arrived from the surgery Celia had five months earlier. Then, in just the last month, her youngest son Andrew was diagnosed with a serious medical condition. It is fortuitous that Celia took her two youngest children in for their immunizations a month ago. At that time, she was able to apply for thirty days of temporary Medi-Cal coverage for children receiving immunizations. Since then, Andrew has undergone an extensive battery of tests. Thanks to the temporary coverage, these medical expenses will be largely or fully covered. Celia is now in the process of applying for permanent coverage for these children, as well as for her oldest child who did not require immunizations at the time and did not get the temporary coverage. She is quite sure they will now qualify for Medi-Cal because in dealing with Andrew's condition, she missed several days of work and lost her job. The family now struggles without her earnings of $2,000 monthly, but ironically, the positive side of this is that now, with the drop in family income, the children should now qualify for state-provided health coverage.

Patricia Ochoa is the only research participant whose family does not currently have access to public or employer-provided coverage. Her employer offers health insurance after six months on the job. She will be eligible for this coverage soon and hopes she will be able to afford it. A recent trip to the emergency room with her twelve-year-old son and a bill of seven hundred dollars has shattered the family budget and created anxiety about her inability to pay medical bills. Finally two families who relocated to the Valley recently have Medi-Cal coverage for their children pending. This becomes effective upon receipt of required records and documentation.

Utility costs in the Valley are very high, due primarily to the high usage of electricity for air-conditioning in this desert climate. For families of limited means, keeping the lights on can be a real challenge. The Imperial Irrigation District (IID), the Valley's publicly administered electric company, offers assistance to low-income households through its Residential Energy Assistance Program (REAP) (Imperial Irrigation District 2010).[7] Low-income households are eligible for reductions of 15 to 25 percent of their bill. Nine families participate in this program. Everyone says the program helps, but that energy costs are still unaffordable. The households of Sylvia Moreno and Rosemary Correa are two that participate in the program. Sylvia tells me that her highest electric bill for the year was $280 (after her 15 percent discount) in August. Rosemary is concerned about her November bill for $122 (a 20 percent reduction) due a few days after the interview. She says, "God knows how I am going to pay it, but . . . [shakes her head]."

How Families Manage

Women and their partners pull together the resources needed to provide for their children with varying degrees of difficulty. Only eleven of thirty-eight households support themselves without directly accessing any public assistance programs. These households—seven married-couple households and four single-mother households—sustain themselves by their waged income and their employer-provided health coverage. But full-time employment in this labor market does not necessarily enable families to be self-sufficient. Five additional families have one or two full-time workers, do not receive cash assistance or food stamps, but still qualify for at least one government program (such as subsidized housing or reduced-price school lunches).

The remaining twenty-two households, more than half of those represented in this research, have considerably more difficulty providing for their families. The following snapshots of sources of support for three families in this group illustrate variation in the degree of reliance on public assistance. Each of these points to the problem of underemployment in the Valley. First is a dual-earner household with low earnings that receives modest assistance. Second is a two-parent household with one low-wage worker and an unemployed partner; this household needs additional assistance and is eligible for it. Third is a single-parent household with vocational training placements in the workforce, but no formal employment; this household receives assistance through a broad array of programs, but little cash.

Both Julie and Roberto Peña are employed. Julie earns $800 monthly at her half-time job as an instructional aide at a local school (a nine-month position). Roberto earns $300 weekly as an auto mechanic. Their joint annual income is approximately $24,000 for a family of six. They receive $247 a month in food stamps and the children are eligible for reduced-price school lunches. The children have health coverage through Medi-Cal. The Peñas lives rent-free with Roberto's parents.

Consuela and Daniel Reyes are parents of one-year-old twins. Daniel has worked for two years as a baker in a local bakery, earning minimum wage for 30 to 35 hours of work weekly. Consuela is looking for a job. Daniel's earnings average $220 weekly; his annual earnings amount to around $11,400. Consuela participates in the CalWORKs program, receiving $500 monthly in cash aid and subsidized child care while she fulfills program requirements. Their annual cash income from earnings and cash aid is approximately $17,600. They also receive $200 monthly in food stamps and an unspecified amount from the WIC program. They live in low-income housing and receive the low-income discount on their electric bill. Their twins have health coverage through the Medi-Cal plan.

Stephanie Ruiz is the twenty-six-year-old mother of Alexis, age five. Stephanie has received cash assistance through CalWORKs for five years. Over this period of time, she has been unable to secure a permanent job. Stephanie receives $555 in cash assistance and $175 in food stamps monthly. With no earned income, Stephanie has just $6,660 in cash coming into her household annually. She receives subsidized child care while she continues to look for a job. Alexis receives free school lunches and has health coverage through Medi-Cal. The family's housing is subsidized through the Section 8 program. Stephanie is the only mother I interviewed whose household is, and has for several years been, entirely reliant on public assistance. A few other women currently depend quite heavily on public assistance programs or have done so in the past. These are typically fairly brief periods of assistance that have been precipitated by family structure change, illness, or unemployment.

Women talked very little about border-based strategies for family survival in the categories analyzed here. A few accessed medical care and some had child care arrangements with women from "the other side." During my time in the Imperial Valley, some residents were suggesting that with U.S. housing prices rising so high locally, the obvious solution was to buy a home in Mexico. U.S. Customs and Border Patrol's SENTRI (Secure Electronic Network for Travel Rapid Inspection) program facilitates transborder residence by providing expedited border crossing for low-risk travelers (U.S. Customs and Border Patrol 2009). This residential strategy is a social class–related option. It is not relevant to poor and working-class families who depend on institutional supports in the United States. Furthermore, it is unlikely to be used by families with school-age children. None of my research participants were considering real estate in Mexico.[8]

A 2001 Urban Institute study of the implementation of TANF in rural areas conducted case studies of a total of twelve rural counties in four states.[9] Imperial County was included in this analysis, and in the classification system used by researchers it was designated as a relatively "more isolated" county with "an urban population of 20,000 or more [in the towns] in poor economic condition" (Pindus 2001, 6). In the study, welfare supervisors in Imperial County reported that in the move from welfare to work, very few clients actually leave assistance because even with their earnings they remain eligible for benefits. This finding illustrates the low earning capacity of many jobs in Imperial County. The desperate need for jobs in this community is demonstrated by local economic development activities. Pindus reports that the county was considering strategies such as bringing in trash dumps, mental health facilities for sex offenders, and a toxic waste disposal site (2001, 19). In most communities, NIMBY (Not in My Back Yard) sentiment would preclude pursuing these initiatives. The willingness to consider socially undesirable projects points to the difficulties rural areas have in attracting new job-producing investment to their communities.

I began this chapter with the observation by Taylor and his colleagues that low-earning farmworkers are a drain on public resources in economically stressed rural communities. In the Imperial County sample, eligibility for public programs goes well beyond low-paid farmworkers. Given the structural realities of this rural area, a significant majority of households need and use public assistance. A key problem is that "work does not pay," that is, as a result of low wage scales, part-time hours, or the seasonal nature of the employment, work does not bring families to economic self-sufficiency.

The families represented by the Imperial County women would prefer to be economically self-sufficient. But even lacking that possibility, most (but not all) households are able to provide a decent home and the necessities of life for their children by relying on a combination of their own earnings, public assistance, and family network support. The government assistance piece in the resource package is vitally important. Support from public programs partially compensates for the structural barriers to self-sufficiency in a community plagued by massive underemployment.

BUILDING A BETTER LIFE

The Imperial County women have humble origins. Farmworkers' daughters arguably began their lives on the lowest rung of American society.[10] Granddaughters of farmworkers also know about the deprivations experienced by their parents growing up in farmworker households. The women in this research are determined to get ahead but face the challenge of trying to accomplish this in an agriculture-reliant border community. Rural residence imposes constraints on upward mobility because rural areas have more than their share of jobs that are low paying, part-time, and seasonal. It is perhaps unsurprising, then, that while work in rural areas has historically provided Mexican immigrants the principal means of initial entry to the United States, most of their children have not remained in rural areas. In discussing urban growth in California's Central Valley, the largest and most productive agricultural valley in the state, Taylor and his colleagues refer to cities as a "magnet" for immigrant farmworkers' children (1997, 53).

Some rural areas do have well-established populations of Mexican Americans, that is to say, some people stay where they are rather than flee to urban places as soon as possible. While considerable scholarly attention has focused on Hispanic immigrants in rural areas, established populations are less visible (see, for example, Lichter and Johnson 2006; Pfeffer and Parra 2009). Second- and third-generation rural Hispanics frequently have improved their economic status, in comparison to the economic situations of new arrivals (Kandel and Newman 2004). Nonetheless, established Hispanic populations in rural counties continue to have high poverty rates.

The earnings for Mexican Americans lag far behind those of all U.S. workers, but generational differences are key to understanding the economic status of this group. In short, second, third, and later generations have improved their situation in comparison to the immigrant generation but fall short of achieving earnings parity with all U.S. workers. Scholars find a high level of generational progress between the first and second generations because the second generation has considerably more education and higher earnings than do than their Mexico-born parents. But because Mexican immigrants overall have little education and low wages, the comparison is to a low standard. Significant gains to educational attainment and earnings still leave the second generation substantially behind national achievement norms. A cause for serious concern is research finding very limited gains to education and wage improvement after the second generation (Grogger and Trejo 2002; Telles and Ortiz 2008).

Research analyzing generational progress typically uses cross-sectional data, that is, it compares characteristics of first-, second-, and third-generation Mexican Americans at a particular point in time. These data are valuable but do not allow for an analysis of earnings and educational attainment across generations. An important longitudinal study by Telles and Ortiz (2008) does permit that analysis, however.[11] This research captures generational change between first-, second-, and third-generation parents (1965 survey) and their children (2000 survey). The study demonstrates the powerful and consistent effect of education in predicting socioeconomic status. It was education that explained variation in earnings within generations, and economic progress between generations of Mexican Americans. Because educational advancement stalls after the second generation, upward mobility is blocked for the third generation and beyond. Telles and Ortiz exhausted many possible explanations for why, over several generations, Mexican Americans are unable to attain the same educational progress as earlier generations of European immigrants. They conclude that low academic achievement for Mexican Americans "derives from a racialized system that stigmatizes Mexican American children in various ways. Racialization through schooling seems to help cement their low status in American society" (2008, 133). These results find racial inequality to be embedded in the structure of the institution of education, which systematically denies equal access and opportunity to all members of society.

Education Is the Key

The Imperial County women are not scholars, but their belief that education is the key to getting ahead is consistent with the Telles and Ortiz study and many others. One of the clearest messages I received from these women was the importance of education. In this labor market, where minimum-wage work predominates, it is education that provides the ticket out of low wage work. Getting an education is understood to be their main chance for upward mobility. What these women mean by "getting an education" varies somewhat. Getting a bachelor's degree is viewed as a major triumph by all, and for most, getting an associate's degree or becoming a registered nurse (R.N.) is also an outstanding achievement.

Rosa Navarra states the alternatives faced by local workers starkly: "Either you get educated, or you fall into everybody else's category: minimum wage." The dilemma is exacerbated by Imperial County's location at the U.S.-Mexico border. Rosa points out that while the Valley is growing, most jobs coming in are minimum wage. "And if we don't take them, the people from the other side are more than willing to take them." Rosa's viewpoint is shared by many other women. Their basic understanding is that if you don't have an education, "you are pretty much going to get paid minimum wage for whatever you do."

A look at the educational attainment of these women tells us something about how successful this group has been in getting an education. Thirty of thirty-eight women have at least a high school diploma or GED. Of those thirty, three have a GED or high school diploma, sixteen have completed "some college" coursework, six have an associate's or technical degree, and five have a bachelor's degree; none have graduate degrees. This leaves eight women who have not completed high school or a GED. The educational attainment of my unrepresentative sample is quite similar to that of other U.S.-born Mexican American women, but with one main difference (Grogger and Trejo 2002). A much larger segment of the Imperial County women have had some college education (without achieving the bachelor's degree).[12] Grogger and Trejo's analysis of Current Population Survey (CPS) data shows that 28 percent of U.S-born Mexican America women have had some college coursework (this includes associate's and technical degrees), while 58 percent of my sample have done so.

Most women have pursued their postsecondary education at Imperial Valley College (IVC), the region's community college. The institution offers associate of arts (A.A.) and associate of science (A.S.) degrees. It also provides vocational and occupational education, offering certificates in a number of occupational fields. IVC added a much-anticipated registered nursing (R.N.) program in 2004; this program was said to have a two-year waiting list. The women participating in this research rely heavily on IVC. Of the five women with bachelor's degrees, all did their freshman and sophomore years at IVC before transferring to a B.A. degree–granting university. Of the six women with associate degrees or technical credentials, four have degrees from IVC. Of the sixteen women with "some college," twelve did their postsecondary work at IVC.

Imperial Valley College's programs are in great demand in the Valley. A majority of the county's graduating seniors, typically 60 percent, become IVC students (Ruth 2010). In addition, many nontraditional-age students come to IVC to work toward degrees. By many accounts, the college is unable to meet the demand for its educational programming. IVC's approximately eight thousand students compete for space in the courses needed to complete their degrees. Several women mention that their progress (and that of others) has been delayed because they are not able to get into required classes. Angelica Perez say that because the classes she needs are always full, she has to "crash her courses." She explains how that process works: "'Crashing your courses' means you didn't get into the course through regular registration and didn't make the waiting list, but you show up at the first class and hope you can get in—either people who are registered don't show up, or the instructor just lets you in. When you go the first day, you sign the 'crashers list.' Sometimes they do it like a raffle."

Imperial County's public university is San Diego State University–Imperial Valley Campus (SDSU-IV). This has traditionally been an upper-division-only campus with a dozen undergraduate degree programs and a few master's degree programs. Since 2003, it has also offered a selective Freshman Scholars Program that provides four-year degree programs in three majors. This satellite campus has a total student body of approximately eight hundred students. Many local students who attend IVC and plan to complete a four-year program transfer to SDSU-IV. This pattern is seen in my research. Four of the five college graduates received their degrees from SDSU-IV. All had transferred from IVC.

The reliance of Imperial County residents on community college education is cause for some concern. The women participating in this research were enthusiastic about pursuing IVC degrees and in some cases eventually transferring to SDSU-IV. A degree from a two-year or four-year institution is how women expect to raise the quality of their employment and their earnings. A look at national statistics finds Hispanic students to be underrepresented at four-year institutions and overrepresented at community colleges nationwide, with Hispanics making up 7 percent of students in four-year college and 14 percent of students in two-year colleges in 2000 (Schneider, Martinez, and Owens 2006). Many choose community colleges because they are convenient and affordable. In reality, transfer and completion rates for Hispanic students at two-year colleges are low. Many Hispanic students spend years at a community college without completing a program, and only 25 percent go on to a four-year institution.[13] At the very least, there are capacity concerns at IVC, with insufficient resources to meet the demands of local students. Ironically, the Imperial County women face stiff competition for both jobs and college coursework.

Higher education proves to be a very local phenomenon. The only college graduate in my sample who did not complete her degree at the Valley did her first two years at IVC and then transferred to California State University San Bernardino. Most women do not even consider attending institutions in other places. Marina Mendez is an exception. She would like to go to school somewhere other than IVC. She thinks it is quite advantageous in the workplace to have your education from "somewhere else." She says, "I tell my boyfriend, 'If I go to IVC, I'm just staying on the same level as everyone else.' I just don't think IVC is that good a school." Marina would like to distinguish herself from the local competition by attending a school outside the Valley.

The women in this research are typically oriented toward one of four degree programs. One is the registered nursing program at IVC. The others are three B.A. programs at SDSU-IV: teacher education, criminal justice, and psychology. The SDSU degrees depend on freshman- and sophomore-level course work at IVC. Women are drawn to these degrees, in part, because they believe they can lead directly to secure jobs with good pay. Women who are interested in social service work typically pursue a psychology degree. I was initially curious at the strong interest in the criminal justice degree. I found that some years earlier county officials had promoted Imperial County as the site for new state prisons as a means of bringing more jobs to the Valley. As a result, the county now has two large prisons, the Centinela and Calipatria state prisons. These prisons employ a total staff of 2,400 to maintain custody of a prison population of 8,500 (California Department of Corrections and Rehabilitation 2010). The California Department of Corrections and Rehabilitation (CDRC) is one of the largest employers in the county. Some women are drawn to the criminal justice degree because they think it will enable them to get one of the better jobs in the prisons.[14] State government jobs are among the best in the Valley.

Some women have come to a fairly recent understanding of their need for more education. In Helen Estrada's case this will mean getting a GED. She tells me that she is coming to realize that without a GED she will really be held back in her job search. She says, "Yeah, that's what I'm thinking about today 'cuz I see that I'm really gonna get nowhere." Cecelia Diaz completed her GED at age thirty-five. The present circumstances of this mother of seven are dispiriting, but she remains proud of this accomplishment. She also sees it will take more education to gain the stability she hopes for. She says, "I believe if you go to college and you have some kind of degree, you can make it out here. You can have a home. Because the living expenses are reasonable. So anyone can have a home out here.

But you have to have some kind of degree. People can work out in the prisons and have a home, you know." Cecilia is divorced and struggling, but even in better days this family never owned a home.

Many more women have been pursuing an educational agenda for several years. They know that the jobs they want require more education or training than they currently have. Many have been attending the local community college, but for more than half of those who pursue post-secondary education, an associate's degree remains an elusive goal. Many women describe circumstances in which they started a program of study, but the complications of day-to-day life, for example, the birth of a child or schedule conflicts with a new job, result in their dropping classes and often stopping their programs. Very few women described lives in which "student" had been their primary role. Most have been workers and students, parents and students, or most likely, parents, workers, and students.

The experiences of four mothers currently seeking degrees suggest the extent to which women's competing responsibilities might slow their progress to degree completion. Angelica Perez began the administration of justice program at IVC at age seventeen. She dropped out at age eighteen when her first child was born. She came back to IVC two years ago as a mother of three and changed her major to business marketing. Angelica is now pregnant with her fourth child. She is working part-time and searching for a better job. Sylvia Moreno is a mother of three who works nearly full-time, cleans her grandmother's house, and is working on an associate's degree in psychology. She is now thinking about switching to the registered nursing program. This will require taking science courses that are prerequisites and then applying for admission. Erica Martinez has three daughters, a full-time job, and is working on a degree but has not taken classes for a while. She has pledged that, while she doesn't know how she will manage it, she will go back next semester. Finally, Cynthia Mateo, mother of a one-year-old, dropped out of IVC during her pregnancy. She has decided to start over at IVC by retaking several courses, hoping to get better grades, and then applying for the R.N. program. The busy family lives of these women often create complications that interfere with their ability to make good progress toward completing their degree programs.

Education and the Legacy of Farm Labor. For some women limited educational attainment is part of the legacy of farm labor. Many immigrant farmworker parents did not encourage their children to study and stay in school. Some of these parents themselves had no education at all or only a few years in Mexico. Likewise, some U.S.-born parents had limited or no formal education. Some parents were barely literate in Spanish and could speak little or no English. These parents generally lacked the cultural knowledge and the confidence to suggest that their children aspire to a college education. And poverty was certainly a factor in parents' emphasis on work over education. Cecilia Diaz's mother is the daughter of Brawley farmworkers. Cecilia says that back in the days when her mother was growing up, everyone in the neighborhood was poor. Her mother worked from a very young age. "They were raised to always work. I don't think education was really too much of a priority back then, you know," explains Cecilia.

Ana Ramirez and her sisters battled their father, a farm laborer who worked in a feedlot since coming to the United States, about going to college. She says, "My parents never encouraged education." The five sisters had worked in their aunt and uncle's Mexican restaurant since they were girls. Their parents assumed the daughters would continue with the extended-family business. This occupation was consistent with women's traditional domestic roles. Ana explains what happened: "My oldest sister wanted out. She knew the only way she could get out of the family business was if she went to school. And we just followed. My sister got accepted to UCSD. But I'm telling you, we had no support. My father said, 'None of you are going to college. There's no way that you can go out there by yourself.' My sister resented my father because he wouldn't sign the papers [the university asked parents to sign]. So she went there anyway. Yeah, he didn't know the world." Ana later followed in her sister's footsteps, contesting her father's disapproval, and going away to college for a teaching credential. It is clear that Julian Ramirez did not understand the value of education. From his standpoint, a parent prepared his children for the workforce by teaching them the importance of hard work. As Ana says, "All we heard when we were growing up was, 'I want you to be a hard worker. You get to work ten minutes before [everyone else] and you're the last one to leave.' That's all I remember my father telling me. And he had the strongest work ethic."

Gloria Espinosa is the granddaughter of Mexican American farmworkers. Her mother is a Mexican immigrant. When Gloria's parents split up early on, it was up to her mother to support the children. Both poverty and her immigrant status made it difficult for her to help Gloria think about her future. Gloria explains, "As a kid, we didn't have money at all. We didn't. It was kind of like a hopeless situation. But I look forward in my adulthood to getting out of that situation and helping my mom financially. And, I worried about a lot of things that I don't think kids should worry about—like am I going to eat tomorrow, you know? And I never want my kid to ever worry about that." There were aspects of American society that Gloria's mother simply did not understand. There were important subjects—like higher education—she could not help her children negotiate. Gloria says that considering how poor they were, maybe it helped her mother to be unaware of some things she arguably "should" be doing as a parent. When food is an issue, "going to college is impossible. It's a luxury. My mom just worked and did whatever she could do. I mean, my mom couldn't really help us on our homework. She was never really there. She couldn't be. You know, she had to put food in our mouths." It was in high school that Gloria learned that she could actually go to college. She did complete two years and hopes to return to finish her degree in the near future.

For Patricia Ochoa, a farm work–related accident in conjunction with a deep sense of obligation to the family functioned to short-circuit her plans to complete a B.A. degree. Her college education ended abruptly at age twenty when she dropped out of school to fulfill what, according to Mexican culture, was her family obligation in the aftermath of a family calamity. Patricia had completed an associate of science degree and was enrolled in SDSU-San Diego for fall. Her father had been the sole earner in the family. She explains the situation:

> He had a truck and he worked in agriculture and stuff. He was a diabetic for many years and it started taking a toll on his body, so he became disabled. And then, I have an older brother—I had an old brother—two years older than myself. He took over my dad's little business. Well, it hadn't been maybe a year, a year and a half at the most, that [long pause]—it was during the sugar beet season here; it's a big time of the year for the Valley. He crashed into another truck and he died. And the truck exploded, and so it was devastating. We lost a family member, we lost our income, you know, so I was next in line. So I put my education and everything on hold, against my dad's will. There were two younger sisters at home and my dad didn't have a source of income anymore. The truck was gone and he was disabled. So what am I supposed to do, just like, you know?

I said the word she couldn't say: "Leave?" Patricia responded, "I couldn't. That's what they instilled in me—how important family is. And so I stepped up and took charge, sort of, you know, with finances." As Patricia interprets this story for me, she says, "Back then, being a Mexican and then, being the oldest, I had to step up and leave my education." This story is a tragic one in many respects. It would have been a tremendous achievement for this bracero-era farmworker's daughter to leave home in 1976 and earn a B.A. degree. Twenty-nine years later, Patricia, now age forty-nine, has not yet been able to complete her degree. She says, "I have my A.S. Before I die, I'm gonna have my B.A. I am."

The Impact of Early Childbearing. Early and unplanned pregnancies have had a significant impact on the educational experience of this sample of women. Early births short-circuited education and vocational training opportunities or placed difficult obstacles in paths of young women with children. Fifteen of these women had teen births; six more had births at age twenty. A total of twenty-one women, more than half of the sample, had a child by age twenty. It is worthy of note that teen pregnancy may interrupt the education of both pregnant young women and the fathers of their children. Frequently what occurred when teen girls "turned up pregnant" (a term I learned from some women in the study) was that couples got married and boyfriends dropped out of high school. This action enables fathers to support the family in the short term but leaves them with too little education to support their families adequately in the long run.

In the United States, early motherhood is more characteristic of the Mexican American population than other Latino groups or the white and African American populations (Landale and Oropesa 2007). The relationship between teen birth, social class, and race/ethnicity is well established. The principal association is between poverty and early childbearing; because racial-ethnics are disproportionately poor, we then find higher rates of early childbearing among young women of color. In general, economically disadvantaged teens have less access to contraception and poor career prospects. These increase the risk of pregnancy and decrease the disincentives associated with early parenting (Musick 2002).

I suggest here how the relationship between social disadvantage and early births might work out for the women participating in this research (Musick 2002).[15] Let me note that the Mexican American population is predominantly an urban population and that I am not speculating on processes operating in urban centers. All of the Imperial County women grew up poor or at the bottom of the working class in an agricultural community. A majority of parents, mostly immigrants, suffered the indignities of farm work as they struggled to provide for their families. Many parents, poorly educated and still learning English, could not help their children very much in finding a path for upward mobility. Often immigrant parents emphasized hard work as the way to get ahead but did not yet have a sense of the importance of education for mobility in the United States. Most women learned, from what their parents said and did, that they did not want to do farm labor; this did not help them much in charting a viable career path. Most parents expected their daughters to be primarily wives and mothers. It seems that the women who participated in my research expected the same. It is in the context of poverty, racial-ethnic disadvantage, and restricted horizons for women, in conjunction with the recentness of family immigration, that young women "turned up pregnant." It seems reasonable to conclude that many of these couples married because, by some calculus, the prospective fathers were "marriageable men" (Wilson 1987; Landale and Oropesa 2006). The young men had access to work (in the form of farm labor) in a way that the urban poor do not, and that allowed them to support their new families marginally. In fact, given the flat structure of compensation in farm labor, creating a pregnancy-precipitated family might be seen as feasible and sustainable. A young man who leaves high school to work in the fields may earn minimum wage, but this may also be the same rate of pay his farmworker father earns after twenty years of field work. In this community, farmworker families have long constructed family life on a very low budget. Dropping out of school might not initially be seen to limit substantially the horizons of either young mothers or fathers.

For most women it is the dual imperative of working and raising a family that now stands in the way of additional education. Many wish they had thought more about their future before having children. Erica Martinez relates a conversation she had with her oldest daughter:

> My daughter was doing an interview of me for school. She asked me, "Mom, if you could go back to some year to change things, what year would you go back to to change things?" I said, "Probably the year before you were born." She said, "You didn't want me?" [I said,] "No, it's not that. It's just the fact that I would probably change the fact that instead of having you back then, I would have gone to school." She said, "Oh, that's nice." I said, "Yes, now with having so many kids, it is hard. . . . I just hope you guys keep going on your education because I don't want you guys stuck like me."

Women frequently discussed their disappointments and regrets with the paths their own lives had taken when answering my question about their hopes for their children. Many said, in effect, "I hope my children do not do what I did."

Marina Mendez thinks that as a twenty-three-year-old mother of two children, it is already too late to "be someone." She says, "I want my kids to think higher than me. I have kids now, but my plan was to have something before I had kids. But, it's too late. I wanted to be someone. It's not just about having a job—anyone can have a job—but to be someone. To have a good paying job. Yeah, I was going to be a correctional officer. I passed my tests. But I got pregnant with my son. That was my fault—I don't blame anybody else but me."

Rosemary Correa is a divorced mother of four. An early birth thrust her into adult responsibilities. She says, "I had my daughter at the age of fourteen. I was like the youngest mother in Brawley, California. They even gave me an award for it. The 19[—] Award from Teen Mothers. But, you know, now I get to enjoy my daughter. I get to go and play softball a bit with her. I'm not saying that it's good for mothers to be young mothers—just wait. Just wait until it's really time. Wait till you're settled down. Wait till you have your school going for you. Wait till you have your husband that works." In fact, Rosemary had four children before she turned nineteen. She is now divorced, and after six years of experience in medical billing, she has struggled to find steady employment. She is now a full-time student at IVC.

A Multigenerational Strategy for Upward Mobility

Many women believe that the paths their lives have taken will not really enable them to get ahead economically. It is already too late for them. For some of these women, upward mobility becomes a multigenerational strategy. They hope their children will move into the economic mainstream and achieve the American Dream. Stephanie Ruiz has been unsuccessful in her own efforts to find a job. With a high school diploma but no significant work experience, she aspires to a job in hotel housekeeping. But she wants much more for her daughter. Stephanie says, "I hope that my daughter gets a very good job—a high-paid job. And a good education. A job that she enjoys, that she loves—not miserable with. Live somewhere where she's happy. Have her own home—not an apartment like me. Have her own car—not be walking like me. Take it different ways than I did." For Stephanie, achieving the American Dream means having a good job, a good education, a car, and owning a home. Stephanie herself currently has none of these.

Christina Gilbert recognizes that traditional gender assumptions have constrained her ability to support herself and her two children. Christina, now thirty-one years old and divorced, is a part-time retail manager. She was nineteen when her first child was born. Christina says, "I want them [children] to do more than I did. I want them to not waste time. I didn't go to school because I had to work while Kevin [ex-husband] was in school, you know. I want them to finish school fast and get it over with. That way they have the rest of their lives to do what they want. Like me now, I can't do much because I'm having to finish school." Christina had a premarital pregnancy and says she wasted her time in a relationship that she now believes was destined never to work. She says, "It was too hard because our cultures were totally different. I was a stubborn Mexican and he was a stubborn white boy."

Some women who have fallen on hard times do not see how their own circumstances can change very much. They would advise their children not to do what they have done. Antonia and Luis Alivar have fallen on hard times and are desperately poor. This farmworker's daughter minimizes her own hardship and says of her three children, "I want them to finish school, go to college. Get a good opportunity. Not be like me. I am happy. I have my three children and I am happy. But I do not want my daughter to be doing housekeeping. I do not want my sons doing field work."

Helen Estrada is a cohabiting mother of four girls; they range in age from Katrina, age eight, to Jasmine, four months old. Helen has worked most recently as a cashier in a convenience store; her partner, Ricky, is a carpet installer. Helen is already presenting herself to Katrina as a negative example of what happens if you do not get a good education. Helen explains, "We [Helen and Ricky] tell her, 'Look at us. Look at what we go through 'cuz we didn't get a good education. No one will pay us good money.' I mean, I tell her, 'If you want to get paid good money, then, you know, you have to get a good education.' We've told her we want her to go to college. That's the best thing for her to do." I ask if Katrina is listening to what she says. Helen replies, "Yes. And she sees how we, how me and him, struggle, you know. And she sees us sometimes stress out, like, 'What are we going to do?' And she knows that there's times that we don't have money like her friends."

Several parents believe they must be positive role models to encourage their children to get the education they know they need to succeed. Rosa Navarra, in the introduction of this book, talked about her path to completing an associate's degree and her hope that her sons would "play it smart" and not end up working in the fields. Rosa says about completing her degree, "It's a good example for them. So that means if mom can do it, they definitely have to do it." Several women echo Rosa's perspective. For example, twenty-one-year-old Francesca Alvarez hopes to return to college to complete a B.A. degree so she can be an example for her now one-year-old son. She says, "Now I'm not a role model for my son to go to school. I want him to go to college. I don't want my son to say, 'Why should I go to college if you didn't?'"

Theresa Romero is an example of a woman who negotiates her farmworker origins and her hopes for a brighter future for her daughter every day. Her U.S.-born father met her mother, Juanita, across the border in Mexicali. He "immigrated her" when they were married. Theresa and her daughter, Crystal, live with her parents. Juanita is a farmworker who packs carrots; Theresa has never heard her speak a word of English. At the same time Theresa is thinking about how she can best encourage Crystal's achievement. She hopes to go back to college to get a B.A. "in something." She says, "I need to do that. I can't ask my daughter to do the same thing if I haven't done it."

Assessing Upward Mobility

The women in this study have been able to improve their economic status relative to the immigrant generation. They have been able to create far more settled lives than were possible for a prior generation that followed the crops. In comparison to their parents or grandparents, many with only a few years of education in Mexico, these women, most of whom have a high school diploma or more, are well educated. But still many struggle. The current reality in this community and across the United States is that a high school diploma is no guarantee of a stable, full-time job. In general, women see that they and their children will need more education to have a comfortable lifestyle. Most have tried to further their own education. Nearly all pledge to encourage their children to complete college degrees.

The economic progress of married and cohabiting women is frequently hindered by the low educational attainment of their partners. By every measure of educational attainment—from high school graduation, some college, to college completion—the partners of the Imperial County women have achieved less. This difference has had, and is likely to continue to have, a detrimental effect on their families' life chances.[16]

The women in this research are doing the hard work of economic integration into U.S. society. Most did not grow up with a road map for achieving upward mobility. For many, the efforts of their farmworker parents were principally focused on survival because they lived so close to the economic edge. Their parents often could not help very much in constructing a path for success in contemporary U.S. society. Education was not a priority in the poor rural Mexican communities where parents grew up. Many parents themselves had little or no education in Mexico. Antonia Alivar told me that her father had no formal education, and as for her mother, she never talked about it, but Antonia thinks she had some education because she has good handwriting. Elena Sanchez says that the only education her farmworker father considers himself getting was (as an adult) going to the library and learning from the children's books. She says this is how he learned to read.

For granddaughters of farmworkers in this sample, the situation is more complicated to assess. At least one parent of each of these women grew up in a farmworker household. The economic progress for those particular parents of research participants was quite limited. Low education and early childbearing shaped the life course of many. But still, most of the granddaughters of farmworkers have improved their economic status in comparison to both their parents and their grandparents. For example, Lisa Cabrillo's mother, Estella, immigrated to the United States with her farmworker parents when she was a child. Estella has a tenth-grade education and worked in one of the school cafeterias. Now Lisa has an associate's degree and is a social worker for the county.

Upward mobility is typically framed in terms of economic advancement. Studies of generational progress usually, but not always, consider earnings as a measure of economic assimilation. But in Imperial County, the first hurdle for "getting ahead" is getting out of farm work. The low status attached to this work, along with difficult working conditions, creates incentives for farmworkers to move into other types of work, even for the same pay. In Imperial County, leaving farm work for a minimum-wage job at a gas station is "getting ahead." Likewise, getting a minimum wage job in hotel housekeeping is also "getting ahead."

In this high-unemployment, high-poverty setting, the Imperial County women explain their economic situation in two different ways. First, nearly everyone would agree with this assertion: "There are no jobs." The labor force participation of women in this research has been facilitated by government-subsidized child care programs and by family-provided care. These private and public supports enable women to work, but even after months or years of searching, some women are not able to find jobs. For women (and their partners) who do find employment, wages may fall far short of allowing them to be self-sufficient. Many of these working families have earnings so low that they remain eligible for substantial additional public supports including food stamps, subsidized housing, and Medi-Cal coverage.

Second, many women blame themselves for being unprepared to create a better life for their children. They recognize that many of the job postings at the One Stop require educational credentials they do not have. Many women express the sentiment: "I messed up." By this, they usually are referring to an early pregnancy that has set the course for their adult lives. Examining the situation through the lens of a race, class, and gender analysis leads us in another direction. It seems clear that local social institutions—school, church, government, and family—failed to support adequately these poor and working-class Mexican American young women. In striving to understand the experiences of Latinas, we must, as Zambrana writes, "examine multiple factors including the intersection of social and family material conditions on the lived experiences of girls in unresponsive school systems, the effect of racialized, gendered identity constructions, and how the confluence of these factors shaped decisions to have children and form families" (2011, 92).

Arguably, the main concern with early births among the Imperial County women is that they interfered with educational achievement.[17] Many teens, without parental and community support, dropped out of school when they became pregnant. Family responsibilities then interfered with further education. Now they see education as key to economic advancement, but they experience substantial barriers to adding education to the mix of an already busy family life. Many see themselves in fairly dead-end situations. In response, some have adopted a multigenerational strategy for upward mobility; that is, they have transferred any substantial hope for upward mobility to their children.

CHAPTER 7

WHY DO THEY STAY?

The conventional wisdom is that farm labor provides Mexican immigrants their entree into the United States, but that the children of immigrants quickly see that the way forward for them is to leave rural areas and migrate to cities where employment opportunities are better. The fact that Mexican Americans are predominantly an urban population reflects, in part, the movement of the children of immigrant farmworkers to urban places. The Imperial County women defy convention by continuing to live in the agricultural area that provided employment to their (or their partners') immigrant parents or grandparents.

This chapter considers the question of why the women I studied and their families remain in the Imperial Valley. In engaging this question, I assume that individuals are more than merely economic actors maximizing economic well-being through their migration decisions. Rural sociologists increasingly point to the need to consider noneconomic along with economic factors in understanding migration to and from rural areas (Brown 2002). A multitude of individual and household-level factors shape decisions to leave or stay (Johnson 2003, 29). To begin to examine women's decisions to continue to live in the Valley, I asked what they think to be the positive and negative aspects of living in Brawley. I also asked if they have considered moving away from the Valley. I also consider structural characteristics of Imperial County that may affect their satisfaction with the community and decisions to stay.

COMMITMENTS TO PEOPLE AND PLACE

The main reasons women continue to live in the Valley are related to people and place. First, women choose to live here because their extended family also lives here; second, they have strong attachment to the community.[1]

The extended family plays a central role in the organization of family life in Imperial Valley. Kin networks serve a vital function by distributing economic resources and care across generations. Household extension is a major economic strategy, with more than 40 percent of women sharing housing with parents, parents-in-law, or siblings. The Imperial County women and their families frequently lack the economic resources necessary to live as freestanding independent households. Some live with and provide care for their disabled parents. The parents of several single mothers provide the emotional and instrumental support that enables their daughters to be both good workers and good parents. This finding is consistent with research finding that reliance on kin is an important survival strategy for working-class and poor families and is especially prevalent among families of color (Blumberg 2005; Stack 1974).

Next I explore the attachment of women research participants to Brawley, specifically, or the Imperial Valley, more generally.[2] The things the Imperial County women say they appreciate most about living in Brawley are its small-town atmosphere, the presence of a strong sense of community, and the positive environment the community provides for raising children. The most frequent comments about Brawley and its small-town atmosphere are that "everyone knows everyone," and "it is calm." Knowing your neighbors and being known in the community are among the benefits of living in this place. Patricia Ochoa appreciates that if you need assistance, people are willing to help, in part because people know each other. Eva Vallejo says that if you go to the grocery store, "You are guaranteed to meet friends. Pretty much anywhere you go you will meet someone you know. It's a comfortable lifestyle." Christina Gilbert says, "It's good because there's not so many people that you get lost [in the crowd]. You can get close as a community with the teachers, with the school." Several women use the word "calm" to describe Brawley. They use "calm" or sometimes "mellow" to refer to their positive experience of Brawley as slow-paced, quiet, relatively safe, rural, and without major traffic issues. Gloria Espinosa says, "It's calm—there's not that much crime. I mean, there's crime everywhere, but you do feel relatively safe in your home." Carmen Silva says, "It's a small town—I like that environment. Transportation is not a big issue. I can't see myself spending hours on the road getting kids to school."

Many women identify a strong sense of community as one of the most favorable characteristics of Brawley. Several women comment on the sense of connectedness in the community. The perspectives of three daughters of farmworkers illustrate this point. Angelica Perez finds that as a lifelong Brawley resident, she feels as though the community is a family. She says, "I feel that I'm a little bit safer here than anywhere else." Monica Rodriguez also refers to the family-like feeling of the community, saying, "Even though everyone is not related to me, we're very together. And I think I like the small-knit togetherness we have. Everybody watches over everybody else. Kind of like in the circle of trust, you know. Everybody watches everybody's back." Theresa Romero points to the social solidarity of the community. She says, "I love Brawley. I love the community. I love the unity of the community. I love the aspect that when there is something going on, the community reacts to it and they participate with any kind of event that is going on. If anything happens, whether it be sports, Little League, Cattle Call, Christmas in the Park, anything. The community supports it."

Nearly all women believe Brawley provides a good environment for raising children. Several describe Brawley as a family-oriented town. Many women appreciate that other people know their children and will watch out for them. In general, they believe small towns are safer, less complicated places where it is easier to monitor your children than in urban centers. Celia Roberts says, "It's safe. I mean, you can send your kids to the park to play and you don't have to worry about them getting mugged or something on the way." Elena Sanchez compares Brawley to Fresno, where she lived previously. She says, "Here everyone knows everyone. You know whose kids they are. If you see kids are getting into trouble, you can go to the parents. In Fresno, it's like, you don't know who it is. Here you can find out who are the bullies. You can know who are the good kids, who are the wrong kids, you know." Perceptions about local schools are not uniformly positive, but women are more likely to say the schools are good or very good than to criticize them. Some women themselves have very positive memories of attending school in Brawley. A part of small-town life they appreciate is that their teachers, even their elementary school teachers, still know them by name.

Next I consider what women find difficult about living in the community. The two top concerns—employment-related issues and drugs—were mentioned by more than half of interviewees. Several women also refer to the lack of local goods and services and the hot summer climate as negative aspects of life in the community.

Employment-related difficulties have been thoroughly analyzed in previous chapters. To recap briefly, the Imperial County women are concerned about the quantity and quality of jobs. Available jobs are not what they call "decent jobs" or "career-type jobs." They describe strong competition for available jobs, mostly from local residents, but also from Mexican border-crossers. Underemployment is pervasive in this agriculture-reliant, border community with the highest unemployment rate in California.

Worries about illegal drugs in the community have also been documented. Major quantities of drugs cross the border routinely from Mexico into Imperial County. Drugs have wreaked havoc in the families of many women participating in this research. One woman's husband is in a residential drug rehab center. One of the research participants has been "clean" for just three months. Several marriages have ended because a partner sold or used illegal drugs. Women point to the association between drugs and crime; that is, increased drug use in the community results in more crime. Women express great concern when crime intrudes into their neighborhoods or when their children are exposed to individuals engaged in drug-related activity. All women would likely agree with Monica

Rodriguez who says, "I think that it is a challenge for all parents to make sure their kids don't get wrapped up [in drugs]." In general, however, women think there is less crime in their community than in large urban centers.

Secondary concerns of the women I interviewed are the lack of local goods and services and the oppressively hot summer weather. With respect to the former, women most frequently mention two areas of concern: first, the need to drive considerable distances to shop for clothing and home goods; second, insufficient activities for children and youth. Some point out that when children's activities are available, families often cannot afford the fees required for participation.[3] While many women find that progress has been made in these areas, they wish more could be done. As for the summer heat, temperatures that rise to more than 120 degrees are both unpleasant and dangerous. Women both express their personal complaints and note that the hot climate shapes their children's lives by restricting their activities.

The women interviewed for this research realize there are pros and cons to living in any community. Overall, women were more positive than negative about life in the Imperial Valley. A few women did say that they could not think of anything good about living in Brawley. But nearly a third said they could not identify anything negative about raising children in the community.

The central dilemma these women negotiate is the tension between family ties and community attachment on the one side and a poor labor market on the other. In many cases interviewees recognize that what they value most about the community comes with a price. The small-town atmosphere they appreciate is associated with a limited job market, less shopping, and fewer entertainment possibilities than in an urban center. For example, Daniela Rosales says, "We have less crime and robbery, but there are better jobs in bigger cities." Marina Mendez hopes there will not be too much commercial development, because it would change the Valley too much. She prefers maintaining the sense of community, "Even if we don't move up too much."

INEQUALITIES OF RACE/ETHNICITY, CLASS, AND PLACE

As a Hispanic-majority place, Imperial County presents a particularly interesting context for exploring relations of race/ethnicity in a small community. I found that many women were quizzical when I asked them if there was ever a time they thought they might not have gotten a job because they were Hispanic. Nearly half of women said that because "almost everyone" in the Valley is Hispanic, this did not happen to them. For example, Rosa Navarra says, "No, because the majority here is Hispanic. So I haven't had any trouble with that." Cecilia Diaz says, "I don't think so, at least not here in the Valley. There's so many Hispanics around here." In fact, these women usually did compete with other Mexican Americans for jobs. Most had Mexican American managers. Mexican-dominated workplaces were not the exception but the rule. Women generally thought of racism in terms of individual acts of discrimination. Institutional discrimination is more difficult to recognize. Rosemary Correa was one of a few women who found discrimination to be institutionally based. In describing her former workplace, she says, "Out of the twenty-two women that did work in our area, all of us were Hispanic, except for the boss and the supervisor. The supervisor has the same work history as me. She has everything the same, but she was a white female. And a white boss. A man. I'm like, 'What's wrong with this picture?' I had noticed that right away." Several women did report discrimination in hiring or in the workplace in other places, such as San Diego and Phoenix. In general, women believe they encounter less racial/ethnic discrimination in the Valley than in places where Latinos are the numerical minority. I do not mean to imply that these women are mostly immune from employment discrimination in the Valley, only that they perceive it to be less prevalent than in Anglo-majority places.[4]

Even though many women struggle to find adequate employment, or any job at all, they observe many Mexican Americans in very responsible jobs in the community. They see that upward mobility is possible. Imperial County has two main industries: government and agriculture. In government institutions, Mexican Americans are employed not only in positions delivering services to county residents but also as administrators and managers in city, county, and state government, including positions of authority in law enforcement, public schools, prisons, and border control. Mexican Americans are also directors of several nonprofit organizations.

Agricultural enterprise, on the other hand, is dominated by Anglo farmers. This industry is obviously stratified by race. Field workers are Mexican Americans, crew leaders and managers might be Mexican American, but wealthy Anglo growers control this industry.[5] Women are well aware of the inequities structured into the organization of labor in agriculture. This explains their profound antipathy for farm work and a deep desire to dissociate themselves and their families from this work. Thus they believe that in exiting farm work they leave highly exploitative work behind.

A fundamental purpose of public schools is to integrate a community's younger members into the community and to consolidate community support for education. The high school experience figures importantly in the life of many small communities, frequently bringing together disparate groups and creating a sense of belonging. Jennifer Castillo is one of the women who is not considering leaving Brawley. She has good memories of growing up in the Valley and hopes for the same experiences for her children. Jennifer says, "I wanted my kids to grow up here too like I did. I wanted my son to be a Wildcat [school mascot] because he plays sports."

Some women tell return-migration stories of people who left the Valley but returned. Lisa Cabrillo says that the community is very important to everyone and that people who move away often return in time for their twenty-year high school reunion. She relates an example from her own family: "I have an uncle who moved away, got his associate's [degree], got married, had children—three boys—and when his oldest reached his sophomore year of high school, the family returned to Brawley so that his boys could go to the same high school as their dad. The boys all went through the football like their dad, achieved all of that, and graduated from Brawley High." Ana Ramirez says, "In Brawley, the community is just very tight." She describes the outpouring of community support the previous year when the football team advanced to the California Interscholastic Federation (CIF) Regional Championship. Businesses closed and people were given the day off. Over 10,000 people from Brawley (population 22,000) traveled to San Diego to support the team.

When the women I interviewed talked about the community as "close" or "united," I tried to discern if they were talking about Anglos and Hispanics as united together or the Mexican American population as a close community. My sense is that most women were referring to the Mexican American community as close. This would be consistent with data finding that U.S.-born Mexicans value living in communities with significant populations of Mexican Americans (Sáenz and Dávila 1992). Some women, however, articulated somewhat different views.

When Celia Roberts refers to the community as united she is referring to the more "Americanized Hispanics" and the white population. "And then," she says, "you've got the other group." Here she refers to immigrants who are less socially integrated into the community and do not speak English. Some Mexican Americans, like Celia, find more connection with Anglos than with newly arrived Mexicans. Social divisions within the Mexican-origin population have been described in the literature and are largely based on length of time in the community (Du Bry 2007; Menchaca 1995). Some Imperial County women think of local post-IRCA (1986) immigrants as newcomers, some of whom are criticized as being too tied to Mexico and Mexican culture.

Strained relations between Anglos and Mexican Americans in small towns and rural places have also been described in the literature (see, for example, Chávez 2005, Menchaca 1995, and Naples 1994). My study of second- and third-generation women uncovers little of this, at least on the surface. It would not always have seemed so harmonious, given the long history of labor disputes in the Valley.[6] Tensions may be especially strong between Anglos and Mexican immigrants, but second- and third-generation Mexican Americans are found to be more integrated into communities (Allensworth and Rochin 1998; Chávez 2005).[7] I recognize that if my study had included immigrant women, the perceptions of the community might have been less positive.

Theresa Romero attempts to deconstruct stereotypical views about Brawley held by residents of other Imperial County communities. She says, "I do think that some people tend to judge Brawley as a white ranchers' community, and it is not. When I worked in Calexico, they said, 'The Brawley people are snobby. They're all white ranchers.' I'm like, 'No, it's not like that.'"

Ana Ramirez acknowledges social divisions in the community. She knows that white ranchers wield disproportionate influence in Brawley. But she maintains that the entire population does come together for community events. She says, "Here in Brawley especially we have some very wealthy people. I mean most of the ranchers, farmers, live here and I don't know if you've cruised by over there [in the southwest quadrant where most ranchers live]. If you look at those houses, you know it's the rich side. And a lot of people, like from Calexico, they'll say, 'Oh there's a bunch of racists in Brawley.' People from El Centro might say the same. But I've been living here for many years and I've never experienced that."

Ana and others mentioned Brawley Cattle Call, a weeklong set of events culminating in a rodeo, as the event that most effectively brings the community together. In this week in November, the town demonstrates the community ethos that is so frequently invoked. During Cattle Call, everyone can feel that this is their town. In 2005, the year I participated in Cattle Call, the Brawley Chamber of Commerce chose the Castro brothers of Holtville to be grand marshals of the Brawley Cattle Call Parade, one of the biggest events of the week. The eight Castro brothers, who grew up following the crops in a migrant farmworker family, have all served in the U.S. military. No other family in the United States has had so many sons serve their country in military service (Hong 2005).

Next, in examining why women and their families choose to stay in the Imperial Valley, I briefly examine their perspectives on urban places. In short, they see that urban areas provide a very different context for jobs. They understand thoroughly that employment prospects are better in larger cities. If they believed urban places provided a favorable environment for family life, certainly many would have already migrated to cities. Instead what we see is that women who are positive about the slower pace of life in Brawley dislike the fast-paced life in cities. Women who celebrate the open space and open roads of Imperial County dislike the population density and congested traffic of cities. Women who appreciate that Brawley is calm talk about San Diego and Los Angeles as "wild."

When women express concern about drugs and crime in the Valley, they reference their apprehensions to more serious problems in urban areas. So, for example, Daniela Rosales says, "If we lived in LA, there would be more crime and killing." Erica Martinez believes the Valley is safe for raising children, "compared to San Diego." Neither Daniela or Erica have lived in the places they mention, but nearly half of the women have lived at least briefly outside Imperial County.[8]

Many women believe that leaving Brawley for an urban place may give them better job prospects, but little else. Women's complaints about inadequate local goods and services and perishingly hot summer weather turn out to be subsidiary concerns and not something they would move to improve.

A central theme in women's perspectives about living in Brawley is that life is lived on a human scale. For women who struggle to gather the resources their families need to survive, this is significant. This group finds they are able to negotiate their personal business and find the help they need in Brawley. They attribute this to the small size of the community and the helpfulness of human service professionals. For example, Rosa Navarra says, "Everybody is always watching out for each other since it's a small community. Everyone practically knows everyone one way or another. Eventually you'll get whatever you're wanting to know." While Rosemary Correa is not particularly tied to Brawley, she appreciates that "there is help out there if you need it. Workers are willing to help you find what you need." Angelica Perez thinks there is less stigma to being poor in a town like Brawley where so many people struggle financially. She says, "If we go to a bigger city, we are categorized as under poverty and stuff. Not everybody's the same. But right here, it's like everybody is equal." Angelica experiences poverty to be less demeaning in a place where everyone understands that it is very hard to be economically self-sufficient and poverty is not attributed to lack of individual effort. In another vein, Angelica notes that while Yuma, Arizona, is a medium-size city just over an hour away, families who are struggling financially receive more assistance in California than in Arizona.

Public supports in California are considerably more generous than in other places to which they might move. The out-of-state places women express the greatest interest in moving to are in Nevada (Las Vegas) and Arizona (Phoenix and Yuma). Economically vulnerable families are better off in California than in either of these states (and most others as well). Better benefits in California can make a critical difference in the extent of deprivation poor families experience. The crucial program for families with children to consider is Temporary Assistance to Needy Families (TANF), the national welfare program. In fact, the United States has fifty welfare programs because states implement TANF differently, according to their own specifications. In 2005 maximum benefit for a family of three was $704 monthly in California, compared to $347 in Arizona and $348 in Nevada. Most important are provisions related to the temporary nature of TANF support. The lifetime limit for benefits to adult recipients is five years. In California, benefits to children continue after parents reach their lifetime limit. In Arizona, Nevada, and most other states, benefits to children do not continue (National Center for Children in Poverty 2010).[9] Remaining in California may be seen as a strategic decision that enables women to fulfill their commitments to others.

LEAVING THE VALLEY?

I now consider the Imperial County women's thinking about moving from the Valley. Women grapple with a difficult predicament—how to resolve the tension between the pull of family and community on the one hand and the necessity of providing for their families on the other. I asked women if they ever think about moving to another community. Eight women have given it little consideration; they simply are not interested in moving. Fourteen women have seriously considered leaving the Valley but have concluded that there are compelling reasons to stay. Six women say "maybe" to moving; they think they may move eventually. Ten women say they are ready and willing to move to a new place.

"Not Interested in Moving!"

Most women who are not considering moving are among the more economically privileged families in the sample. Either they or their partners (or both) have stable full-time jobs. They have been able to achieve what other women strive for—a steady job at decent wages in a community they enjoy. Many of these women, including Lisa Cabrillo, Ana Ramirez, and Monica Rodriguez, have educational credentials that led to jobs that placed them in positions of respect in Brawley. These are the women who are most integrated into the community and arguably have the most to lose in leaving. Some of them have a strong sense of their historical family connection to the Valley. Lisa Cabrillo articulates her sense of belonging in this community: "Both my husband's family and my family live here. Generation to generation, we've all been here."

"I Think We Should Stay Here"

More than one-third of the Imperial County women have thought seriously about leaving the Valley, but their best judgment for now is that they should or must stay. Nearly all of these women mention family-related reasons for not moving. Considerable ambivalence underlies the decisions of many of these women. Several women who provide care for parents do not think they can move. Christina Gilbert says, "I think about moving all the time. But I can't, because of my parents." Celia Roberts expresses a similar thought, "I think about it all the time. But family keeps us here. We'd like to move for more opportunity, but family keeps us here."

In other circumstances women decide to stay both because of extended-family relationships and because they think it will be better for their children. Antonia Alivar and her husband could go back to live with her mother-in-law in Beaumont. She says there is more opportunity there, but she does not want to take her children out of school here. Her children are doing well in school. She is particularly relieved that her son in high school is not in trouble and he does not go out at night. She fears putting him in a new situation. She also wants to be near her family in Mexicali. The problem with staying in Brawley, however, is that she and her husband do not have work. Antonia says, "I pray every night for a job."

Patricia Ochoa has two daughters in college in Imperial County. She stays to support her children in their education. She tells her children, however, that the

Imperial Valley would be a nice place to raise their children, but to be successful, they need to move to a bigger city where there are more job opportunities.

A few women recognize the challenges of moving to a new place. Esther Valdez has thought about moving out of the Valley but notes that other areas of California are very expensive. She also recognizes that she has built up considerable social capital in the Valley. She says, "I think that here I can change one job to another because I already know so many people. And over there where I would go? I wouldn't have anybody. You get roots in a place and it is hard to go." Angelica Perez thought about moving to Los Angeles County but decided "it's bigger city, bigger problems."

Rosa Navarra, newly employed in border security, wants to have a stable life. She says, "I know that I can make my home here in the Valley. I have dealt with the heat and everything else." She notes that she is likely to always have a job because Homeland Security is growing and there are a lot of people illegally crossing the border.

"Maybe"

Women who said "maybe" to moving away from the Imperial Valley usually said they might eventually move. Erica Martinez says, "It crosses my mind every day." The support her parents provide in raising her children is the primary reason she stays. "The fact that I am with my parents, I have security in that sense. I don't have to deal with babysitters. Or if my kids go sick, that I can't take them to a child care provider because they are sick. I guess it's because of that." Erica has a full-time job with the county but might like a new start in a new community later on.

Lucia Hernandez and her husband want better opportunities for their children and would like to move to San Diego, but the children want to stay in the Valley. They are trying to convince the children that it is in their best interest to move eventually. Lucia explains their situation: "We are struggling and so much of that is where we live. There are not good jobs around here and the only thing that they can do is move to a place where they have more opportunity. The only good jobs here are prison, county, school district, and hospital jobs."

"I Am Ready to Move"

The ten women who said they were prepared to leave the Valley were interested in relocating for a job or, more generally, relocating to a new place. None of these women has a stable, full-time job. Most are unemployed. Claudia Gomez says, "I would be willing to move anywhere that I can go to as long as I can know that I can get a job that I can count on, and I can do what I love to do, and I can support my family." Rosemary Correa has been searching for State of California jobs online at the One Stop. She is interested in a prison job, but there are currently no openings in Imperial County. She has found that a prison in Orange County is taking applications. She says that if she could find a good opportunity, like a prison job in Orange County, she would move. She believes God has something in store for her that could very likely require her to relocate.

Marina Mendez and Gloria Espinosa are interested in relocating. Marina's first choice is to move to the state of Washington. Gloria is not sure where she is going but says, "I think I am going to go." She acknowledges that this would be a big transition because she currently lives with her mother who helps a lot with her two-year-old son. She says, "My mom is really close to him. He thinks my mom is his mom. That I'm his grandma and that's his mom [laughs]."

To sum up women's perspectives on moving from the Imperial Valley, the first group of women does not need to move. Women in the second group have decided either that family trumps better prospects somewhere else or that they will probably gain little by moving. Those who say "maybe" suggest that leaving the Valley is more a matter of timing than anything else. When circumstances shift, they will strongly consider a move. Finally, among those prepared to move, some are mostly interested in moving to a new place for a new start and will need a job to make it happen. Others are more intent on a job and will move to a place where they secure employment.

Why They Stay

It seems paradoxical that most women have had little labor market success but plan to stay in the Valley. They encounter strong competition for both "good" and "bad" jobs. They live in a high-poverty, high-unemployment county. Yet most are reluctant to leave. In comparison to their fellow Californians and fellow Americans, the families represented by these women are economically disadvantaged. Family responsibilities are undoubtedly central in the decision to stay. I suggest that other factors explaining why women remain in Imperial County are related to the isolation of the Valley, the recentness of their family's immigration experience, stark differences in life chances between Mexicali and Imperial County, and the determination to avoid moving to an urban center.

The Imperial Valley is isolated from the rest of California. It is also isolated from the rest of the United States. Brawley is 132 miles across desert and mountains from San Diego, 75 miles from Indio, and 70 miles from Yuma. Most women had traveled little outside of Southern California. The metropolitan center that is the nearest and most obvious city of reference is Mexicali, just over the border from Calexico. Although Mexicali is a relatively prosperous city in Mexico, women are well aware that Mexicali's standard of living is considerably lower than that of the United States. In particular, women who live at or near the poverty line in the United States have a standard of living that is higher than is typical across the border. Patricia Zavella found that Mexican immigrant food-processing workers in Watsonville, California, "imagined their work situations and their family lives in terms of a comparison with what was on *el otro lade* (the other side)—across the U.S.-Mexican border." She calls this "peripheral vision" (2002, 238–239). In similar fashion, the Imperial County women who struggle to create the best lives they can for their families in the United States are—out of the corners of their eyes—looking back across the border to Mexicali and concluding that they are not doing so badly.

The recentness of the immigrant experience also shapes women's perspectives about their lives in the United States. The immigration stories of their parents and grandparents often included accounts of tragic circumstances and, in some cases, severe deprivation. For example, Celia Roberts told me she had recently found out that as children back in Mexico her mother and her mother's sisters wore potato sacks as dresses. It was all they had. Celia, a smart dresser, was touched by this information. She said, "Wow, I didn't know it was that bad."

Border dwellers quite understandably compare their own living conditions to those on "the other side." Pablo Vila studies social relations at the El Paso/Juarez border (2000, 2003). The Mexican American women Vila interviewed in El Paso discuss how the U.S. government helps its population more than the Mexican government does. One interviewee says, "Here one does not die of hunger, right? It's because there are food stamps." Another says, "In Mexico, people get nothing from the government" (2000, 156–157). My interviewees did not make statements as stark as these, but they know that a social safety net in the United States provides supports to the extent that they will never live as impoverished an existence as did many of their parents and grandparents in Mexico.

As the out-migration of Mexican Americans from the Southwest (California, Arizona, New Mexico, Colorado, and Texas) increased substantially in recent decades, the percentage of all Mexican Americans living the Southwest has declined. Many immigrants who initially entered the United States and came to urban centers in the Southwest left for better opportunities in the Midwest and Southeast (Crowley, Lichter, and Qian 2006). Second- and third-generation Mexican Americans typically fill different jobs than immigrants, so their employment situation varies from that of immigrants, but still, many U.S.-born Mexicans also left the Southwest for other regions of the country. However, moves within the Southwest rather than moves from the region are more common among the families of the women I interviewed. It is relevant to my research to note that living in a community with a relatively large Mexican-origin population lowers the odds of leaving the Southwest (Sáenz, Cready, and Morales 2007, 205).

In considering those who have stayed in the Imperial Valley, it is right to acknowledge that many second- and third-generation Mexican Americans have indeed left the Valley, the site of their parents' or grandparents' first permanent home in the United States. Obviously, I could not ask those people why they left. A maxim of immigration studies is that it is individuals with the most human capital, particularly in the form of education, who leave (Foulkes and Newbold 2005; Sáenz, Cready, and Morales 2007). Sáenz and his colleagues (2007) note, however, that the Mexican-origin population, as a group, has limited human capital. They suggest this means that social capital, in the form of network-based resources, is likely to figure importantly in migration decisions. Their research confirms the importance of both education (human capital) and household ties to destination regions (social capital) in explaining out-migration by Mexican Americans. Familism functions, as we have already seen, to keep people where they are. It also can function to facilitate moves to other destinations.

Women's decisions about whether to leave or stay in the Valley bring agency into clear view. The preference of the Imperial Valley women for rural areas and small towns over urban centers has precedent. Rural women, whatever their race or ethnicity, generally experience barriers to adequately providing for and caring for their families. The deficits they encounter are related to the structural characteristics of rural places and include limited economic opportunities and the lack of basic amenities. Nonetheless, "based on the belief that rural communities offer safety, security, and quality of life for their families, many women make conscious decisions to continue living in rural areas even when other options are available" (Tickamyer and Henderson 2003, 112).

The women I interviewed were in many cases very critical of urban places, where they feared crime, congestion, and drugs. In reality, it is not entire metropolitan areas that are unsafe or overly busy, but it is more likely to be the case in neighborhoods available to low-income families. These women did not have the economic resources to move to safe, uncrowded neighborhoods in big cities, but they were able to experience lower population density and a safer environment living in this rural area. Concerns about urban life are also a factor in the recent trend of Mexican migration to the Midwest and Southeast. Those who move in response to poor economic prospects in urban centers in the Southwest may also leave behind poor schools, high crime rates, and crowded neighborhoods (Crowley, Lichter, and Qian 2006, 346; Dohan 2003).

Sáenz and his colleagues address how ethnic concentration might discourage out-migration. They write, "[T]he sense of community, solidarity, and mutual obligation often emanating from a preponderance of co-ethnics in the home region may discourage individuals from leaving" (2007, 196). Strong attachment to the community is one of the most obvious reasons the Imperial County women in this study want to stay. An associated point is that many women think employment discrimination in the Valley is reduced because "everyone is Hispanic." This belief may also deter them from moving to an Anglo-majority labor market.

The racialization of Mexican American schoolchildren continues to the present. Jessica Vasquez (2011) found that many second- and third-generation students experienced school as a site of discrimination and disempowerment. Many are educated in Anglo-centric contexts in which Mexicans are assumed to be intellectually deficient and Mexican culture is disparaged or ignored. In embracing

Brawley as a positive place to raise children and affirming local schools, I wondered if the Imperial County women believed the Hispanic-majority community setting protected their children from mainstream stereotypes.

Women's decisions to stay also reflect their intentions to fulfill their family responsibilities to the best of their ability. The long shadow of farm labor limits their perceived options here. Relations of race/ethnicity and class embedded in the structure of labor-intensive agriculture have left many of their farmworker parents disabled and on the edge economically. Women stay to provide economic or other assistance for their parents.

Further, many women decide that staying in Brawley is the best thing they can do for their children. Social class is significant in their decision-making process. Women who have managed to get stable, year-round jobs maintain family and community associations by staying. They are enthusiastic about the community as a positive environment for raising their families.

For women who are poor or at the lower end of the working class, the calculus is different. Here women face the challenges of assisting parents and gathering resources for sustaining themselves and their children. These families survive by a combination of working unstable, part-time jobs, sharing resources with extended kin, and relying on public supports. The extent of reliance on public assistance depends, in part, on whether women and partners are unemployed or marginally employed. What women experience is that public assistance provides a social safety net that will never require them or their children to suffer the deprivations of many of their parents. This usually implicitly made comparison to "the other side" is another example of the peripheral vision referred to earlier.

While a majority of women plan to stay in the Valley, and more are likely to do so, many women recognize that their children will need to leave. This understanding connects to their multigenerational strategy for upward mobility. These women are willing to stay in the Imperial Valley. They have parents to attend to. They regret that in many cases teen pregnancies short-circuited their own educational attainment and that of their partners. They now encounter barriers to getting the degree that would likely lead to one of the stable public sector jobs in the county. But they stay because they think this is good place to raise their children. They may struggle, but in this small-town environment they believe they can monitor their children better, keep them away from drugs and gangs, and promote their success in school. Many hope that things will get better. Some expect a life of scarcity; some are resigned to it. Ironically, they stay in an agricultural community but want nothing to do with agricultural employment.

To say they want more for their children is to recognize that their children will need to leave the Valley. There are not enough stable jobs everyone wants now, and certainly there will not be enough for the next generation of better-educated workers. Many of the women are encouraging their children to leave the Valley for college. In general, most young adults who leave rural areas to pursue bachelor's or advanced degrees do not return to live and work there (Lichter et al. 1993). The same is true in the Imperial Valley (and holds for all racial and ethnic groups there). Alternatively, Mexican Americans who attend IVC and then SDSU in Calexico are more likely to stay, perhaps reflecting family circumstances that did not permit them to leave, a personal unwillingness to leave, or a lack of exposure to other places in the United States.

A perennial dilemma surrounding small towns and rural areas is that they are perceived to be family-friendly environments, but limited labor markets in these spatial contexts make it difficult to earn a living. Deciding to stay in Brawley means not only living in a fairly isolated agriculture-reliant community but also living in one with a large Hispanic-majority population. Research consistently shows a negative relationship between minority concentration and the economic well-being of the minority population. Further, counties with minority concentration at the U.S.-Mexico border are among those most disadvantaged. Minority disadvantage in these communities is principally explained by the lack of opportunities (Albrecht, Albrecht, and Murguia 2005). The Imperial County women, so many in pursuit of a good job, understand this problem well. Still, for the interconnected, mostly family-related reasons described above, they stay. Other Mexican Americans exited farm work when they left the Imperial Valley for better work in urban places. The strategy for most of the families represented in this research is moving out of farm work without, for now, leaving behind the community and all it means to them.

✤

CONCLUSION

The women I interviewed sometimes wondered why in the world I had chosen to come to do research in Brawley, California, and what could possibly explain my interest in interviewing them. Brawley was personally significant to them because they had grown up there or they had family in the area, but they did not believe it to be an intrinsically interesting place. They did not believe their lives to be particularly noteworthy.

But by another way of thinking, their lives provide a valuable angle of vision into the experience of Mexican-origin people in the United States. Their perspectives and experiences shed light on current questions about the organization of Mexican American families and the incorporation of immigrants into American society. Certainly, the agricultural community context is significant. The history of Mexican immigration to the United States is closely tied to the story of the reliance of western agriculture on Mexican labor. And in the present, the needs of agribusiness continue to be a driving force in sustaining Mexican immigration. The fact that the Imperial County women have remained close to the rural, agricultural setting that brought their families to the United States is noteworthy. Their family immigration stories and their personal experiences illumine the ways in which the organization of agriculture has shaped both family life and local community life over two or three generations. My conclusions center on these subjects.

This book is fundamentally about how the incorporation of the children and grandchildren of immigrant Mexican farmworkers into U.S. society is working out. As Karen Pyke notes, scholarly neglect of this subject accounts for "a profound gap in our knowledge of the long-term adaptation processes and outcomes among immigrant families" (2004, 262). My purpose is to contribute to knowledge in this area by exploring the work and family lives of second- and third-generation Mexican Americans in California's Imperial Valley. I explored women's viewpoints and decisions about labor force participation and child care–related issues. I considered the organization of gender in their families and examined how they manage to sustain their families.

I have used a structural approach in this research, assuming that these families are not primarily manifestations of Mexican culture but, like other families, are shaped by macrosocial forces. I have examined how macrolevel historical, economic, social, and political forces have shaped opportunities and constraints experienced by these individuals. Further, I have considered how race/ethnicity, social class, gender, and space allocate access to valued social resources. This approach is guided by the assumption that contextual factors shape experience and expects to find diversity within and between social groups. This research examines the lives of the research participants in all their particularity, recognizing that their perceptions, actions, and experiences are influenced by living in an agriculture-reliant, Hispanic majority, mostly rural border community.

I quickly found that farm labor, the work that brought their families to the United States, both shaped the experience of their immigrant parents and grandparents and continues to cast a shadow that extends well beyond the immigrant generation. In fact, the lives of the Imperial County women could not be understood outside the bounds of farm labor. California agriculture depends heavily on Mexican labor and provides employment for many Mexican-origin men and women. But it is more than that. In this community, agriculture is experienced as an oppressive social structure that is deeply implicated in the social disadvantage of Mexican-origin farmworkers and contributes to the long-term diminishment of life chances for their children.

THE LONG SHADOW OF FARM LABOR

Agriculture is a big business that has realized enormous profits by paying poverty-level wages to vulnerable workers. The political clout of agribusiness was seen in the exclusion of agricultural workers from minimum wage, Social Security, and other legislation protecting and supporting workers. The Bracero Program (1942–1964) institutionalized existing inequities and further commodified the people who did this work. This program functioned to establish Mexicans as the default category for California farmworkers.

The low wage structure, the seasonal nature, and the physically debilitating character of farm labor have had a particular impact on the Imperial County women. They believe the low wages paid by local growers to their partners and parents are exploitative. The highest wage paid to a family member in farm labor was eight dollars an hour. Field workers earned around minimum wage whatever their level of skill or years of experience, and more specialized jobs in agriculture paid slightly more. Monica Rodriguez's statement about her father-in-law captured well women's sensibilities about the fundamental unfairness of flat wages in this industry and points to exceedingly unequal power relations in agriculture. She said, "I just think, he was out there in the summer, at 120 degrees, and never complained about it. Never put up a fight, nothing, because he knew he needed to take care of his family. But he's been there thirty years with that shovel and he still gets paid seven dollars an hour." The impact of low wages on the family economy is compounded by the seasonality of agriculture, which makes work unpredictable and creates income insecurity. California agriculture, as presently constituted, shifts the risks and costs of seasonality to minimum-wage workers. So, for example, when Carmen Silva's partner goes "up north" to pick onions, but it rains, the work stops, and he waits. The family absorbs the cost of his gas, food, and housing with no offsetting earnings.

Farm labor is dangerous and debilitating work. Women occasionally mentioned on-the-job accidents, but the most frequently described problem is disabling musculoskeletal injuries. The manual labor farmworkers do is concentrated in lifting and carrying heavy loads, stooping, and clipping or cutting. All of these expose farmworkers to ergonomic risk and when done repeatedly over time may result in injury. Some have parents who were "hurting" for many years as they worked in the fields and their injuries worsened. Many are now disabled.

The Imperial County women are outspoken in their aversion to farm work. They view it as a physically grueling, dead-end job that will leave you, after thirty years of employment, broken down physically and financially insecure. Women respect and are grateful for the family members who immigrated to toil in the fields, but they are not nostalgic about the work. In fact, no one wants to do farm work. Women who have done it have gotten out of it. Partners who are farmworkers would like a better job. Most of all, women want to ensure their children will never end up in farm labor.

Part of the legacy of farm labor is restricted opportunities and options for many of the women I studied. Low wages and work-related infirmity have left many of their farmworker parents financially insolvent and unable to work in their fifties. Some women have taken responsibility for the economic support and care of their parents, which most often involves coresidence. Some women have been unable to pursue an educational credential or relocate to a better labor market because of these responsibilities.

The concept of "linked lives" proves to be helpful in understanding the strong bonds of care and support evident among the families represented in this research. As Umberson and her colleagues write, "The concept of linked lives—positing that historical events and individual experiences are interrelated through the linked fates of family members (Bengtson and Allen 1993)—has been influential in research on parenthood at all stages in the family life course, although it is particularly prominent in studies of older parents and their adult children. Recent research clearly shows that parents and children affect each other over the life course, and the events and transitions in the lives of one generation have repercussions for the other generation" (Umberson, Pudrovska, and Reczek 2010, 623). This concept, which captures the theoretical point of the "intertwined trajectories of parents and children" (623), helps us understand why so many of the Imperial County women are committed to remain in Brawley. Growing up in a farmworker household links the lives of two-thirds of the women to the poor physical and economic outcomes of their parents' work in agriculture.

Another aspect of the legacy of farm labor is related to the low wage structure of the community. Many agriculture-reliant communities, including Brawley, are typed as "low wage–high public assistance" in structure. This pattern is attributable to the structure of California agriculture (Taylor, Martin, and Fix 1997). The structure of agriculture and the structure of local economies are necessarily interrelated. The undesirability of seasonal minimum-wage agricultural employment results in an oversupply of workers competing for low-skill, nonfarm service work, depressing wages in these jobs as well. In this research, many working families, with or without a worker in agriculture, were eligible for assistance from several public programs. Further, many relied on support from extended family networks. In the case of Brawley, low wage scales were also related to proximity to the border.

One of the most frequently recurring themes in the literature on the status of Mexican Americans today centers on their racially disadvantaged position in U.S. society. For example, López and Stanton-Salizar note that Mexicans cannot escape racial stereotyping (2001, 273). Waldinger and his colleagues refer to Mexicans as "stigmatized labour migrants" (Waldinger, Lim, and Cort 2007, 4). Vélez-Ibáñez and Sampaio refer to "Mexican" as a "word of opprobrium" (2002, 1). Telles and Ortiz (2008) contend that the association of Mexican Americans with cheap labor has resulted in the racialization of the entire Mexican American population. These scholars and others believe that the dirty and degrading work that Mexicans have done in the U.S. economy contributes to this status.

This direction of thought suggests that western agriculture is deeply involved in constructing Mexican American's place at or near the bottom of the U.S. social class hierarchy. The development of California (western) agriculture in the direction of labor-intensive specialty crops represents the development of a labor system that depends on the backbreaking work of Mexicans and other Latinos. The ability to deploy an army of "cheap" and willing workers as needed is a labor strategy that has proved very profitable for growers but created destitution for many workers' families. Further, the peon labor model has disadvantaged countless Mexican Americans who never were farmworkers but encounter barriers to joining the social and economic mainstream.

CONTINUING QUESTIONS ABOUT MEXICAN AMERICAN FAMILIES

Two historic themes in the literature on Mexican American families are family traditionality and familism. The traditional family can be typified as having gender role segregation and a patriarchal structure. In Mexican culture, the ideal representation of the traditional family entails a sharply divided gender system in which men are providers and decision makers and have authority over their wives and children while women are submissive, domestic, and sacrifice themselves for their husbands and children. Questions about family traditionality are fundamentally about the organization of gender. Scholarly inquiry on familism, a construct of considerable complexity, has centered on the maintenance and operation of kinship networks in the Mexican-origin population.

Reconstituting Gender

The Imperial Valley proves to be an intriguing setting in which to observe gender assumptions and associated patterns of behavior in families. Immigration is associated with a reconfiguration of gender relations as couples adapt to the new social reality of their adopted home. Typically gender relations become more egalitarian as women gain status and men lose status in this process (see, for example, Grassmuck and Pessar 1991; Hondagneu-Sotelo 1994; Kibria 1993). At the same time, family change is shaped by structural features of particular places. I have examined gender ideology and practices in a majority Hispanic, border, high-poverty, agricultural setting. The particularities of this setting shape the reconstitution of gender in this place.

The second- and third-generation Mexican American women in this study answered family history questions and told stories about their extended family relationships over the course of my interviews. To the extent that immigrant farmworkers moved into nonfarm work, it was much more likely that men did so. Men increased their marital power by working more stable jobs at better wages while wives remained responsible for domestic work and continued in seasonal farm work. English proficiency varied by gender, with fathers and grandfathers more likely to know English, the language of the public sphere. Meanwhile many mothers and grandmothers remained monolingual in Spanish, the language of farm labor and the home. Gender relations are reconstituted (or not) in particular social and economic contexts. Part of the legacy of farm work in the Imperial Valley appears to be that these second- and third-generation Mexican American women grew up with more traditional gender norms than might be the case in more urban settings.

Most of the Imperial County women have created family lives that deviate in some significant measure from the gender assumptions of traditional Mexican culture. A large majority of women, but certainly not all, grew up in working poor households. The lives of many of their parents were constrained by the deprivations of farm labor and the burden of basic survival. Few women had the support or encouragement to plan systematically for the future by developing educational and career goals. Most had ample opportunity to learn conventional assumptions about women's and men's roles at home, church, and school. Consistent with convention, most assumed they would be mothers and primarily responsible for the domestic sphere.

Many women have subsequently created lives that reveal major transformations in gender expectations and experiences. Most of them have observed the more traditional assumptions of parents and have found these are not feasible for their own lives. In other cases, women observe that their parents have adapted their own patterns of gendered behavior in the context of difficult circumstances. Sometimes women implemented traditional assumptions in their own lives but could not sustain them. The narratives of the Imperial County women demonstrate agency in overcoming patriarchy and forging better lives for their families. The example of Esther Valdez is illustrative here.

Esther Valdez, whom I introduced in chapter 2, is the daughter of immigrant farmworker parents who were ages thirteen and fifteen when she was born. As a young woman, Esther was herself a farmworker and then, after marrying, stayed home with her children. Her efforts were confined to the domestic sphere, while the family depended on the earnings of her husband, Alberto. Esther baked cakes and cupcakes to sell but stayed at home while her husband and children went up and down the streets of Brawley selling them. Esther was pushed out of the domestic sphere by her farmworker husband's injury. In the intervening years, she has developed into a strong leader in this family. Alberto's injury was a traumatic event for the Valdez family. It was also the event that provided an opportunity for Esther to exercise agency. This potentially tragic injury compelled Esther to challenge and overcome the patriarchal assumptions that defined her responsibilities as domestic. Her leadership and hard work have enabled this family to construct a more stable life than ever before with steady wages, health insurance, and even a stock portfolio.

In this research, I find that women take responsibility for both the care and economic support of their children. Some women began motherhood with fairly traditional views of women's and men's roles. But their circumstances, either as single mothers or as women married to men with bad jobs or other misfortunes, led them to see employment as part of their care for their children. In many cases women's work has been a more stable source of income than that of husbands or partners. This is not to say that patriarchal norms do not guide some couples' interactions and family decisions. Although women were sometimes critical of a husband's desire to move as a family away from or back to Brawley, they did not question his prerogative to make that decision. Implied in their narratives was the assumption that their partners had the authority to make important family decisions. On the other hand, many women were willing to divorce or separate from husbands they believed were a negative influence on their children, frequently for reasons related to substance abuse.

Familism

Familism remains an important concept in understanding the integration of Mexican-origin families into U.S. society. While familism has, in the past, been seen as cultural characteristic implicated in producing poverty in Mexican American families, it is increasingly seen as an important survival strategy that represents "a structural response to poverty rather than a cultural antecedent" (Pyke 2004, 258). A structural approach to analyzing family patterns in a diverse society requires taking racial-ethnic disadvantage into account. I treat racial stratification as a macrostructural force that creates and sustains family diversity (Baca Zinn 1990, 75).

Although some research suggests a decline of familism among Mexican Americans, this research finds something very different. For the Imperial County women, kin networks constitute both an important resource and a significant responsibility. Extended families facilitated women's labor force participation by providing child care. They absorbed the inadequacies of the local labor market by providing housing for family members whose earnings do not allow them to sustain independent households. Despite social norms that promote independent nuclear families as the ideal, pooling resources represents a vital strategy for families who cannot make ends meet.[1] In a majority of instances of extended-family households, parents brought a son or daughter's family into their household. In some cases, siblings provided housing that enabled a brother or sister's family to try out a better labor market at some distance from the Imperial Valley. In other cases, the women I interviewed had themselves taken in parents who were infirm or, in their work as farm laborers, had been unable to accumulate the savings and Social Security benefits needed to survive economically. In the experience of these research participants, family connection not only creates economic interdependence but also provides networks of care for young and old.

The Imperial County women and their families survive economically by relying on earnings, institutional assistance and family support. Many struggle to find, and indeed cannot find, adequate employment. In this context, family support and institutional assistance serve as their safety net. While familism characterizes Mexican American families, we expect to find diversity within this population in the extent of familistic behavior. Sarkisian and her colleagues calculate and explain differences in extended family integration by race/ethnicity. Most relevant to my analysis is their finding that structural variables—especially social class—are more important in explaining differences in kin ties than are cultural variables (Sarkisian, Gerena, and Gerstel 2006, 341). If familistic behaviors are, in significant measure, an adaptation to economic strain, then this research setting should prove, and did prove, to be a good place to observe them. It follows then, that in a poor place like the Imperial Valley, familism may be more prevalent than would be the case in a more prosperous community.

Upward Mobility

The examples of Esther Valdez and many other women prompt the question of what constitutes upward mobility. The convention in the literature is to analyze upward mobility for Mexican Americans in terms of generational progress and measure it by gains in educational attainment and earnings. Upward mobility is defined somewhat differently for the women I studied. For them, upward mobility is, first and foremost, leaving farm work. They think this is the most undesirable work anyone could do and most have experienced personally and directly the hardships it imposes on family lives. In this community, moving out of dangerous, low-paid, seasonal work for a job as a maintenance worker or a cashier in a Mexican market represents upward mobility. This is not to say the Imperial County women are not interested in more education and higher earnings. They are. But the first hurdle is moving up and out of farm labor. None of the women were currently employed in farm labor; however, most had not fulfilled the goal of achieving economic well-being.

In looking to the future prospects of the Mexican American women who participated in this research and the families they represent, I cite two relevant perspectives in the literature. López and Stanton-Salazar (2001) conclude that the economic role of the children of Mexican immigrants is not clear. They write, "Certainly they will be dissatisfied with and will reject the poorly paid dirty work done by their fathers and mothers . . . Inevitably, they will occupy some middle status between the largely white and Asian middle and upper classes and the dirty work the fresh waves of poor immigrants will eagerly embrace" (2001, 86). Waldinger, Lim, and Cort (2007) believe that "deeply entrenched" educational disparities between the Mexican-origin population and whites predict that "good jobs" will elude U.S.-born Mexican Americans just as they elude other workers without college degrees. Thus, status gains for most Mexican Americans are likely to bring them only into the working class (2007, 32).

My own perspective on the subject of future prospects draws a somewhat different conclusion than the scholars I cite above. The farmworker parents and grandparents of these women came into the U.S. economy on the bottom rung of the social class ladder. For many, if not most of these women, aspiring to a stable working-class life was like reaching for the stars. It was hard for them to conceive of anything more. Many of the women I interviewed have already surmounted significant obstacles. Education is the prime example. Among the thirty-eight research participants, only eight had a parent with a high school diploma or GED. Nine women had at least one parent who had never gone to school, and eight more had a parent with a third grade education or less. Many parents did not speak English well and some did not it speak it at all. For a few, basic literacy (in Spanish) was an issue. Most parents lacked the cultural knowledge to help their children make decisions about higher education. None of these women had gone through the conventional process in which a prospective college student and her parents examine a number of alternatives before selecting the "right college." Neither of Rosa Navarra's parents attended school (including her U.S.-born father). Rosa says, "That's why it was hard for us. Because you usually need a parent to guide you through something like that."

As a result of the circumstances of their lives, the strategy for upward mobility adopted by Imperial County women is one of incremental progress. They have moved out of farm work, but most have transferred their hopes for substantial status gains to their children. They advance this multigenerational mobility strategy by promoting their children's educational achievement and trying to keep them away from involvement in drugs. The degree to which the next generation will achieve what their mothers hope for is, of course, impossible to know. The literature consistently shows that intergenerational progress stalls after the second generation.

Education is one of the most significant challenges for Latinos today and an important policy issue in U.S. society. Addressing educational disadvantage means reducing the structural barriers that impede educational progress. One important issue to address is the low rate of college graduation among Latinos. Richard Alba (2006) points out that this issue looks somewhat different if the analysis shifts to Latinos who have "some college." Alba notes that "some college" is the category where most Mexican American college students stop their education. In his analysis of education attainment among the 1971–1975 birth cohort using 2000 U.S. Census data, he found that among Mexican Americans, 13 percent of this group has a B.A. or more, while 33 percent have some college credit but are short of a B.A. degree (2006, 290).

My qualitative data suggest microlevel contexts in which many Mexican-origin women do not complete college. The lives of the Imperial County women, more than half with some college coursework, including associate degrees, demonstrate the difficulties of trying to complete college credentials as workers, parents, and sometimes family caregivers. My research suggests that Mexican Americans do not need to be convinced that college education is important. They already know that education is the key to getting ahead. Public policies that reduce barriers to college completion for this population would promote upward mobility and also represent a positive outcome for society at large. As the proportion of the U.S. population in their prime working years decreases in coming decades, it is in everyone's best interest that the Latino population (a young population) is well educated and able to make an optimum contribution to the U.S. economy.

BORDER-BASED DISCOMFORTS AND CONTRADICTIONS

The U.S.-Mexico border is a dynamic transnational region. It is more accurate to describe the border as an integrated region than as a boundary between nation states. However, a possible consequence of conceptualizing the border as an integrated system is that massive border-based inequalities may be invisible in this construction. The life chances of border dwellers depend in large measure on whether they live on the United States or Mexico side. Americans crossing to Mexico for cheap prescription drugs have a different relationship with the border than do Mexicans crossing to the United States for work to provide for their impoverished families. Relations of power are deeply embedded in the borderlands. I believe we can better communicate that transborder exchanges and interactions do not occur on equal terms. For example, the commonly used reference to pairs of border cities such as Calexico-Mexicali or El Paso-Juarez is as "twin towns" or "sister cities." Vila contends that this language contributes to what he calls "the construction of sameness" to be found on both sides of the border (2000, 124). This construction, in all cases, obscures dramatic inequalities.

One of the scholarly themes in narrating life at the border is agency. Mexican women and men are often described as exercising agency as they cross the border into the United States for work, medical care, or education. I do not intend to adjudicate here the moral dilemmas of border crossing, especially those at a border separating a developing nation from a developed nation. Of course I celebrate women who manage by extraordinary measures to, for example, feed their children adequately. But I found that my study of social relations on the U.S. side of the border increased the complexity of this matter in my thinking. The Imperial County women are trying to get ahead, trying to achieve the American Dream, defined as a stable job, a home, and decent prospects for their children. But many are poor people in a poor place. They experience competition with unauthorized workers as a zero sum game: the number of jobs is limited and every job that goes to someone from "the other side" is one that will not benefit a particular family in this community. They also fear that their hospital will close and their children's education will suffer. The Imperial County women negotiate multiple macrosystems of inequality that include the local and the global. In U.S. society they experience disadvantage on the basis of their race/ethnicity, social class, gender, and place. However, in respect to relations of inequality in the transnational border region, they are socially privileged.

PEOPLE AND PLACE

The women I studied have gone against the grain of expectations for the lives of daughters and granddaughters of Mexican farmworkers. The conventional wisdom assumes that the revolving door of agriculture leads to the city, where better opportunities await (Taylor, Matin, and Fix 1997). Most migration theories use an economic model assuming that migration is a rational choice based on a cost-benefit analysis. Individuals are expected to move if there are economic advantages (generally measured as wage differentials) in doing so (Lyson et al. 1993, 132).

The challenges to getting ahead in rural places are well documented. The barriers for people of color are especially daunting. The Imperial Valley women experience formidable challenges to economic stability. I admit to being surprised initially at the loyalty and affection many women had for the community and the desire of most to stay. Questions about the community were near the end of my interview schedule. By the time I asked about the community, I would have already heard about women's farmworker origins and their struggles to secure a decent job. But despite pervasive underemployment, oppressive heat, and concerns about drugs, most women thought the Imperial Valley was a good place to raise a family. In comparing rural and urban environments for family life, they chose rural, and they chose staying where they are.

These women make problematic the assumption that a better life awaits in urban places. Migration scholars and demographers may have statistical models showing they will be better off in urban areas. But statistical models do not capture quality of life matters that concern them deeply. In fact, the women I interviewed stayed in the community for reasons very similar to those documented in rural populations across the United States, that is, a sense of safety and security along with strong community and family ties (Lyson et al. 1993).

For many of these daughters and granddaughters of farmworkers, Brawley is the only place in the United States that their family has called home. They know the people and the place. They experience themselves to be part of a community they view as united. They can negotiate the local schools and know the teachers. They feel secure, in part because they believe "everybody watches everybody's back." They believe their children are safe in local parks because other community members will look out for them. They think their children can succeed in local schools. They see Mexican Americans holding positions of authority in the community, providing ample role models for their children and evidence for them that the American Dream can be achieved.

As these women forge their adult lives, they reject the farm labor that brought their families to the United States. But most who grew up in the Valley have a strong sense of community attachment. In some respects, they remain in the shadow of farm labor for as long as they continue to live here. Yet they have determined that, at least for now, this is the place where they can best fulfill their responsibilities to their parents and encourage the upward mobility of their children.

In the end, this book is about the people of the Imperial Valley—mostly women in this case—and the lives that can be constructed for ensuing generations after their parents or grandparents made the momentous decision to migrate to the United States as farmworkers. I mentioned before that the range of livelihood strategies available to these women turned on how their lives were linked to the people of their extended families. For me, with the privilege and responsibility of telling the story of the Imperial County women, it is also a matter of linkage. We are all linked to a community of people who, because of the structure of agriculture, are not able to escape the shadow of the work that brings food to our tables. Their lives and those of their families are linked to those of us in the majority population, despite our distance from that remote agricultural valley. These women said that their lives were unremarkable and perhaps didn't matter much. But they do matter to their families, their community, and to all who would like to believe in the promise of American life. The question remains, however, if they will be able to achieve the modest success that, for them, would be the goal of all descendents of immigrants—to achieve "the American Dream."

METHODOLOGICAL
APPENDIX

The general goals of qualitative research are to gain a comprehensive overview of the research setting and to come to understand how people explain and manage their everyday activities (Greenstein 2001). My overarching goal in this research was to understand how Mexican American women made sense of their work and family lives in a disadvantaged, rural place. The main challenge for me, then, in this research was to understand the perspectives of the individuals I interviewed in the particular social and economic context in which they raised their children and sustained their families.

One of the truisms of rural research is that "place matters" or "space matters." As the United States has become increasingly urban and suburban, it is understandable that some find the study of rural spaces to be less and less relevant to a careful analysis of contemporary U.S. society. It is in this context that rural scholars assert the continuing significance of spatial analysis and many include a strong spatial component in their work (Lobao, Hooks, and Tickamyer 2007). In my research, this has meant studying the work and family lives of Mexican American women in a particular spatial setting. A work and family analysis that failed to take into account the macrostructural features of the Imperial Valley would have limited explanatory power. Specifically pertinent to my research have been its agriculture-reliant economy, its geographically remote location, and its position at the border. Bringing these into clear focus served to illumine the external forces that shaped the work and family lives of the women I studied. In short, taking spatial context into account proved to be an important tool in understanding how "micro situations are shaped by wider structures" (Burawoy 1991, 282).

During my time in the Valley, I was a research associate at the California Center for Border and Regional Economic Studies (CCBRES) at the San Diego State University-Imperial Valley (SDSU) campus in Calexico. This association was important to me in several ways. CCBRES facilitated my work by providing me with office space, a computer, a phone, and more. The staff willingly answered my questions, responded to my hunches, and helped me understand a complex research setting. My affiliation with the center also functioned to give me a measure of initial creditability in the community. The university in general and CCBRES in particular are well respected in the community. I believe my association with CCBRES helped open the doors of community professionals I hoped to talk with and went far in allaying the possible reservations of potential research participants.

My principal data-gathering activities surrounded recruiting and interviewing women willing to participate in my research. Because I was interested in women's experiences with child care, especially the degree to which child care concerns might impede labor force participation, I limited my sample to U.S.-born Mexican American women who were mothers of at least one child, elementary school age or younger. I recruited interviewees mostly by posting and distributing a flyer that described my research. Flyers were distributed by a local elementary school and were posted in the local Boys and Girls Club and in a municipal office building. Interviewees sometimes passed along flyers to other women who might be interested in participation; one interviewee posted flyers in her place of employment on Main Street. Flyers provided contact information for either my local cell phone number or my office number at the San Diego State University-Imperial Valley campus in Calexico. I was most successful in recruiting interviewees at the Brawley One Stop Career Center. In California, many state services are administered through these local centers; among these services are job services, vocational education and rehabilitation, and youth services. At the One Stop I was able to approach women personally to introduce my research and interview interested individuals in a private interviewing room on-site. Other interviews were conducted at an elementary school and in women's homes. Each interviewee received a twenty-dollar gift card to a local supermarket in thanks for her participation.

My methodology included a protocol for both English- and Spanish-language interviews. Because my population of interest was U.S.-born women, I expected that most women would be comfortable interviewing in English, but I also supposed that some would prefer an interview in Spanish. Because I am not fluent in Spanish, I had located a Latina student at SDSU who was willing to serve as my research assistant on this project. She created a Spanish-language flyer and planned to translate for me as needed for Spanish-language interviews. To my surprise, all interviews were conducted in English. I simply did not find U.S.-born Latinas who were not comfortable in English. Most second-generation women attributed their English language proficiency to their U.S. school experience. Simply stated, it was because they had attended school in the United States that they could speak "good English."

This research used a semistructured interview format. I asked questions related to household composition, employment, work history, child care, family of origin characteristics and immigration experiences, and living in the community. Responses provided factual information (such as household composition and children's dates of birth), personal experiences (such as types of child care utilized), and the perspectives of research participants (such as viewpoints about the community as a place to raise a family). While specific questions were asked, these questions did not place rigid limits on the data. The interview schedule provided a good deal of latitude for research participants to speak to their individual concerns as women, parents, partners, extended family members, workers, and community members. Interviews were tape-recorded and transcribed. Transcripts have been coded and analyzed using the ATLAS.ti computer-assisted qualitative data analysis software.

The concept of human agency has been important in analyzing the data for this book. This concept "views humans as creative and probing creatures who are coping, dealing, designating, dodging, maneuvering, scheming, striving, struggling, and so forth—that is, as creatures who are actively engaged in and attempting to negotiate their social settings" (Lofland et al. 2006, 166). I assume that women are competent actors in their own lives. I use women's responses as a source of data that illumines the values, expectations, and assumptions that underlie their actions and strategic inactions in constructing work and family life. This is not to say that women necessarily believe they have options or choices in all situations or that every woman I talked with felt empowered to affect her circumstances very much. Yet most women had found ways to improve, at least incrementally, their own situations or those of their children when they were especially difficult.

I take seriously the responsibility to represent accurately the perspectives and experiences of the women participating in the research. I make ample use of quotes from the interviews in order to give women a platform from which to speak in their own voices. These passages allow the reader to listen directly to the speakers without the intrusion of or mediation by the researcher. I believe that readers who "hear" the passion, resolve, or desperation in the voices of research participants are better able to understand their actions within the broad context of their family lives.

This book centers on the narratives of thirty-eight Mexican American women who were born in the United States and were daughters or granddaughters of farmworkers. In planning this research project, I did not intended to write a story centered on farm labor. But qualitative research sometimes takes the researcher in unexpected directions. In recruiting research participants, I did not seek women with a family background of farm work. I had three principal screening criteria for inclusion in the sample. I was interested in interviewing: Mexican American women who (1) were born in the United States, (2) lived in or around Brawley, and (3) were mothers of at least one child, elementary school age or younger. In fact, thirty-eight of the forty Mexican American women who met the criteria for inclusion in the sample were daughters or granddaughters of farmworkers. The story I had to tell from this research emerged over the course of the project. Discovering how prominently farm work figured in the memory and experience of these women, I oriented my analysis toward understanding the continuing significance of farm work in their lives.

I engaged in additional research activities to provide clarification and contextualization for this analysis. In screening potential interviewees, I met some women who fit all but one criterion for inclusion in my sample: that is, they were born in Mexico instead of the United States. I interviewed a few of these women to get a sense of how their perspectives and experiences might vary from those of the U.S.-born women. Other research-related activities included attending public and community events; interviewing community professionals (both white and Mexican American) in education, business, and social services; interviewing or engaging in informal conversations with growers about the organization of agriculture in the county, both current and retired farmers (all were white); and interviewing or talking informally with other long-term community residents (both white and Mexican American).

NOTES

INTRODUCTION

1. The old assimilation model also fails to apply to those bracero-era families in this research who settled permanently in the United States prior to 1965. It was the Immigration Act of 1965 that was largely responsible for transforming the racial and ethnic composition of the immigrant stream by discontinuing the old national origin quota system that had maintained the European character of the immigrant stream (Mitchell 1992).

2. Race, social class, and gender have been the systems of structural inequality most often included in analyses of social location. The concept of social location may also be extended to other systems of inequality, including sexual orientation, immigration status, language, and religion.

3. In presenting descriptive statistics in this book, my overall strategy has been the following: first, I describe the research setting using 2005 statistics where possible, thereby providing contextual information about Imperial County for the year the interviews were conducted; second, I have used more current statistics in describing contemporary U.S. society, for example, rates of women's labor force participation. For all population statistics in this particular section, I use the U.S. Census Bureau's annual estimates for 2005 (U.S. Census Bureau 2010).

4. Overall, 14 percent of U.S. counties have farming-dependent economies. As to their social characteristics, 15 percent of U.S. counties are categorized as low-employment and 20 percent are low-education, while 17 percent experience housing stress. The definitions used in categorizing U.S. counties are summarized as follows. Farming-dependent: either 15 percent or more of average annual labor and proprietors' earnings derive from farming or 15 percent or more of employed residents work in farming occupations. Low-employment: less than 65 percent of residents 21–64 were employed. Low-education: 25 percent or more of residents 25–64 had neither a high school diploma nor a GED. Housing stress: 30 percent or more of households had one of these housing conditions: lacked complete plumbing, lacked complete kitchen, paid 30 percent or more of income for housing, or had more than 1 person per room (Parker 2005).

5. This situation changed with the opening of a Walmart in Brawley in 2008. Audi (2010) reports that 10,000 people applied for the 200 jobs at this store.

6. In some cases, personal details have been altered to protect the identity of research participants.

7. A reasonable supposition might be that the parents of third-generation women were not farmworkers and that all third-generation women would likely be granddaughters of farmworkers. This is not the case. In fact, among the twelve women who are third-generation Mexican Americans, nine have a parent (or parents) with a work history that includes farm labor.

8. Research participants were presented with a card with income categories in $10,000 increments and asked which category described their annual family income. I verified their answers to the degree possible by comparisons to hourly wage rates provided elsewhere. The annual income results are as follows: ten (26 percent) earning less than $10,000, six (16 percent) earning $10,000–$20,000, eight (21 percent) earning $20,000–$30,000, three (8 percent) earning $30,000–$40,000, four (11 percent) earning $40,000–$50,000, four (11 percent) earning $50,000–$60,000, and three (8 percent) earning more than $60,000. I did not attempt to calculate the poverty status of this sample. Poverty is a household status. Because so many women had extended household arrangements and did not know how much other household members earned, it was not possible to calculate whether a large segment of my sample had household incomes above or below government-established poverty thresholds.

CHAPTER 1 — THE STRUCTURE OF AGRICULTURE
AND THE ORGANIZATION OF FARM LABOR

1. A family farm is commonly defined as a farm that uses less than 1.5 person-years of hired labor annually (Martin and Mason 2003, 192).

2. Using 2005 data, Martin, Fix, and Taylor demonstrate how seasonal farm work produces low earnings for workers. The average wage for private-sector U.S. workers was $16 hourly and totaled $32,000 annually for full-time, year-round workers. Because farmworkers' hourly wages are about half as much as those for non-farmworkers and they work half as many hours, their total annual income amounted to around $8,000 annually (2006, 20).

3. In fact, in the 1980s, some growers found it cost-effective to discontinue mechanical weeding, pruning, and tree harvesting, and return to hand labor (Palerm 1984, cited in M. Wells 1996). An additional impediment to mechanization was a 1979 lawsuit against the University of California that claimed that the use of public funds to finance mechanization research was illegal because labor-saving machines displaced small farmers and farm workers. The lawsuit, filed by the United Farm Workers and California Rural Legal Assistance, served to reduce the scale of this type of research and move it to the private sector (Martin and Mason 2003, 197).

4. In the case of the NLRA, agricultural interests, who were politically powerful in Washington, argued that agriculture was sufficiently different from other sectors of employment to warrant an exception from national legislation. The two principal arguments for exclusion centered on harmony in agriculture and hardship to the farmer (Morris 1966, 1968). First was the contention that worker protections were unnecessary because relationships between farmers and their field hands were generally personal and harmonious and would be compromised by the bureaucratic process of collective bargaining (Rawls and Bean 2003). Second was the argument that labor protections placed an undue burden on growers already challenged by perishable commodities, unpredictable weather, and lack of control over volatile commodity markets (Morris 1966, 1971).

5. The agreement instituting what is typically known as the Bracero Program was titled "Agreement between the United States of America and Mexico Respecting the Temporary Migration of Mexican Workers."

6. The agreement initiating the Bracero Program stipulated a number of conditions for the employment of Mexican nationals, including standards for work hours, wages, housing, food, and healthcare. These terms were largely ignored by the growers and the U.S. government (Carrasco 2005, 220). The Bracero Program created a system in which power relations were extremely unequal. Mexican workers conformed to growers' demands and were silent in the face of contract violations because they recognized that they could be deported for complaining or showing resistance. With an oversupply of willing workers just over the U.S.-Mexico border, workers knew, and were frequently told, that they were easily replaced. Ronald Mize Jr.'s interviews with ex-braceros provide evidence of a "despotic" system, as seen in the organization of the work day, work hazards, and coercion (2006, 100). The total number of temporary labor contracts filled by guest workers was 4.6 million. Because many workers returned (on new contracts) year after year, it is estimated that 1 to 2 million Mexicans worked in U.S. agriculture under the Bracero Program (Martin and Mason 2003, 199).

7. Wages rose immediately as the program ended (M. Wells 1996, 195). By the mid-1970s, California farmworkers were covered by minimum wage legislation, standards for overtime pay, unemployment insurance, and workers' compensation. Especially important was the enactment of California's Agricultural Labor Relations Act (ALRA) of 1975, which guaranteed the rights of farmworkers to organize and engage in collective bargaining (M. Wells 1996, 73). Finally, the rise of the United Farm Workers gave many reason to believe that the farm labor market would develop into a heavily unionized industry administered by the UFW (Martin 2002, 1130). This hope was not realized and only 10 percent of farm workers were ever under union contract. Nonetheless, the wages and working conditions for a large majority of farmworkers were positively affected by UFW activities and pro-labor legislation (M. Wells 1996, 94).

8. A significant increase in illegal migration by the late 1970s is principally explained by an economic crisis in Mexico that fueled labor migration, and also by the resistance of U.S. farms to meeting union demands for higher farm worker wages (Escobar et al. 2006, 710).

9. This program requires Department of Labor certification that a shortage of domestic workers for particular agricultural jobs exists and that the wages and working conditions of domestic workers will not be negatively affected by using guest workers in those positions. Employers are required to offer a guaranteed minimum wage and provide housing and transportation for their workers. The number of H-2A visas issued annually has held steady at approximately 30,000 in recent years (Congressional Digest 2005, 164–165).

10. According to National Agricultural Workers Survey (NAWS) data for 2003–04, approximately 18 percent of all U.S. crop workers were hired by farm labor contractors. The situation in California was quite different, with 37 percent of California crop workers hired by labor contractors (Aguirre International 2005, 8). California provides both conditions necessary for a labor contracting system to thrive: first, the need for unskilled labor, and second, seasonal variation in demand for labor (Vaupel and Martin 1986). The concentration of California agriculture in high value–labor intensive crops requiring large infusions of temporary workers for harvest explains the greater proportion of crop workers employed by labor contractors in the state.

11. The U.S. Department of Labor (DOL) sponsors this nationally representative random sample survey of the U.S. crop workforce. This survey, begun in 1988, gathers data

through face-to-face interviews with farmworkers. Since its inception, more than 50,000 farmworkers have been interviewed (U.S. Department of Labor 2010). In recent years, major reports from DOL have not been published from these data. The last DOL research report using NAWS data, *Findings from the National Agricultural Workers Survey (NAWS) 2001–2002: A Demographic and Employment Profile of United States Farm Workers*, was published in 2005. The most relevant report on California farm workers, *The California Farm Labor Force: Overview and Trends from the National Agricultural Workers Survey*, also published in 2005, uses data from the 2003–2004 NAWS. The California report is from Aguirre International, the research company that conducted the survey for the DOL.

12. According to the NAWS 2001–2002 report, the survey interviews workers in "seasonal agricultural services," a USDA designation for workers "who perform 'field work' in the vast majority of nursery products, cash grains, and field crops, as well as in all fruits and vegetables. The NAWS also includes persons who work in the production of silage and other animal fodder. As such, the population sampled by the NAWS consists of nearly all farm workers in crop agriculture, including field packers and supervisors . . ." (U.S. Department of Labor 2005, 1).

13. According to the NAWS (U.S. Department of Labor 2005), 53 percent of California crop workers spoke no English and 35 percent could speak a little English. As to immigration status, 57 percent are not authorized to work in the U.S., 33 percent are legal permanent residents, 10 percent are U.S. citizens, and 1 percent have temporary work permits.

14. The seasonal nature of agricultural employment comes into view when we note fluctuations in the number of farmworkers directly hired by California farm operators over the 2005 calendar year. In mid-January, 2005, 128,000 farmworkers were employed, while in mid-July, the numbers rose to 206,000 (U.S. Department of Agriculture National Agricultural Statistics Service 2005).

15. Specialty crops are sometimes referred to as F-V-N (fruits and nuts, vegetables, and nursery and greenhouse) products. In 2003–2004, 46 percent of California farmworkers were employed in fruits and nuts, 40 percent in vegetables, and 8 percent in horticulture. The remainder worked in field crops (5 percent), and other crops (1 percent) (Aguirre International 2005, 7).

16. What Palerm (2002) considers to be a "good job" in agriculture may well be lower in quality than other good job–bad job typologies that assume good jobs to be full-time, year-round, stable jobs with reasonably good wages and benefits (see, for example, Nelson and Smith 1999).

17. Martin's (2009) analysis uses data reported by agricultural employers when paying their unemployment insurance taxes in California. Employers report the Social Security numbers and earnings of their workers to the state quarterly. Martin examined records for 1991, 1996, and 2001. The data have some limitations because some workers share a single Social Security number and other individuals use more than one Social Security number (in the latter case, to enable them to draw unemployment compensation while working another job). Martin attributes increasing numbers of unique Social Security numbers over the period to rising farm labor contractor employment. Contractors typically hire more workers, but for shorter periods of time (2009).

CHAPTER 2 — FARMWORKER ORIGINS

1. Because this research focuses on the experience of second- and third-generation Mexican Americans, I do not subdivide the first-generation parents or grandparents into "decimal generations," an analytic strategy that differentiates immigrants by their age and

entry into the U.S. For example, the 1.5 generations refers to individuals who immigrated between the ages of five and thirteen (Rumbaut 1997; Fry and Lowell 2006)

2. The migration of indigenous families from central and southern Mexico has been precipitated by both Mexican and global events that have made it more difficult for rural peasants to sustain their families. Elizabeth Maier summarizes a complex situation: "Land privatization resulting from the constitutional revision of the Agrarian Reform Act (Article 27) in 1993, farm-subsidy deregulation of basic grain production, financial loan ineligibility for peasant farmers, drastic reductions of federal social welfare budgets and consequent diminished access to previous social-service support systems, reduced world-market agricultural prices, conservation of farm subsidies in the developed nations, and overly competitive agricultural importations have all forced Native Mexicans' flight from ancestral homelands" (2006, 21).

3. Although family members were not authorized to accompany bracero men, some migrant families secured employment (with both women and men in field work) in the United States through informal channels. During this period, braceros frequently facilitated the legal or illegal migration of their relatives and friends, including women. Of course, the end of the Bracero Program in 1964 did not signal the end of demand for Mexican farmworkers among Southwestern growers. Both daughters and sons of former braceros frequently followed in their fathers' footsteps, migrating from Mexico to the U.S. for work (Massey and Liang 1989).

4. The negative characteristics of farm work identified by research participants are corroborated in the sources cited in chapter 1.

5. Beatrice Padilla was born in the Brawley hospital to migrant farmworker parents who returned to Mexicali after the harvest cycle. They later made a permanent move to Imperial County. Beatrice was less fluent in English than other women because she completed several years of school in Mexicali before the move and had fewer years to develop English proficiency in U.S. schools.

CHAPTER 3 — LIFE IN A BORDER COMMUNITY

1. This would be comparable to depositing someone in Calexico whose home was in Minneapolis, Minnesota, or Memphis, Tennessee.

2. In 2005, 320,212 commercial trucks entered through Calexico East (U.S. Department of Transportation 2009).

3. Prior to August of 2004, Border Crossing Card regulations enabled Mexicans to remain in the United States for only seventy-two hours. The *Federal Register* notes that extending the period to thirty days accomplishes two things: first, it creates greater parity between policies for Mexican and Canadian nationals; second, it promotes commerce and tourism near the southern border of the United States (U.S. Department of Homeland Security 2004, 50051).

4. Visa applicants must also demonstrate their intention to return to their home country. According to the U.S. State Department, "The presumption in the law is that every visitor visa applicant is an intending immigrant. Therefore, applicants for visitor visas must overcome this presumption by demonstrating that: The purpose of their trip is to enter the U.S. for business, pleasure, or medical treatment; That they plan to remain for a specific, limited period; Evidence of funds to cover expenses in the United States; Evidence of compelling social and economic ties abroad; and That they have a residence outside the U.S. as well as other binding ties that will insure their return abroad at the end of the visit" (U.S. Department of State 2010a).

5. The significance of the cross-border shopper became especially clear to me in March 2010, when on a return research trip to Imperial County, I happened to visit Imperial Valley Mall on a Monday afternoon. Rather than finding it quiet, as I had expected, it was bustling with customers. I later found that this day, March 15, 2010, was a public holiday in Mexico in celebration of the birthday of Benito Juarez, the famous president of Mexico and national hero. Apparently many Mexicans decided to spend part of their holiday shopping in the United States.

6. An intriguing point here is that Walmart is also an important retailer in Mexico; in fact, it is the largest private employer in that country with 702 stores in 64 cities in 2005 (Walmart Mexico 2010). Further, Mexicali, just over the border from Calexico, has two Walmarts. The reasons Mexican shoppers bother to cross the border to patronize this establishment are related to quality and selection. Walmart Mexico, with headquarters in Mexico City, stocks its stores with merchandise oriented toward the Mexican consumer. Mexicans who shop the Calexico Walmart do so for products oriented toward the American consumer and deemed to be more desirable and of higher quality than those available in their local Walmarts.

7. The term "close relative" refers to a spouse, child, parent, grandparent, or sibling.

8. Historian Patricia Limerick (1987) points out that it was European and not Mexican immigration that was an intensely debated public issue in the early twentieth century. The Immigration Act of 1924 restricted immigration by imposing numerical quotas for European immigration, but not for immigration from Western Hemisphere nations. The only stipulations for Mexican immigration were literacy, the prohibition of contract labor, and an eight-dollar head tax. None of these requirements was strictly enforced. A public outcry marked by nativism followed the omission of Mexico from the quota system. Concerns about an unrestricted number of Mexican immigrants were countered by southwestern growers and others who emphasized the need for Mexican labor (Limerick 1987, 246).

9. My own experience of the Imperial Valley as a border region was reinforced almost daily in a way I did not anticipate. I was a research associate at San Diego State University in Calexico and had chosen Brawley, approximately twenty miles north, as my primary research setting. I lived in El Centro, midway between Brawley and Calexico, and a modest drive to both. To be specific, I lived on the far south side of El Centro, just south of and in sight of Interstate 8. What I did not anticipate was low-flying border control helicopters patrolling the area along I-8 after dark most nights. Helicopter patrols were initially startling, and their noise was always disruptive.

10. A fundamental shift in border control strategy occurred in 1993 and 1994 as the Clinton administration adopted a "concentrated border enforcement strategy." This strategy concentrated border enforcement resources in areas with the highest numbers of illegal crossings (Cornelius 2001, 661). The strategy was first implemented with Operation Hold-the-Line in El Paso, Texas, in 1993 and then with Operation Gatekeeper, an operation addressing illegal immigration in the San Diego area in 1994. Operation Gatekeeper reframed the task of border control in Imperial County and reshaped life in the community. The San Diego area had historically been the site of heaviest illegal crossing activity into the United States from Mexico. Operation Gatekeeper used a "prevention and deterrence" strategy, preventing many prospective migrants from crossing at the San Diego border (Nieves 2002). The illegal immigrant stream would necessarily shift eastward, where migrants would encounter rough mountain terrain and vast deserts. This strategy assumed that harsh geography would serve as a natural deterrent to immigration

(Berestein 2004a). What happened instead was that the policy mostly channeled illegal immigration to more hazardous areas.

11. The All-American Canal is an eighty-two-mile long irrigation canal that carries water from the Colorado River to the Valley. At its widest point, the canal is two hundred feet wide, and its greatest depth is twenty feet. It originates at the Imperial Diversion Dam, eighteen miles northeast of Yuma, Arizona. Fifty-three miles of the canal run parallel to and just north of the U.S.–Mexico border (NASA 2009).

CHAPTER 4 — NEGOTIATING WORK AND FAMILY

1. I am sure there were disadvantages to being an Anglo researcher in this setting. There were also advantages. One is that women sometimes provided explanatory frameworks for their experiences or actions. That is, they said to me, "This is why we [Mexican Americans] do this," or "This is how we think about that," and the like. An example from the current chapter is when Denise Ortiz explained to me why her family moved back to Brawley after her mother-in-law died. The explanation was that because her husband is the youngest child in his family, it is really his responsibility to step in when a parent needs help. It is part of Mexican culture. I think she and others wondered if I would "get it" if they did not explain these matters.

2. As of 2008, 56 percent of Latinas (ages sixteen and over) were in the labor force, compared to 59 percent of all U.S. women. Latinas with children are significantly less likely to be employed than are other U.S. women, however. Among mothers with children under the age of eighteen, 61 percent of Latinas are in the labor force, while 71 percent of all U.S. women are in the force; for mothers with children under the age of six, 52 percent of Latinas are in the labor force, compared to 6 percent of all U.S. women (U.S. Department of Labor 2009). In examining patterns of women's labor force participation, it is relevant to note that the U.S. Department of Labor's statistics on this matter generally measure the labor force participation rate of women age sixteen and over. These statistics also include elderly women who are unlikely to be employed. Some statisticians examine the labor force participation of women sixteen through sixty-four. These statistics actually provide a better snapshot of contemporary women's employment by focusing on the group of women most likely to be in the labor force.

3. Esther has been very deliberate about her strategy to secure health insurance for her family. I asked her if she thought the pay for her job was pretty good. She replied, "No, I think it is bad. It is very hard on our back and we're standing up the whole eight hours on our feet. But the reason I am working there is not because of the money. I'm working because of the insurance—for my family."

4. Hansen's (2004, 2005) research studied networks of care for children among white families of varied social class locations.

5. Despite diverse cultural origins, most contemporary immigrants to the United States originate from countries with patriarchal gender relations. Immigrant-sending countries in Asia, Latin America, the Caribbean, and the Middle East typically have sharply divided gender divisions of labor, male dominance in the family, and discourage women's employment (Pyke 2004, 260).

6. Working mothers are not alone in describing their lives as stressful. Marta Lujan, who has stayed home with her children for the past eight years, repeatedly says that she is "stressed out." She is now at the point that she wants to go back into the workforce, which she believes will reduce her stress. Marta's husband has a full-time, year-round

federal government job; his stable earnings have enabled Marta to take some time out of the labor force.

7. Marjorie's husband's lack of involvement with the children may be partially explained by the fact that he is the father of only the youngest child and stepfather to the older two children. He may view himself as not very responsible for the parenting of the older children.

CHAPTER 5 — THE LEGACY OF FARM LABOR

1. Nonmetropolitan areas are areas outside Metropolitan Statistical Areas (MSAs). They are designated on a county-by-county basis using U.S. Office of Management and Budget (OMB) criteria. Imperial County, California, was a nonmetropolitan county until 2003, when a new classification of counties as metropolitan and nonmetropolitan was released. This reclassification reflected both a decade of urban growth and extensive modification of the rules governing metro and nonmetro status. Under the new guidelines, 298 formerly nonmetro counties—including Imperial County—became metro counties. The terms "nonmetropolitan" and "rural" are frequently used interchangeably, but they have different meanings. Urban and rural places are designated on the basis of the population density of territory, unrelated to municipal boundaries. Rural places include open country and settlements with populations of less than 2,500. Metropolitan and nonmetropolitan counties typically have both rural and urban areas (Cromartie 2003, 2007). While Imperial County is now classified as a metropolitan county, the vast county is overwhelmingly rural.

2. Juanita Lopez contacted me because she saw the flyer for my research and wanted to participate. I asked her if she had been born in the United States and explained that I was interviewing Mexican American women who were U.S-born. She told me that she was a U.S. citizen and was Mexican American; she thought that should be enough to participate in the research. My original intent with the flyer was not to locate immigrant women to interview, but I did interview some immigrants who I found by other means. I did interview Juanita, an interview precipitated by her interest in my project. In talking with her, I found out that she was very proud to be a U.S. citizen. She makes a distinction between herself and her husband. She refers to herself as a Mexican American because she is a citizen. But she says her husband is not a Mexican American, but a Mexican immigrant, because he is not a citizen.

3. The minority concentration literature has been focused on African Americans in central cities. As a general conclusion, this research finds the residential concentration of African Americans in urban places to be associated with concentrated poverty and the disadvantage that accompanies it (see, for example, Wilson 1987).

4. For several decades the trend in the distribution of income in the United States has been in the direction of increasing economic inequality. Research finds greater income inequality in U.S. counties at the Mexico border than is the case in either border states or the United States overall. Peach (1997) uses the Gini coefficient as a measure of income distribution. He found, for example, that in 1989, Imperial County's Gini coefficient was 0.435 in comparison to 0.398 for the United States overall. Higher coefficients indicate greater inequality.

5. This research provides varied analyses of earnings in the border region, with nonborder comparisons. Scholars have calculated wage differentials between, for example, border and nonborder MSAs in Texas (Smith and Newman 1977), select border MSAs and interior U.S. MSAs (Dávila and Mora 2008), and U.S. counties at the southwestern border

(including Imperial County) and U.S. interior counties (Mollick, Mora, and Dávila 2007). Research on this subject consistently finds an earnings penalty for U.S. workers near the Mexico border. The size of the earnings gap varies between studies depending on sample characteristics, control variables, and timeframe. The analysis by Mora and her colleagues found the border penalty to be approximately 13 percent for Mexican immigrants, 10 percent for U.S.-born Mexican Americans, and 5 percent for U.S.-born non-Hispanic whites, net of control variables (2008).

6. The body of research on the effects of immigration on the wages of U.S. workers has mixed results. Some research finds immigration lowering the wages of U.S.-born workers, while other shows no wage effects (Murray, Batalova, and Fix 2006). Spatial context is relevant in assessing the impact of immigration on the wages of native workers. For native-born workers in the interior of the United States, the impact may be negligible.

7. The concepts of employment hardship and underemployment are closely related. The principal difference is that underemployment is generally defined to include discouraged workers in addition to the unemployed, involuntarily part-time workers, and the working poor. Discouraged workers, those who want a job but have given up on finding one because they believe none are available, are not included in government-provided unemployment statistics.

8. Alex Ortega's job is in commercial trucking, not in agricultural transport.

9. This means the county has determined that with nineteen hours and seventeen hours of care per month respectively, Maria's father and mother will be able to avoid out-of-home care, such as a nursing home. Some women mentioned that the authorized hours were inadequate to provide the care the disabled individual actually needed.

10. An ongoing point of controversy in the county is the structure of compensation associated with the work. Many women contend that they are, in fact, county employees and should receive wages and benefits according to county compensation schedules.

CHAPTER 6 — SURVIVING NOW AND BUILDING A BETTER LIFE FOR LATER

1. Affordable housing in the Imperial Valley was a key factor enabling many migrant Mexican farmworkers to settle permanently in the United States rather than returning to Mexicali at the end of the agricultural season. Palerm's research found that in the 1990s, most of the lettuce workers (lechugueros) in California's Santa Maria Valley owned homes in the U.S.–Mexico border area (2002).

2. Some Imperial Valley homes were indeed purchased by San Diego residents, many on speculation. For the price of a one-bedroom condominium in San Diego, one could buy a new three- or four-bedroom home in the Valley. One of my most astute community contacts suggested that many who bought these houses, once they became fully aware of the lack of amenities in this rural area and the summer heat (in comparison to San Diego), would never actually move to the Valley.

3. The national "housing bubble" that burst in 2008 occurred with force in Imperial County. A USA Today analysis found that the foreclosure problem was most severe in a few areas. In fact, in 2008, thirty-five U.S. counties accounted for half of all U.S. foreclosure actions. Sparsely populated Imperial County, California, was one of those counties (Heath and Merrill 2009).

4. These householders paid between $345 and $900 for rent. These properties vary significantly from $345 for a two-bedroom mobile home to $600 for a two-bedroom apartment to $900 for a three-bedroom house.

5. Antonia Avilar has applied for welfare but is required to provide information on her husband's health status before the application can be processed. At issue is whether his medical records from the hospital that treated him for cancer show that he is now able to work. Antonia says she has no money to go to this hospital near Los Angeles—nearly 150 miles from home—to get the needed paperwork.

6. Under HUD programs that subsidize rent, the amount a family pays is based on its annual income and family size. So, for example, Rosa Navarra had Section 8 housing when she was out of the labor force and attending college. Her family of three paid $174 for a three-bedroom house. Christina Gilbert now lives with her two children in a low-income housing development. With an income of over $20,000 annually, including child support, her rent is $434 for a three-bedroom apartment.

7. The Imperial Irrigation District's responsibility goes beyond managing the All-American Canal and the system of irrigation canals in the Imperial Valley. This entity also serves as the water company and the electric company for the Valley.

8. I did meet a woman who currently lived and worked in Calexico whose family was in the process of buying a house in Mexicali.

9. The Urban Institute conducted this study for the Economic Research Service (ERS) of the USDA in 2001. Some of the TANF program specifics have changed since this study was completed, but the description of the community and the challenges in moving from welfare to work continue to be relevant.

10. Toussaint-Comeau (2004) developed a measure of socioeconomic status based on the education and experience requirements of particular occupation categories. The assignment of a "socioeconomic status score" provides a means of measuring occupational mobility. The lower the score, the less education and experience are needed for the occupation. Jobs in the category of Farming, Fishing, and Forestry have a socioeconomic status score of "14," the lowest score on the scale (compared to, for example, Construction and Extraction with a score of "27," and Management with a score of "54").

11. In *Generations of Exclusion: Mexican Americans, Assimilation, and Race* (2008), Edward Telles and Vilma Ortiz present the results of their follow-up study to the research on which Leo Grebler, Joan W. Moore, and Ralph C. Guzman based their *The Mexican-American People: The Nation's Second Largest Minority* (1970). The original research was a survey of nearly 1,600 households in Los Angeles County, California, and San Antonio, Texas. The sample for the research was entirely urban. Thirty-five years later, the follow-up study located and interviewed nearly 700 of the original research participants and approximately 750 children of the original participants.

12. My sample size did not allow for a comparative analysis by generational status. Grogger and Trejo presented results by generational status, which I recalculated to create a U.S-born category for consistency with my data. Their data are not directly comparable to mine, but provide a general basis for comparison. According to 1996–1999 Current Population Survey (CPS) data used by Grogger and Trejo, the educational attainment of U.S.-born Mexican American women ages twenty-five to fifty-nine is the following: 26 percent have no high school diploma or GED; 34 percent have a high school diploma or GED; 28 percent have some college; 8 percent have a bachelor's degree; and 3 percent have a postgraduate degree (2002, 12).

13. Schneider and Stevenson (1999) refer to this scenario as an "ambition paradox"; that is, very ambitious students sometime choose an educational path that provides little likelihood of success (cited in Schneider, Martinez, and Owens 2006, 213).

14. Women begin this major with the administration of justice coursework at Imperial Valley College. Some stop with the associate's degree in administration of justice as Rosa Navarra did. Priscilla Ortega, who completed the criminal justice B.A., decided she did not really want to do prison work.

15. In her article about nonmarital births, Kelly Musick (2002) proposes how the association between social disadvantage and nonmarital births might work. I have used her analytic strategy to examine another association, that of social disadvantage and early births in a particular social context.

16. Twenty of the Imperial County women live with partners. Among these men, ten do not have a high school diploma or GED, four have a high school diploma, four have some college, one has an associate's degree, and one has a B.A. In contrast, among the women partnered with these men, three do not have a high school diploma or GED, one has a high school diploma only, twelve have some college, two have an associate's degree, and two have a B.A.

17. Another way of viewing this situation is that Latinas may leave school and start a family when parents and school personnel have low expectations for their educational attainment (Zambrana 2011, 92).

CHAPTER 7 — WHY DO THEY STAY?

1. Community attachment is a complex construct that has been interpreted in various ways (Fernandez and Dillman 1979; Ryan et al. 2005; Theodori 2001). Ryan and his colleagues quote a well-known article in which McMillan and Chavis discuss this concept, "[C]ommunity attachment in the sociological literature parallels what community psychologists call 'sense of community,' or 'a feeling that members matter to one another and to the [community], and a shared fate that members' needs will be met through their commitment to be together' (McMillan and Chavis 1986, 9)" (2005, 292). The concept of community satisfaction is less useful for this analysis because measurements of community satisfaction typically include economic variables such as "satisfaction with employment." The women in my research might, for example, be very satisfied with local friendship and kinship ties, but most were dissatisfied with their employment situations (Filkins, Allen, and Cordes 2000).

2. A number of qualitative studies consider community life in rural California. See, for example, Allensworth and Rochin (1998), Chávez (2005), and Du Bry (2007). The communities featured in these studies vary considerably along dimensions of size, spatial isolation, ethnic concentration, and economic well-being. None of the studies centers specifically on second- and third-generation Mexican Americans, but some references are made to these groups in each.

3. This set of concerns is common in rural communities (MacTavish and Salamon 2003).

4. Three women described incidents of workplace discrimination in their Imperial Valley workplaces, and two others wondered if recent job losses resulted from racial bias.

5. The valley has a few prosperous Mexican American farmers. Women told me that these farmers are excluded from informal gatherings of the (white) agricultural power structure.

6. As agriculture in the Imperial Valley expanded in the 1920s and thereafter, growers became increasingly reliant on Mexican workers. Historical analyses find that racial/ethnic relations in the Imperial Valley have been marked by social exclusion in communities and contentious and sometimes violent interactions between growers and farmworkers. See, for example, Martin 2003, Starr 1996, and Wollenberg 1969.

7. Allensworth and Rochin suggest that U.S.-born Mexican Americans function as a social buffer between Anglos and new immigrants in rural California. They typically have family and social ties with both groups, economic connections with both groups, and language facility in English as well as some Spanish (1998, 43). Allensworth and Rochin did their research in the San Joaquin Valley. The women in my research had very few family ties to Anglos, although a few were married to Mexican immigrants. I attribute this difference to the spatial isolation of the Imperial Valley from areas with greater concentrations of Anglos and its position at the U.S.-Mexico border.

8. Most of these have remained in Southern California, living in Riverside, Los Angeles, or San Diego counties. Seven have lived in urban areas in other states including Las Vegas, Phoenix, Yuma, Philadelphia, Honolulu, and Detroit, sometimes for a very short time of, for example, two months.

9. California also provides better unemployment insurance benefits and a higher minimum wage than Arizona and Nevada. In addition, California is one of a handful of states that provides partial wage replacement for up to six weeks of family leave, usually used as maternity leave (California Employment Development Department 2008).

CONCLUSION

1. The postindustrial economy has dealt a blow to the financial security of many families, including white families who would likely have had stable resources in the industrial economy. Judith Stacey (1991) writes about "postmodern families," products of the postindustrial economy, for whom extended family households are a principal survival strategy. The relationship between residential arrangements and economic standing became starkly evident in the Great Recession of 2008–2009 when job loss and home foreclosures resulted in a large increase in extended family households (Fleck 2009).

REFERENCES

Acker, Joan. 1992. "Gendered Institutions: From Sex Roles to Gendered Institutions." *Contemporary Sociology* 21 (September): 565–568.

Aguirre International. 2005. *The California Farm Labor Force Overview and Trends from the National Agricultural Workers Survey*. www.agcenter.ucdavis.edu.

American Immigration Lawyers Association [AILA InfoNet]. 2006. *Summary of the Secure Fence Act of 2006*. Doc. No. 06091368. http://www.aila.org.

Alba, Richard. 2006. "Mexican Americans and the American Dream." *Perspectives on Politics* 4 (2): 289–296.

Albrecht, Don E., Carol Mulford Albrecht, and Edward Murguia. 2005. "Minority Concentration, Disadvantage, and Inequality in the Nonmetropolitan United States." *Sociological Quarterly* 46:503–523.

Allensworth, Elaine M., and Refugio I. Rochin. 1998. "Ethnic Transformation in Rural California: Looking Beyond the Immigrant Farmworker." *Rural Sociology* 63 (1): 26–50.

Amato, Paul R., Alan Booth, David R. Johnson, and Stacy J. Rogers. 2007. *Alone Together: How Marriage in America is Changing*. Cambridge, MA: Harvard University Press.

Andreas, Peter. 2000. *Border Games: Policing the U.S.-Mexico Divide*. Ithaca, NY: Cornell University Press.

———. 2003. "A Tale of Two Borders: The U.S.-Canada and U.S.-Mexico Lines After 9–11." In *The Rebordering of North America*, edited by P. Andreas and T. J. Biersteker, 1–23. New York: Routledge.

Audi, Tamara. 2010. "Bypassed by the Recovery." *Wall Street Journal*. June 17. http://www.wsj.com.

Baca Zinn, Maxine. 1980. "Employment and Education of Mexican American Women: The Interplay of Modernity and Ethnicity in Eight Families." *Harvard Educational Review* 50:47–62.

———. 1982. "Familism among Chicanos: A Theoretical Review." *Humboldt Journal of Social Relations* 10 (1): 224–238.

———. 1990. "Family, Feminism, and Race in America." *Gender & Society* 4 (1): 68–82.

Baca Zinn, Maxine, D. Stanley Eitzen, and Barbara Wells. 2011. *Diversity in Families*. 9th ed. Boston: Allyn and Bacon.

Baca Zinn, Maxine, and Barbara Wells. 2000. "Diversity within Latino Families: New Lessons for Family Social Science." In *Handbook of Family Diversity*, edited by D. H. Demo, K. R. Allen, and M. A. Fine, 252–273. New York: Oxford University Press.

Barton Amy E. 1978. *Campesinas: Women Farmworkers in the California Agricultural Labor Force*. Sacramento: California Commission on the Status of Women.

Beale, Calvin L. 2004. "Anatomy of Nonmetro High-Poverty Areas: Common in Plight, Distinctive in Nature." *Amber Waves* (February): 21–27. http://www.ers.usda.gov/amberwaves.

Bean, Frank D., Roland Chanove, Robert G. Cushing, Rodolfo de la Garza, Gary P. Freeman, Charles W. Haynes, and David Spener. 1994. "Illegal Mexican Migration & the United States/Mexico Border: The Effects of Operation Hold the Line on El Paso/Juarez." Washington, DC: U.S. Commission on Immigration Reform.

Becker, Andrew, and Jackie Bennion. 2008. Map: Securing the Border. PBS. http://www.pbs.org/frontlineworld.

Bengtson, Vern L., and Katherine R. Allen. 1993. "The Life Course Perspective Applied to Families Over Time." In *Sourcebook of Family Theories and Methods: A Contextual Approach*, edited by P. G. Boss, W. P. Doherty, R. LaRossa, W. R. Schumm, and S. K. Steinmetz, 469-499. New York: Plenum Press.

Berestein, Leslie. 2004a. "Rugged Routes, Deadly Risks: Migrants Push East to Avoid Fortified Border, with Tragic Results." *San Diego Union-Tribune*. September 29. http://signonsandiego.com.

———. 2004b. "Tightened Border in San Diego Shifts Strain to Areas East." *San Diego Union-Tribune*. August 1. http://signonsandiego.com.

Bianchi, Suzanne M., and Melissa A. Milkie. 2010. "Work and Family Research in the First Decade of the 21st Century." *Journal of Marriage and Family* 72 (June): 705–725.

Blumberg, Rae Lesser. 2005. "Gender, Economy and Kinship in Complex Households among Six U.S. Ethnic Groups: Who Benefits? Whose Kin? Who Cares?" In *Complex Ethnic Households in America*, edited by L. Schwede, R. L. Blumberg, and A. Y. Chan, 248–279. Lanham, MD: Rowman & Littlefield.

Brown, David L. 2002. "Migration and Community: Social Networks in a Multilevel World." *Rural Sociology* 67 (1): 1–23.

Burawoy, Michael. 1991. *Ethnography Unbound: Power and Resistance in the Modern Metropolis*. Berkeley, CA: University of California Press.

Calexico Mission School. 2010. Our Mission Story. http://www.cams-education.com.

California Department of Corrections and Rehabilitation. 2010. Institutional Statistics. www.cdcr.ca.gov.

California Department of Education. 2010. DataQuest: English Learners. http://dq.cde.ca.gov/dataquest.

California Department of Finance. 2007. *2006 California Statistical Abstract*. www.dof.ca.gov.

California Department of Social Services. 2007. Child Care: CalWORKS Child Care Program. http://www.cdss.ca.gov.

California Employment Development Department. 2008. Paid Family Leave. www.edd.ca.gov.

Camarillo, Albert M. 2007. "Mexico." In *The New Americans: A Guide to Immigration since 1965*, edited by M. C. Waters and R. Ueda, 504–517. Cambridge, MA: Harvard University Press.

Carrasco, Gilbert Paul. 2005. "Bracero Program." In *Oxford Encyclopedia of Latinos and Latinas in the United States*, edited by S. Oboler and D. J. González, 220–224. New York: Oxford University Press.

CBS. 2010. The Deadly Passage of the All-American Canal. http://www.cbsnews.com/ stories.

CCBRES (California Center for Border and Regional Economic Studies). 2003. "Mexicali-United States: Selected Indicators." *CCBRES Bulletin* 4 (12): 7. www.sci.sdsu.edu/ccbres.

———. 2005. "Quarterly Workforce Indicators for Imperial County." *CCBRES Bulletin* 6 (12): 7. www.sci.sdsu.edu/ccbres.

Chapman Larry, and James Meyers. 2001. *Ergonomics and Musculoskeletal Injuries in Agriculture: Recognizing and Preventing the Industry's Most Widespread Health and Safety Problem*. National Ag Safety Database (NASD) [Centers for Disease Control (CDC)].

Chávez, Sergio. 2005. "Community, Ethnicity, and Class in a Changing Rural California Town." *Rural Sociology* 70 (3): 314–335.

Collins, Kimberly. 2004. "The Imperial Valley and Mexicali: An Introduction to the Region and its People." In *Imperial-Mexicali Valleys: Development and Environment of the U.S.-Mexican Border Region*, edited by K. Collins, R. Ganster, C. Mason, E. Sánchez López, and M. Quintero-Núñez, 3–8. San Diego, CA: San Diego State University Press.

———. 2007. Personal communication. March 22.

Congressional Digest. 2005. "Guest Worker Program Overview: Current Policy and Issues for Debate." *Congressional Digest* (June): 164–168.

Cornelius, Wayne A. 2001. "Death at the Border: Efficacy and Unintended Consequences of US Immigration Control Policy." *Population and Development Review* 27 (4): 661–685.

Cromartie, John. 2003. Measuring Rurality: New Definitions in 2003. U.S. Department of Agriculture. http://www.ers.usda.gov.

Crowley, Martha, Daniel T. Lichter, and Zhenchao Qian. 2006. "Beyond Gateway Cities: Economic Restructuring and Poverty among Mexican Immigrant Families and Children." *Family Relations* 55 (July): 345–360.

Dávila, Alberto, and Marie T. Mora. 2008. "Changes in the Relative Earnings Gap between Natives and Immigrants Along the U.S.-Mexico Border." *Journal of Regional Science* 48 (3): 525–545.

De Anda, Roberto M. 2005. "Employment Hardship among Mexican-Origin Women." *Hispanic Journal of Behavioral Science* 27 (1): 43–59.

De Genova, Nicholas. 2005. "Immigration Policy, Twentieth Century." In *Oxford Encyclopedia of Latinos and Latinas in the United States*, edited by S. Oboler and D. J. González, 352–358. New York: Oxford University Press.

Del Castillo, Adelaida R. 1996. "Gender and its Discontinuities in Male/Female Domestic Relations: Mexicans in Cross-Cultural Context." In *Chicanas/Chicanos at the Crossroads: Social, Economic, and Political Change*, edited by D. R. Maciel, and I. D. Ortiz, 207–230. Tucson: University of Arizona Press.

Dill, Bonnie Thornton. 1988. "Our Mothers' Grief: Racial Ethnic Women and the Maintenance of Families." *Journal of Family History* 13 (4): 415–431.

Dohan, Daniel. 2003. *The Price of Poverty: Money, Work, and Culture in the Mexican American Barrio*. Berkeley: University of California Press.

Du Bry, Travis. 2007. *Immigrants, Settlers, and Laborers: The Socioeconomic Transformation of a Farming Community*. New York: LFB Scholarly Publishing.

Ducheny, Denise Moreno. 2004. "Foreword: Two Valleys, Two Nations-One River, One Region." In *Imperial-Mexicali Valleys: Development and Environment of the U.S.-Mexican*

Border Region, edited by K. Collins, R. Ganster, C. Mason, E. Sánchez López, and M. Quintero-Núñez, xi–xii. San Diego: San Diego State University Press.

Duncan, Brian, V. Joseph Hotz, and Stephen J. Trejo. 2006. "Hispanics in the U.S. Labor Market." In *Hispanics and the Future of America*, edited by M. Tienda and F. Mitchell, 228–287. Washington, DC: National Academies Press.

Dye, Jane Lawler. 2005. *Fertility of American Women: June 2004*. Current Population Reports, P20–555. U.S. Census Bureau.

Edin, Kathryn, and Maria Kefalas. 2005. *Promises I Can Keep: Why Poor Women Put Motherhood before Marriage*. Berkeley: University of California Press.

Ellingwood, Ken. 2004. *Hard Line: Life and Death on the U.S.-Mexico Border*. New York: Random House.

England, Lynn, and Ralph B. Brown. 2003. "Community and Resource Extraction in Rural America." In *Challenges for Rural America in the Twenty-First Century*, edited by D. L. Brown, and L. E. Swanson, 317–328. University Park: Pennsylvania State University Press.

Escobar, Agustín, Kay Hailbronner, Philip Martin, and Liliana Meza. 2006. "Migration and Development: Mexico and Turkey." *International Migration Review* 40 (3): 707–718.

Fernandez, Richard R., and Don A. Dillman. 1979. "The Influence of Community Attachment on Geographic Mobility." *Rural Sociology* 44:345–360.

Filkins, Rebecca, John C. Allen, and Sam Cordes. 2000. "Predicting Community Satisfaction among Rural Residents: An Integrative Model." *Rural Sociology* 65 (1): 72–86.

Fimbres Durazo, Norma. 2004. "Capitalist Development and Population Growth in the County of Imperial, California, and Mexicali, Baja California." In *Imperial-Mexicali Valleys: Development and Environment of the U.S.-Mexican Border Region*, edited by K. Collins, R. Ganster, C. Mason, E. Sánchez López, and M. Quintero-Núñez, 43–54. San Diego: San Diego State University Press.

Fitchen, Janet M. 1981. *Poverty in Rural America: A Case Study*. Boulder, CO: Westview Press.

Fleck, Carole. 2009. "All Under One Roof." *AARP Bulletin* (May): 24–25.

Foner, Nancy, and Philip Kasinitz. 2007. "The Second Generation." In *The New Americans: A Guide to Immigration since 1965*, edited by M. C. Waters and R. Ueda, 270–282. Cambridge, MA: Harvard University Press.

Foulkes, Matt, and K. Bruce Newbold. 2005. "Geographic Mobility and Residential Instability in Impoverished Rural Illinois Places." *Environment and Planning A* 37:845–860.

Fry, Richard, and B. Lindsay Lowell. 2006. "The Wage Structure of Latino-Origin Groups Across Generations." *Industrial Relations* 45 (2): 147–168.

Garey, Anita I. 1999. *Weaving Work and Motherhood*. Philadelphia: Temple University Press.

Gelles, Richard, and Murray A. Straus. 1988. *Intimate Violence*. New York: Simon and Schuster.

Gibbs, Robert M. 2002. "Rural Labor Markets in an Era of Welfare Reform." *Rural Dimensions of Welfare Reform*, edited by B. A. Weber, G.J. Duncan, and L. A. Whitener, 51–75. Kalamazoo, MI: W. E. Upjohn Institute for Employment Research.

Glick, Jennifer E. 2010. "Connecting Complex Processes: A Decade of Research on Immigrant Families." *Journal of Marriage and Family* 72 (June): 498–515.

González, Arturo. 2002. *Mexican Americans and the U.S. Economy: Quest for Buenos Días*. Tucson: University of Arizona Press.

González-López, Gloria. 2005. *Erotic Journeys: Mexican Immigrants and Their Sex Lives.* Berkeley: University of California Press.

Grasmuck, Sherri, and Patricia R. Pessar. 1991. *Between Two Islands: Dominican International Migration.* Berkeley: University of California Press.

Grebler, Leo, Joan W. Moore, and Ralph C. Guzman. 1970. *The Mexican-American People: The Nation's Second Largest Minority.* New York: Free Press.

Greenstein, Theodore N. 2000. "Economic Dependence, Gender, and the Division of Labor in the Home: A Replication and Extension." *Journal of Marriage and Family* 62 (May): 322–335.

———. 2001. *Methods of Family Research.* Thousand Oaks, CA: Sage Publications.

Grogger Jeffrey and Stephen J. Trejo. 2002. *Falling Behind or Moving Up? The Intergenerational Progress of Mexican Americans.* San Francisco: Public Policy Institute of California.

Hansen, Ellen R. 2006. "Women's Daily Mobility at the U.S.-Mexico Border." In *Women and Change at the U.S.-Mexico Border: Mobility, Labor, and Activism*, edited by E. R. Hansen and D. J. Mattingly, 36–52. Tucson: University of Arizona Press.

Hansen, Ellen R., and Doreen J. Mattingly. 2006. "Women at the Border: Foundations and Frameworks." In *Women and Change at the U.S.-Mexico Border: Mobility, Labor, and Activism*, edited by E. R. Hansen and D. J. Mattingly, 3–16. Tucson: University of Arizona Press.

Hansen, Karen V. 2004. "The Asking Rules of Reciprocity in Networks of Care for Children." *Qualitative Sociology* 27 (4): 421–437.

———. 2005. *Not-so-Nuclear Families: Class, Gender, and Networks of Care.* New Brunswick, NJ: Rutgers University Press.

Heath, Brad, and Dave Merrill. 2009. "Confined Crisis." *USA Today.* March 6. www.usatoday.com.

Helburn, Suzanne W., and Barbara R. Bergman. 2002. *America's Child Care Problem: The Way Out.* New York: Palgrave.

Hochschild, Arlie R., with Anne Machung. 1989. *The Second Shift.* New York: Viking Penguin.

Holden, Christopher. 2001. *Monograph Series: Housing.* Buda, TX: National Center for Farmworker Health. www.ncfh.org.

Hondagneu-Sotelo, Pierrette. 1994. *Gendered Transitions: Mexican Experiences of Immigration.* Berkeley: University of California Press.

Hong, Robert S. 2005. "Veterans Tapped as Grand Marshals." *Imperial Valley Press* A1.

Imperial County. 2007. Department of Social Services: Adult Services. http://www.co.imperial.ca.us.

———. 2008. Benefits Details. http://www.co.imperial.ca.us.

Imperial Irrigation District [IID]. 2010. Residential Energy Assistance Program (REAP). www.iid.com.

Jensen, Leif, Jill L. Findeis, Wan-Ling Hsu, and Jason P. Schachter. 1999. "Slipping into and Out of Underemployment: Another Disadvantage for Nonmetropolitan Workers?" *Rural Sociology* 64 (3): 417–438.

Jensen, Leif, Diane K. McLaughlin, and Tim Slack. 2003. "Rural Poverty: The Persisting Challenge." In *Challenges for Rural America in the Twenty-First Century*, edited by D. L. Brown, and L. E. Swanson, 118–131. University Park: Pennsylvania State University Press.

Jepson, Lisa K., and Christopher A. Jepson. 2002. "An Empirical Analysis of the Matching Patterns of Same-Sex and Opposite-Sex Couples." *Demography* 39 (August): 435–453.

Johnson, Kenneth M. 2003. "Unpredictable Directions of Rural Population Growth and Migration." In *Challenges for Rural America in the Twenty-First Century*, edited by D. L. Brown, and L. E. Swanson, 19–31. University Park: Pennsylvania State University Press.

Kandel, William, and Constance Newman. 2004. "Rural Hispanics: Employment and Residential Trends." *Amber Waves* 2 (3): 39–45. www.ers.usda.gov/amberwaves.

Kandiyoti, Deniz. 1988. "Bargaining with Patriarchy." *Gender & Society* 2 (3): 274–290.

Kibria, Nazli. 1993. *Family Tightrope: The Changing Lives of Vietnamese Americans*. Princeton, NJ: Princeton University Press.

Lamphere, Louise, Patricia Zavella, and Felipe Gonzales. 1993. *Sunbelt Working Mothers: Reconciling Family and Factory*. Ithaca, NY: Cornell University Press.

Landale, Nancy S., and R. S. Oropesa. 2007. "Hispanic Families: Stability and Change." *Annual Review of Sociology* 33:381–405.

Larson, Alice. 2001. *Monograph Series: Environmental/Occupational Safety and Health*. Buda, TX: National Center for Farmworker Health. www.ncfh.org.

LeDuff, Charlie. 2004. "Just this Side of the Treacherous Border, Here Lies Juan Doe." *New York Times*. September 24. http://www.nytimes.com.

Lichter, Daniel T., Lionel J. Beaulieu, Jill L. Findeis, and Ruy A. Teixeira. 1993. "Human Capital, Labor Supply, and Poverty in Rural America." In *Persistent Poverty in Rural America*, edited by Rural Sociological Society Task Force on Persistent Poverty, 36–67. Boulder, CO: Westview Press.

Lichter, Daniel T., and Kenneth M. Johnson. 2006. "Emerging Rural Settlement Patterns and the Geographic Redistribution of America's New Immigrants." *Rural Sociology* 71 (1): 109–132.

Limerick, Patricia N. 1987. *The Legacy of Conquest: The Unbroken Past of the American West*. New York: W. W. Norton.

Lobao, Linda M., Gregory Hooks, and Ann R. Tickamyer. 2007. "Intoduction: Advancing the Sociology of Spatial Inequality." In *The Sociology of Spatial Inequality*, edited by L. M. Lobao, G. Hooks, and A. R. Tickamyer, 1–25. Albany: State University of New York Press.

Lofland, John, David Snow, Leon Anderson, and Lyn H. Lofland. 2006. *Analyzing Social Settings: A Guide to Qualitative Observation and Analysis*. Belmont, CA: Wadsworth.

López, David E., and Ricardo D. Stanton-Salazar. 2001. "Mexican Americans: A Second Generation at Risk." In *Ethnicities: Children of Immigrants in America*, edited by R. G. Rumbaut and A. Portes, 57–90. Berkeley: University of California Press.

Lorey, David E. 1999. *The U.S.-Mexican Border in the Twentieth Century: A History of Economic and Social Transformation*. Wilmington, DE: Scholarly Resources.

Lowenthal, Abraham, and Katrina Burgess, eds. 1993. *The California-Mexico Connection*. Stanford, CA: Stanford University Press.

Lyson, Thomas A., William W. Falk, Mark Henry, Jo Ann Hickey, and Mildred Warner. 1993. "Spatial Location of Economic Activities, Uneven Development, and Rural Poverty." In *Persistent Poverty in Rural America*, edited by Rural Sociological Society Task Force on Persistent Poverty, 106–135. Boulder, CO: Westview Press.

MacTavish, Katherine, and Sonya Salamon. 2003. "What do Rural Families Look Like Today?" In *Challenges for Rural America in the Twenty-First Century*, edited by D. L. Brown and L. E. Swanson, 73–85. University Park: Pennsylvania State University Press.

Maier, Elizabeth. 2006. "The Unsettling, Gendered Consequences of Migration for Mexican Indigenous Women." In *Women and Change at the U.S.-Mexico Border: Mobility,*

Labor, and Activism, edited by E. R. Hansen and D. J. Mattingly, 19–35. Tucson: University of Arizona Press.

Martin, Philip. 2002. "Mexican Workers and U.S. Agriculture: The Revolving Door." *International Migration Review* 36 (4): 1124–1142.

———. 2003. "AgJobs: New Solution Or New Problem?" *International Migration Review* 37 (4): 1282–1291.

———. 2009. *Importing Poverty? Immigration and the Changing Face of Rural America*. New Haven, CT: Yale University Press.

Martin, Philip L., Michael Fix, and J. Edward Taylor. 2006. *The New Rural Poverty: Agriculture and Immigration in California*. Washington, DC: Urban Institute.

Martin, Philip, and Bert Mason. 2003. "Hired Workers on California Farms." In *California Agriculture: Dimensions and Issues*, edited by J. Siebert, 191–214. Information Series No. 03-1. Giannini Foundation of Agricultural Economics, University of California. http://giannini.ucop.edu.

Martínez, Oscar J. 1998. *Border People: Life and Society in the U.S.-Mexico Borderlands*. Tucson: University of Arizona Press.

Massey, Douglas S., and Zai Liang. 1989. "The Long-Term Consequences of a Temporary Worker Program: The US Bracero Experience." *Population Research and Policy Review* 8:199–226.

McLaughlin, Diane K., and Alisha J. Coleman-Jensen. 2008. "Nonstandard Employment in the Nonmetropolitan United States." *Rural Sociology* 73 (4): 631–659.

McLoyd, Vonnie C., Ana Mari Cauce, David Takeuchi, and Leon Wilson. 2000. "Marital Processes and Parental Socialization in Families of Color: A Decade Review of Research." *Journal of Marriage and Family* 62 (4): 1070–1093.

McMillan, David W., and David M. Chavis. 1986. "Sense of Community: A Definition and Theory." *Journal of Community Psychology* 14:6–23.

Menchaca, Martha. 1995. *The Mexican Outsiders: A Community History of Marginalization and Discrimination in California*. Austin: University of Texas Press.

Mitchell, Christopher. 1992. *Western Hemisphere Immigration and United States Foreign Policy*. University Park: Pennsylvania State University Press.

Mize, Ronald L., Jr. 2006. "Mexican Contract Workers and the U.S. Capitalist Agricultural Labor Process: The Formative Era, 1942–1964." *Rural Sociology* 71 (1): 85–108.

Mollick, André Varella, Marie T. Mora, and Alberto Dávila. 2007. "Changes in the Earnings of Mexican Americans Along the U.S.-Mexico Border between 2000 and 2005." Paper presented at the 87th Annual Meeting of the Southwestern Social Science Association (SSSA), Albuquerque, NM, March.

Morris, Austin P. 1966. "Agricultural Labor and National Labor Legislation." *California Law Review* 54 (5): 1939–1989.

Murray, Julie, Jeanne Batalova, and Michael Fix. 2006. *The Impact of Immigration on Native Workers: A Fresh Look at the Evidence*. MPI Insight No. 18. Migration Policy Institute. www.migrationpolicy.org.

Musick, Kelly. 2002. "Planned and Unplanned Childbearing among Unmarried Women." *Journal of Marriage and Family* 64 (November): 915–929.

Naples, Nancy. 1994. "Contradictions in Agrarian Ideology: Restructuring Gender, Race-Ethnicity and Class." *Rural Sociology* 59 (1): 110–135.

NASA. 2009. All-American Canal, California-Mexico Border. http://earthobservatory .nasa.gov.

National Center for Children in Poverty (NCCP). 2010. Data Tools: 50-State Policy Wizard. Columbia University. www.nccp.org.

Nelson, Margaret K. 2000. "Single Mothers and Social Support: The Commitment to, and Retreat from, Reciprocity." *Qualitative Sociology* 23:291–317.

Nelson, Margaret K., and Joan Smith. 1999. *Working Hard and Making Do: Surviving in Small Town America*. Berkeley: University of California Press.

Nieves, Evelyn. 2002. "Illegal Immigrant Death Rate Rises Sharply in Barren Areas." *New York Times*. August 6. http://www.nytimes.com.

Noriega-Verdugo, Sergio. 2004. "Economic Overview: Employment Patterns in the Municipality of Mexicali." In *Imperial Mexicali Valleys: Development and Environment of the U.S.-Mexican Border Region*, edited by K. Collins, R. Ganster, C. Mason, E. Sánchez López, and M. Quintero-Núñez, 113–131. San Diego, CA: San Diego State University Press.

Palerm, Juan Vincente. 1984. "The Transformation of Rural California: Agribusiness, Farmworkers, and the Making of Chicano/Mexican Enclaves in the Agricultural Communities of Kern, Santa Barbara, San Luis Obispo, and Ventura Counties." Grant proposal submitted to the University of California, Santa Barbara.

———. 2002. "Immigrant and Migrant Farmworkers in the Santa Maria Valley." In *Transnational Latina/o Communities: Politics, Processes, and Cultures*, edited by C.G. Vélez-Ibáñez and A. Sampaio, 247–272. Lanham, MD: Rowman & Littlefield.

Parker, Tim. 2005. Measuring Rurality: 2004 County Typology Codes. U.S. Department of Agriculture. http://www.ers.usda.gov.

Peach, James. 1997. "Income Distribution Along the United States Border with Mexico: 1970–1990." *Journal of Borderlands Studies* 12 (1 & 2): 1–15.

Pedraza, Silvia. 1996. "American Paradox." In *Origins and Destinies: Immigration, Race, and Ethnicity in America*, edited by S. Pedraza and R.G. Rumbaut, 479–491. Belmont, CA: Wadsworth.

Pfeffer, Max J., and Pilar A. Parra. 2009. "Strong Ties, Weak Ties, and Human Capital: Latino Immigrant Employment Outside the Enclave." *Rural Sociology* 74 (2): 241–269.

Pindus Nancy M. 2001. *Implementing Welfare Reform in Rural Communities*. Urban Institute. www.urban.org.

Portes, Alejandro, and Richard Schauffler. 1996. "Language Acquisition and Loss Among Children of Immigrants." In *Origins and Destinies: Immigration, Race, and Ethnicity in America*, edited by S. Pedraza and R.G. Rumbaut, 434–443. Belmont, CA: Wadsworth Publishing.

Pyke, Karen. 2004. "Immigrant Families in the US." In *The Blackwell Companion to the Sociology of Families*, edited by J. Scott, J. Treas, and M. Richards, 253–269. Malden, MA: Blackwell.

Quintero, Cirila. 2005. "Border Industrialization Program." In *Oxford Encyclopedia of Latinos and Latinas in the United States*, edited by S. Oboler and D. J. González, 213–215. New York: Oxford University Press.

Ramírez, Oscar, and Carlos H. Árce. 1981. "The Contemporary Chicano Family: An Empirically Based Review." In *Explorations in Chicano Psychology*, edited by J. Baron Augustine, 3–28. New York: Praeger.

Rawls, James J., and Walton Bean. 2003. *California: An Interpretive History*. New York: McGraw-Hill.

Roschelle, Anne R. 1997. *No More Kin: Exploring Race, Class, and Gender in Family Networks*. Thousand Oaks, CA: Sage Publications.

Rumbaut, Rubén G. 1997. "Introduction: Immigration and Incorporation." *Sociological Perspectives* 40 (3): 333–338.

Ruth, Brooke. 2008. "8,000 Sought 250 Brawley Wal-Mart Jobs." *Imperial Valley Press.* October 10. www.ivpressonline.com.

———. 2010. "Students Fight for Classes at Imperial Valley College as State Funding Dwindles." *Imperial Valley Press.* February 16. www.ivpressonline.com.

Ryan, Vernon D., Kerry A. Agnitsch, Lijun Zhao, and Rehan Millick. 2005. "Making Sense of Voluntary Participation: A Theoretical Synthesis." *Rural Sociology* 70 (3): 287–313.

Sáenz, Rogelio, Cynthia M. Cready, and Maria Cristina Morales. 2007. "Adios Aztlan: Mexican American Out-Migration from the Southwest." In *The Sociology of Spatial Inequality,* edited by L. M. Lobao, G. Hooks, and A. R. Tickamyer, 189–213. Albany: State University of New York Press.

Sáenz, Rogelio, and Alberto Dávila. 1992. "Chicano Return Migration to the Southwest: An Integrated Human Capital Approach." *International Migration Review* 26 (4): 1248–1266.

Sarkisian, Natalia, Mariana Gerena, and Naomi Gerstel. 2006. "Extended Family Ties among Mexicans, Puerto Ricans, and Whites: Superintegration Or Disintegration?" *Family Relations* 55 (3): 331–344.

Sayer, Liana C., Philip N. Cohen, and Lynne M. Casper. 2005. "Women, Men and Work." In *The American People: Census 2000,* edited by R. Farley and J. Haaga, 76–106. New York: Russell Sage Foundation.

Schenker, Marc B. 2004. "Hired Farm Labor: The California Experience." *AgConnections* 2 (2): 1, 3.

Schneider, Barbara, Sylvia Martinez, and Ann Owens. 2006. "Barriers to Educational Opportunities for Hispanics in the United States." In *Hispanics and the Future of America,* edited by M. Tienda and F. Mitchell, 179–226. Washington, DC: National Academies Press.

Schneider, Barbara, and David Stevenson. 1999. *The Ambitious Generation: America's Teenagers, Motivated but Directionless.* New Haven, CT: Yale University Press.

Schneider, Linda, and Arnold Silverman. 2010. *Global Sociology: Introducing Five Contemporary Societies.* New York: McGraw-Hill.

Slack, Tim, and Leif Jensen. 2002. "Race, Ethnicity, and Underemployment in Nonmetropolitan America: A 30-Year Profile." *Rural Sociology* 37 (2): 206–233.

Smith, Barton, and Robert Newman. 1977. "Depressed Wages Along the U.S.-Mexico Border: An Empirical Analysis." *Economic Inquiry* 15:52–66.

Snipp, C. Matthew. 1996. "Understanding Race and Ethnicity in Rural America." *Rural Sociology* 61 (1): 125–142.

Spagat, Elliot. 2011. "Buoys Strung on Border Canal to Prevent Drownings." Associated Press. January 4. http://www.nbcnews.com.

Stacey, Judith. 1991. *Brave New Families: Stories of Domestic Upheaval in Late Twentieth Century America.* New York: Basic Books.

Stack, Carol B. 1974. *All Our Kin: Strategies for Survival in a Black Community.* New York: Harper and Row.

Starr, Kevin. 1996. *Endangered Dreams: The Great Depression in California.* New York: Oxford University Press.

Steffen, David. 2009. "Economy Decreases Valley Private School Enrollment, Public Schools Grow." *Imperial Valley Press.* October 9. http://www.ivpressonline.com.

Taylor, J. Edward, Philip L. Martin, and Michael Fix. 1997. *Poverty amid Prosperity: Immigration and the Changing Face of Rural California*. Washington, DC: Urban Institute Press.

Telles, Edward E., and Vilma Ortiz. 2008. *Generations of Exclusion: Mexican Americans, Assimilation, and Race*. New York: Russell Sage Foundation.

Theodori, Gene L. 2001. "Examining the Effects of Community Satisfaction and Attachment on Individual Well-being." *Rural Sociology* 66 (4): 618–628.

Thorne, Barrie. 1992. "Feminism and the Family: Two Decades of Thought." In *Rethinking the Family: Some Feminist Questions*, edited by B. Thorne and M. Yalom, 3–30. Boston: Northeastern University Press.

Tickamyer, Ann R., and Debra A. Henderson. 2003. "Rural Women: New Roles for the New Century?" In *Challenges for Rural America in the Twenty-First Century*, edited by D. L. Brown and L. E. Swanson, 109–117. University Park: Pennsylvania State University Press.

Tickamyer, Ann, Julie White, Barry Tadlock, and Debra Henderson. 2002. "Where All the Counties Are Above Average: Human Service Agency Director's Perspectives on Welfare Reform." In *Rural Dimensions of Welfare Reform*, edited by B. A. Weber, G. J. Duncan, and L. A. Whitener, 231–254. Kalamazoo, MI: W. E. Upjohn Institute for Employment Research.

Timothy, Dallen J. 2005. *Shopping Tourism, Retailing, and Leisure*. Tonawanda, NY: Channel View Publications.

Tirman John. 2006. Immigration and Insecurity: Post–9/11 Fear in the United States. Social Science Research Council. http://borderbattles.ssrc.org/Tirman.

Toussaint-Comeau Maude. 2004. *The Occupational Assimilation of Hispanics in the U.S.: Evidence from Panel Data*. WP 2004–15. Federal Reserve Bank of Chicago. www.chicago fed.org.

Turner, Margery Austin, and G. Thomas Kingsley. 2008. *Federal Programs for Addressing Low-Income Housing Needs: A Policy Primer*. Urban Institute. www.urban.org.

U.S. Census Bureau. 2007. American FactFinder: Imperial County, California. www.fact finder.census.gov/.

———. 2010. Statistical Abstract of the United States: 2010. www.census.gov.

U.S. Centers for Disease Control. 2008. Agricultural Safety. National Institute for Occupational Safety and Health. www.cdc.gov/niosh.

U.S. Customs and Border Patrol. 2009. El Centro Sector: Welcome. U.S. Deptartment of Homeland Security. http://www.cbp.gov.

———. 2009. SENTRI. U.S. Department of Homeland Security. www.cbp.gov.

U.S. Department of Agriculture. 2004. 2002 Census of Agriculture. National Agricultural Statistics Service (NASS). www.agcensus.usda.gov.

———. 2005, 2006, 2007, 2008. Farm Labor. National Agricultural Statistics Service (NASS). http://usda.mannlib.cornell.edu.

U.S. Department of Homeland Security. 2004. "Extension of Time Limits on Admission to Certain Mexican Nationals." *Federal Register* 69 (156): 50051–50053.

———2009. Immigration Enforcement Actions: 2008. Office of Immigration Statistics Annual Report. www.dhs.gov.

U.S. Department of Labor. 2005. Findings from the National Agricultural Workers Survey (NAWS) 2001–2002: A Demographic and Employment Profile of the United States Farm Workers. http://www.doleta.gov.

———. 2007. Local Area Unemployment Statistics. www.bls.gov/lau/.

————. 2009. Women in the Labor Force: A Databook. Report 1018. www.bls.gov.

————. 2010. National Agricultural Workers Survey. www.doleta.gov.

U.S. Department of State. 2010a. Border Crossing Card. http://travel.state.gov.

————. 2010b. Visitor Visas: Business and Pleasure. http://travel.state.gov.

U.S. Department of Transportation. 2009. U.S. Border Crossings/Entries by State/Port and Month/Year. RITA: Research and Innovative Technology Administration; Bureau of Transportation Statistics. http://www.transtats.bts.gov.

U.S. Government Accountability Office. 2006. Illegal Immigration: Border-Crossing Deaths Have Doubled Since 1995; Border Patrol's Efforts to Prevent Deaths Have Not Been Fully Evaluated. GAO-06–770. Washington, DC: Government Accountability Office.

U.S. Immigration and Customs Enforcement. 2012. About ICE: Enforcement and Removal Operations. http://www.ice.gov/about/offices/enforcement-removal-operation.

Umberson, Debra, Tetyana Pudrovska, and Corinne Reczek. 2010. "Parenthood, Childlessness, and Well-being: A Life Course Perspective." Journal of Marriage and Family 72 (June): 612–629.

Uttal, Lynet. 1999. "Using Kin for Child Care: Embedment in the Socioeconomic Networks of Extended Families." Journal of Marriage and Family 61: 845–857.

Valdes, Dionicio. 2005. "Migrant Workers." In Oxford Encyclopedia of Latinos and Latinas in the United States, edited by S. Oboler and D. J. González, 146–150. New York: Oxford University Press.

Vasquez, Jessica M. 2011. Mexican Americans Across Generations: Immigrant Families, Racial Realities. New York: New York University Press.

Vaupel, Suzanne, and Philip L. Martin. 1986. Activity and Regulation of Farm Labor Contractors. Information Series No. 86–3. Giannini Foundation of Agricultural Economics, University of California. http://giannini.ucop.edu.

Vélez-Ibáñez, Carlos G. 1996. Border Visions. Tucson: University of Arizona Press.

Vélez-Ibáñez, Carlos G., and Anna Sampaio. 2002. "Introduction: Processes, New Prospects, and Approaches." In Transnational Latina/o Communities: Politics, Processes, and Cultures, edited by C.G. Vélez-Ibáñez and A. Sampaio, 1–38. Lanham, MD: Rowman & Littlefield.

Vila, Pablo. 2000. Crossing Borders, Reinforcing Borders: Social Categories, Metaphors, and Narrative Identities on the U.S.-Mexico Frontier. Austin: University of Texas Press.

————. 2003. Ethnography at the Border. Minneapolis: University of Minnesota Press.

Villarejo, Don. 2006. "Farm Labor Research Needs: How do Workers Fare when Production Increases?" Changing Face 12 (4).

Waldinger, Roger, Nelson Lim, and David Cort. 2007. "Bad Jobs, Good Jobs, No Jobs? The Employment Experience of the Mexican American Second Generation." Journal of Ethnic and Migration Studies 33 (1): 1–35.

Walmart Mexico. 2010. http://www.walmart.com.mx.

Wells, Barbara. 2002. "Women's Voices: Explaining Poverty and Plenty in a Rural Community." Rural Sociology 67 (2): 234–254.

Wells, Miriam J. 1996. Strawberry Fields: Politics, Class, and Work in California Agriculture. Ithaca, NY: Cornell University Press.

Wilson, William J. 1987. The Truly Disadvantaged. Chicago: University of Chicago Press.

Wollenberg, Charles. 1969. "Huelga, 1928 Style: The Imperial Valley Cantaloupe Workers' Strike." Pacific Historical Review 38 (1): 45–58.

Ybarra, Lea. 1982. "When Wives Work: The Impact on the Chicano Family." Journal of Marriage and the Family 44:169–178.

Zambrana, Ruth E. 2011. *Latinos in American Society: Families and Communities in Transition.* Ithaca, NY: Cornell University Press.

Zavella, Patricia. 1987. *Women's Work and Chicano Families: Cannery Workers of the Santa Clara Valley.* Ithaca, NY: Cornell University Press.

———. 2002. "Engendering Transnationalism in Food Processing: Peripheral Vision on both Sides of the U.S.-Mexican Border." In *Transnational Latina/o Communities: Politics, Processes, and Cultures,* edited by C. G. Vélez-Ibáñez and A. Sampaio, 225–245. Lanham, MD: Rowman & Littlefield.

Zhou, Min. 1997. "Segmented Assimilation: Issues, Controversies, and Recent Research on the New Second Generation." *International Migration Review* 31 (4): 975–1008.

INDEX

Page numbers for figures are in italics; the suffix *T* indcates a table.

abuse, *see* partners: abuse of; substance abuse
accidents, workplace, 89, 90. *See also* injuries
acculturation, 15
African Americans: concentrated poverty of, in urban settings, 176n.3; rural, outside U.S. social and economic mainstream, 98–99
agency: in aftemath of partner's injury, 158; of border crossers, 162; human, 167; in relocation decisions, 162
Agricultural Labor Relations Act of 1975, 171n.7
agriculture, industrial, 8; California's high-value labor-intensive crops, 171n.10; driving Mexican immigration, 153; "good job" in, 172n.16; "harmony" in, 170n.4; inequality embedded in structure of, 113; labor-intensive model of, 112; occupational risks and injuries, 26, 35, 41 (*see also* disabling injuries); as oppressive structure, 5; organization of, 20–22; percentage of U.S. counties dependent on, 169n.4; in post-bracero period, 22–24; and present-day farmworkers, 24–26; specialty ("F-V-N") crops, 172n.15
alcohol, abuse of, 89, 90, 92
alfalfa, 8
All-American Canal, 7, 58, 61–62, 175n.11, 178n.7

amenities, lack of, in Imperial Valley, 177n.2. *See also* goods and services
Anglos: Dust Bowl migrants, 21; growers, 10, 113, 142, 143–144; pioneer settlers, 9; social buffer with new immigrants, U.S.-born Mexican Americans as, 180n.7; tensions with Mexican Americans, 143
apprehensions, of illegal border crossers, 59, 62
Arrington, Gloria, x
"asking rules," 78
asparagus, 37
assimilation: becoming "too Americanized," 52–53; standard model, and bracero-era families, 169n.1
associate's degrees, 126–127
authority: men's, in Mexican culture, 82, 91, 158; patriarchal, women's disillusionment with, 84–85, 92; women's, through parenting, 87, 89
auto mechanics, 106, 122

Baca Zinn, Maxine, ix, 4
bakery work, 123
BCC. *See* Border Crossing Card
behavioral familism, 68
bilingualism: and retail work opportunities, 52–53; of teachers, 109
"binational consumers," 50
biometric identifier, in BCC, 49
birth control, absence of knowledge regarding, 35. *See also* early pregnancy

ABOUT THE AUTHOR

Barbara Wells is a professor of sociology at Maryville College in Maryville, Tennessee, where she is also vice president and dean of the college. She is coauthor (with Maxine Baca Zinn and D. Stanley Eitzen) of *Diversity in Families*.